IT Best Practices

Management, Teams, Quality, Performance, and Projects

IT Best Practices

Management, Teams, Quality, Performance, and Projects

TOM C. WITT

CRC Press
Taylor & Francis Group
Boca Raton London New York

CRC Press is an imprint of the
Taylor & Francis Group, an **informa** business

AN AUERBACH BOOK

CRC Press
Taylor & Francis Group
6000 Broken Sound Parkway NW, Suite 300
Boca Raton, FL 33487-2742

First issued in paperback 2019

© 2012 by Taylor & Francis Group, LLC
CRC Press is an imprint of Taylor & Francis Group, an Informa business

No claim to original U.S. Government works

ISBN-13: 978-1-4398-6854-6 (hbk)
ISBN-13: 978-1-138-37456-0 (pbk)

Library of Congress Cataloging-in-Publication Data

Witt, Tom C.
    IT best practices : management, teams, quality, performance, and projects / Tom C. Witt.
        p. cm.
    Includes bibliographical references and index.
    ISBN 978-1-4398-6854-6 (hardback : alk. paper)
    1. Information technology--Management. 2. Knowledge management. 3. Project management. I. Title.

HD30.2.W58 2012
004.068'4--dc23   2011046673

Visit the Taylor & Francis Web site at
http://www.taylorandfrancis.com

and the CRC Press Web site at
http://www.crcpress.com

Contents

1

Introduction

The current thinking among companies is that in order to be success-ful in today's global marketplace, they need to be able to do more with less, with "less" often translating into reducing the cost of labor by either downsizing employees or outsourcing work. Since these companies have no idea how (or have given up trying) to get large savings through internal performance increases by improving existing processes, it's really easy for them to plug in cheaper labor costs into their business model rather than looking internally for savings by reducing the waste that occurs. But as companies are finding out, simply having cheaper labor costs does not automatically lead to large savings. The expected savings are frequently offset by new negative factors such as low worker engagement, increased time to create a unit of work, more defects, and additional resources being expended to check for and fix defects. Consequently, with slower produc-tion, fewer quality units of work are being produced. Then there is the factor of the customer: With slower delivery and more defects, customer satisfaction decreases, which in turn leads to decreased revenue. In the end, it becomes unknown what the savings are, if any.

But what if a company could consistently have success in reducing expenses by 15% and shorten delivery time of a product by 25% across the enterprise? Imagine a project that takes only 3,000 hours instead of 4,000 hours to do. What about improving everyday productivity by 20% with little additional cost to accomplish that goal? These would be very good results for a company.

Consistent success just does not randomly happen. It occurs by hav-ing an understanding of what is happening in the environment and then having the skills and knowledge to execute the necessary changes. In the handful of companies I worked for, a few people understood these things. They could adapt to and be successful with any assignments given to them.

They had the respect of upper management and were frequently asked to either lead or to give input and feedback on important changes. Most companies classified these types of people as high performers. Remember this: People get a pay raise when they do their current duties and responsibilities well, but when they can successfully handle tasks outside of their current job duties they normally get promoted to a new title.

It's not complicated to obtain a performance increase if a person understands what to look for. In a company, many things can be classified as waste that robs employee performance. The waste could occur in a company's processes and procedures or with managers who are complacent in both development of their own skills and of their subordinates that report to them. There is the waste that occurs with assigning the wrong people to a task. There is also waste when the wrong tool is used, such as with projects if the wrong project methodology is used. What high performers mostly do is identify the waste that is occurring and address it by either removing or lowering it. This in turn increases both quality and performance.

Whether trying to improve quality and performance at the enterprise level or trying to be promoted ahead of everyone else, the learning path is the same. It all starts by understanding common factors in the everyday business world that affect outcomes. These factors include positive ones required to complete the tasks and negative (waste) ones that add little or no value to the tasks. The most common factors are the processes put in place to make things happen and the human resources that are needed to get things done. Thinking of work in the simplest form, it's about doing a series of actions in a predefined process to create a beneficial outcome for both the worker and the company. With correct knowledge, the right processes, and the right team, quality and performance are the outcome.

The more common way to think about the material to be covered in this book is: What does it take to bring about change successfully—not just small changes in one specific area but also large changes across an entire enterprise? Individuals can think of changes and drive the execution of the change but rarely bring about change on their own. They need other resources with different skills to help with the design, development, and implementation of the changes. It's the coordination and leverage of these resources, along with understanding the environment (barriers, wastes, processes, limitations, capabilities), that sets a high performer apart from everyone else.

In the everyday workplace, there are common knowledge areas that affect everyone, such as management best practices, project methodology, project management, quality, process engineering, and high-performance team (HPT). How people understand and execute these knowledge areas affect whether something is a success or a failure. Each area is dependent on the others. For example, a high-performance team cannot function without knowledge of management best practices, quality, and process engineering.

If training is given on only HPT, when these concepts are implemented the performance increases will be very small most of the time. But what is also robbing performance is there could be waste in the management process, wrong people being assigned and waste with using a process that does not fit the needs. This book covers Lean management, wherein obtaining maximum gains involves looking at the entire process and not just one single part. Yet so often training is based around learning one knowledge area at a time and does not involve a full understanding of how each area ties into all the others. Thus, individuals see very little increase in performance. In addition, understanding HPT will help to reduce the waste that occurs in a normal team, but performance increase will be impeded by waste in other processes such as in the management process, with wrong people being assigned, and with possibly using a process that does not fit the needs. Shortly, people will lose interest, and the effort to improve something disappears. Often, people revert to what they were doing before the training.

In information technology (IT), everything is tied into bringing about change. Even maintenance deals with making small changes to improve things or to continue to keep things running. In companies that are unable to successfully bring about change consistently, words like *descoping, additional phases, missed deadlines, over budget,* and *poor quality* are often used when any type of medium to large change is being attempted. Very rarely are heard words like *stretch goals, early delivery, under budget,* and *zero defects.* A company using the first set of words is working in a *reactive* mode and normally has a shortage of resources to do work and never enough money to get all the work done. It can't react quickly to business needs, so there is a backlog of work always needing to be done. But a company that commonly uses the second set of words is normally near the top in its field and is in a *proactive* mode. It can react quickly to market changes with quality output and a cheaper product than its competition.

Morale, pride, and overall engagement are also higher in a company that commonly uses the second set of words.

The goal of this book is to help readers be aware and understand the many factors that come into play in their everyday work environment that make a difference in both performance and the outcome of the work being done. This will give them a good chance of being able to control things in their environment and thus to be in a proactive versus a reactive mode. This is what makes high performers so good: They understand concepts and processes in their environment that allow them to work in a proactive mode most of the time. Members of upper management would love to issue a memo to everyone stating that on a certain day people all need to start working in a proactive mode; however, this occurs only if individuals make the effort to learn the knowledge that will make it happen.

A small sample of the material covered in this book, with the effect it has on performance outcomes can better be explained using three similar projects I worked on with most of the same core team members each time. For the first project, the team had to create the process from scratch. To invent the process and implement it, the final cost was $350K, and there were two defects. A year later, the exact same project team was asked to do something very similar. This time it was slightly more complicated. The team leveraged what was done in the prior project, and the final cost was $178K with one defect. The following year, with most of the same project team as the first two efforts, a third project was assigned very similar to the first two. The end result was a cost of around $900K and with more than ten defects.

Since the first project cost $350K and the second cost $178K, the cost of the third project would be expected to be between the other two. Nobody would have guessed that it would cost $900K. So what caused the cost increase? The same project methodology was used for all three projects, but how it was applied was changed. The first two times the core project team talked and agreed that the project approach was based around the three key factors: (1) quality; (2) reusability; and (3) what was truly needed to accomplish the project successfully. The third time the project was still based around quality and reusability, but the third key factor was changed from what was truly needed to accomplish the project successfully to *following the project methodology*. Because of this, countless meetings were held and tons of paper was generated, and most of it was never needed for the project's success.

Even though the approach for the first two projects had been explained, the project manager for the third project followed the company's methodology roadmap. The first two times the project methodology was changed to fit what was required of the project, but the third time the project was changed to meet the project methodology. And even though most of the core team members were the same, changing just a few people resulted in going from a high-performance team that worked together, to eliminate tasks that had no bearing on the outcome of the project, to a team following a standard plan, requiring doing tasks with no bearing on the final solution. Those changes led to higher cost (probably over $500K) and poor quality that could be measured in multiple factors based on prior similar projects.

Even though most of this book is geared around change, which translates mostly into doing projects, many of the concepts and knowledge discussed here can be used in companies and organizations in their day-to-day activities. I know of one dental office that used the concepts of high-performance team when looking to employ someone. Before hiring they looked not only at the person's qualifications but also tested for his or her personality attributes. They wanted to make sure the new employee would fit in with the existing workers. The end results were all positive. The dentist's office always had high morale and little conflict, provided friendly customer service, and was very efficient.

Until the late 1970s, there was little material or formal training on the market dealing with how to manage businesses successfully. Managers developed only through trial and error from their own experiences. If they succeeded, they got promoted. If they failed, they got demoted or fired. In the latter situation, they normally never understood what they could have done differently to be successful. Managers developed following nature's concept of survival of the fittest.

In the mid-1980s, the concept of *quality* in business was widely introduced. Up to that time only a few companies, such as Toyota, had formal quality processes in place. Shortly after quality became common in business so did the concepts and ideas of *new best practices, project methodology*, HPT, and *process engineering*. Businesses realized that success or failure can occur based on whether a set of rules and principles were being followed. They no longer wanted to use blind luck for a project's success or find a natural-born leader for management positions. Instead, they wanted to use training, guidelines, procedures, and processes to develop their own leaders. Things became more of a science than guesswork.

Most front-line management members will be familiar with the topics covered in this book, but few will have a detailed understanding of them. It's not that they don't want to learn; it's that many of them are working in crisis mode, with little time outside of their normal tasks to devote to it. One manager I know has only 15 minutes to himself every morning—while his PC boots up—so he reads books during this time for personal development. Once on the system, he's bombarded with e-mails, chat sessions, phone calls, and meetings that fill up his entire day. Because of the lack of time for personal development in the normal work day, it's even important that the personal development material is obtained in a high performance format. It's not efficient to read one book on quality, another on best practices, another on team building and then try to tie all these together into how they relate to a person's job. A more efficient method for personal development would be to have most all the knowledge in one spot.

For readers not yet in management but interested in moving in that direction, the material covered here will help them understand and work on the processes, different knowledge areas, and skills needed for management success. Then when a management position opens up they will be better prepared for their new role. The topics covered here will also help front-line workers in a team or project environment, who should understand the chemistry and teamwork necessary for reducing the risk of failure and stress. The front-line workers and managers actually execute the work in an organization, so when looking to adding quality into a process they are an invaluable resource in terms of knowledge on how things work and what needs to be changed to improve performance.

Today, most companies realize that not all high performers should go into management, where their time and talents will be wasted on daily human resource duties, status reports, and countless meetings. Instead, companies are leveraging the talent of high performers by putting them into such roles as consultant—with the same pay as management. This allows their skills and knowledge to be used across the company without being weighed down by paperwork and clerical work that comes with managing people. In this book when the word *management* is used, think of persons who manage change, such as directors, project managers, technical leads, architects, analysts, and even developers. All of these people manage change in some shape or form.

This book will help readers bridge existing gaps in learning gleaned from seminars and other business books. For example, if a reader understands quality, then maybe it's unclear how to incorporate it into project management or management best practices. Maybe the reader understands the steps to build a high-performance team but is unfamiliar for what tasks an HPT should be used. Or how about when to use linear (waterfall) project methodology versus spiral (agile/rapid application development [RAD]) project methodology? All of these topics and knowledge can come into play for a single task such as a project. Not understanding just one of these knowledge areas for a task can add waste and possibly ultimately result in failure.

ACQUIRING KNOWLEDGE

I'm old enough to remember when the only available televisions were black-and-whites. Man had not yet walked on the moon. Cell phones, personal computers (PCs), networks, word processing, spreadsheets, e-mail, the Internet, project methodology, and management best practices were just a few of the things not yet invented. I have been fortunate to be in the right place at the right time with the right job duties as many of these new concepts and inventions were being implemented into the business world. Naturally, as with anything brand new, none of these things worked perfectly when introduced. To be successful and to achieve maximum quality output in these early days, a person had to question everything and to be able to make modifications to processes and procedures.

The first company I worked for was like a race car on a race track. It could make changes fast and accurate with minimum resources. Even though it was mid-sized ($400 million), each year it was one of the market leaders in profitability in the industry. Other companies I have worked for were more like a race car on a gravel road. The gravel road limits how fast the company can react to its own needs. These other companies had the potential to be market leaders but never could reach that status because of the waste that occurred with bad process, procedures, and barriers that they had implemented. Even though these other companies' staff members were as skilled and knowledgeable as the first company I worked for, they never reached their maximum performance—just like driving a racing car down a gravel road where it cannot reach its top speed.

I started to research different knowledge areas when I first started in business. In my first job I lived four blocks from the office. Between home and the office was the local library. Twice a week I would stop in and read every article I could find on management and human behavior. Things I would encounter in my career had been happening for decades, and by reading and researching why things succeeded or failed in the past would allow me to recognize and hopefully bypass many of the common mistakes and pitfalls that occur in the everyday workplace that others had already experienced. Why not learn from other's mistakes? When I finally got my first management position after four years in business, all this information helped enormously. Did I make mistakes when I first started? Absolutely! But one of the early knowledge areas I obtained was problem solving, and with that skill I was able to identify how to change my behavior and actions to get improved results.

It's very good to get training, but to understand it and retain it a person should apply it right away. I have been very fortunate to be put into a wide range of situations that have allowed me to apply my knowledge as I have learned it. Past experiences range from projects dealing with implementing image systems and their workflow to restructuring a business organization to building PC networks to being responsible for finding and implementing any new technology that would improve performance in an organization.

CONTENT MATERIAL

At times, this book will jump into topics that seem to stray away from the core message. The purpose of this is to try to make readers think a different way and to come up with their own conclusions. If you take every one of my words and thoughts and then try to execute them, you will probably never truly learn what is being taught. What this book offers is guidance and understanding of individual parts in the everyday work environment a person encounters. It's a variance of the 80–20 rule: 80% of what and why things are happening around you and your specific environment is going to be explained; for the other 20% you need to modify the knowledge to how it applies to your specific environment and job.

Do not be discouraged if some of the information presented here does not make sense right away. Many subject matter experts (SMEs) and high performers ran into problems understanding some topic when they were first introduced to it. For example, regarding understanding quality, earlier in my career members of upper management every so often would say to add "quality" or "raise the bar" in our department. But when I asked them how to do that, they would just say, "Do your job better." I was already trying my hardest to do a good job, so I never really understood what that meant. To get a better understanding of quality, I attended countless seminars and read many books, including material from the expert Dr. William Edwards Deming. Still, I could not grasp it. Then one day I came across an article that talked about the concept of *generalist* versus *specialist*. This concept originated from a book called *The Wealth of Nations* written by Adam Smith, which was first published in 1776. Grasping the concepts in this book helped me to begin to understand what quality is. Sometimes, all the information needs to be gathered and merged together where it can sit for awhile, where something later on will trigger full understanding of some complex subject.

The book is broken down into different topics, such as project management, high-performance teams, quality, and management best practices. More time is spent on the subject of projects. It's probably the easiest function within business to put together a team to do a project, yet at the same time it's the most complex to understand all the parts and factors that can cause a project to fail or to exceed expectations. In addition, in projects a great deal of waste can occur. Quality and performance can be dramatically increased if the waste is identified and removed from the project process.

The beginning of the book deals with simple, everyday topics. Reading some of these might seem boring, but the purpose is to build a common knowledge base so that the more complex items in the business world, such as the execution of large projects, are simple to understand. Think of it as how a person learns math. It's a progression process. First we learn addition, subtraction, multiplication, and division, which then lead into the possibility of learning algebra and trigonometry. After that comes the ability to learn calculus and statistics. Finally, after learning all this, a person can learn theory of numbers and differential equations. Business knowledge is much like that. To understand the more complex items in business, we first need to learn and understand the simple things first.

Let's get started.

2

Management Best Practices

A person's title as manager means very little in getting results—it's how the manager acts, reacts, and leads. A common set of attributes defining the best way managers need to act to get the best results is called *management best practices.*

In the handful of organizations I have worked for, all have had formal training classes on the topic, but most of them did nothing else. There are no processes and procedures incorporated into the company's review process guaranteeing that the managers had to spend time working on improving their skills. Most companies let their managers evolve, or stay the same, with little guidance or structure to monitor their development. They hold the usual classes for management improvement, but there is no process in place to measure if managers are applying any of it.

Let's step back and understand what occurs in the real business world. In a perfect scenario, everyone is working together toward a common goal. In reality, though, that is not the case. Some 20% of the staff members (including management) are working to make the company better. Let's call them the *performers.* They take all the training and try to apply it. Another 60% are called *fence sitters.* They take the training and might apply some of it—only if they feel like it. The other 20% are called *cave dwellers.* If they take the training, they do it only to get away from their daily tasks and subordinates. Unless forced to make changes, they have no intent of applying any of the training in their workspace. In their opinion, they already know just enough to get by. Even though everyone in an organization receives excellent training, it does not mean everyone is going to apply it. Processes need to be incorporated into the company to ensure that all staff members (fence sitters and cave dwellers) are at least attempting to apply the training they received.

When I hear someone use a buzzword like *adding quality, speed to market,* and *best practices*, I like to ask what he or she means and how it is implemented. Rarely will a direct answer come back because they themselves do not know. Most people use these phrases because they sound sophisticated. Upper management contributes to the confusion by using the phrases without defining or explaining them. Adding quality and speed to market will be covered later in the book, but this chapter covers management best practices.

Best practices are a proven set of successful processes, procedures, or characteristics that have been tried thousands of times and work almost every time. (Note: There is never a sure thing.) Management best practices, then, are a group of behaviors (sometimes called disciplines) that management should adhere to.

When the same management best practices are not incorporated across a company, inconsistency in management skills occurs—not only from one department or division to another but also between different managers in the same department. Think of it like having skilled basketball players on a team but letting each one do whatever he wants on offense and defense. Some players will be great, and others will look bad. The team overall will lose most games because there is no game plan to pull everyone together. In the same way, large corporations without all its management consistently following and applying the same management concepts will have waste occur for performance and quality. Well-known business leaders like Dr. W. Edwards Deming, who is known for quality, and Jack Welch, from General Electric, understood the waste that can occur without having best practices in place, so they devised plans with a set of action points from which all management can follow. These points help all members of management work together because they all have the same game plan. Later in the book the action points of Dr. Deming (Chapter 13) and Jack Welch (Chapter 7) will be covered. Small corporations tend to not experience as much waste because management from different areas tend to work together closely with one another all the time. In turn, management members tend to adapt to one another to create a common management style.

Early in my management career, to help define and improve my management skills, I learned about and started to apply a concept called "the five building blocks" (sometimes referred to as "disciplines"). These five disciplines were defined as: (1) leadership; (2) negotiation; (3) problem solving; (4) ability to influence the organization; and (5) communication. Understanding these five disciplines has been invaluable to me on projects in my career. Many times during my career, I have been asked to help on projects that were not on track. My approach is always to first review the five disciplines and see what is missing on the project team. Then, based on what is missing, sometimes I would fill that void and other times I would find someone else to fill it. Part of being a good manager is to leverage others who are better than you in certain subjects. Most of the time, by finding out which disciplines were lacking and filling that void, I was able to get the project back on track.

While working on one project, I seemed to discover, by accident, another discipline. I was asked to step in and help on a project that seemed to be going nowhere. Within a month, the project was back on track. One of the project team members mentioned that they liked that I did just not step right in and start to make decisions but instead seemed to create steps and plans on how to get a decision made. The person said that was the turning point in the project. Not only were decisions being made, but they were also the best decisions because the right people were being brought in to discuss the different options and then they were also used to help make the final decision. Before I came on the project, one person was making most of the decisions on the project, merely because of title, and did not include anyone else in the decision-making process.

Based on my observations on this project, I thought I had uncovered a sixth discipline: decision making. After reviewing past development projects, I realized that decision making was actually another key discipline. In the past I had thought that decision making was under the discipline of leadership. Rethinking this in my type of work, leadership is about delegating to others to arrive at the correct decision. Decision making is the process around selecting the best option and getting approval. Both are different yet equally important when trying to complete a project on time and within budget.

With making the small modification of making decision making one of the disciplines by itself, I was applying the concept of continuous improvement, which is to always to make things better to fit the needs. As you read the book, think not only about the material being covered but also your past experiences. Never take anything for granted or face value. Think about past projects or conflicts that have occurred. Don't look at the superficial excuses that people gave for why things failed or dates were missed. Instead, consider the core reason for the failure. Was it because one or more of the disciplines were weak or not there?

Secrets to Success
   Leadership
   Negotiation
   Problem solving
   Decision making
   Ability to influence the organization
   Communication

If you can remember the names of these disciplines then you will be a great manager because you know management best practices. And this is where many seminars and books leave you: You walk away with the very high level understanding of what management best practices are but are never given any instructions on how to implement, execute, and, most importantly, how to improve upon them. There will be very little performable improvement until the person obtains the detail information behind early discipline. Success does not happen just from knowing buzzwords, so let's explore each of these disciplines fully.

LEADERSHIP

In every corporation and organization, we can find examples of people with great leadership skills. Normally, they end up in upper management someplace. They are always the people out front, trying to give direction and setting a vision. If there is an issue, people turn to them immediately to help resolve it. Leaders will probably not solve the problem directly but instead will supply a plan to get the issue resolved. Leaders are often used as a sounding board. Employees will know the answer but will want verification from a leader. Leadership is a key attribute for individuals promoted to top positions in an organization. But how do we tell what makes a good leader?

Leadership can be seen in people who are old, young, tall, short, fat, skinny, male, female. Leaders are found in all ethnic and religious groups. One leader can be the life of the party, and another leader can be as quiet

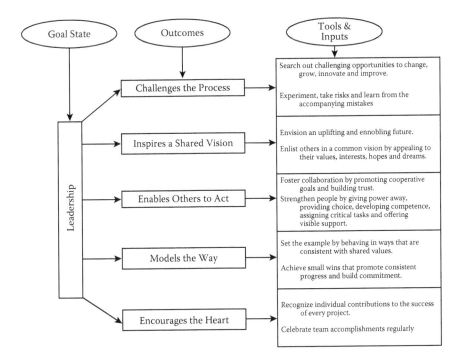

FIGURE 2.1
Leadership components. (Reprinted with permission of John Wiley & Sons, Inc.)

as a mouse. So how can such a diverse group of people have leadership, and how can it be obtained?

One of the better books I have come across that has helped define leadership for me is *The Leadership Challenge—How to Keep Getting Extraordinary Things Done in Organizations* (Kouzes and Posner, 1995). In Chapter 1, "The Practices and Commitment of Exemplary Leadership," it gives structure to what leadership is by defining it as five separate parts, each of which is broken down further and further into smaller and smaller tasks as necessary (Figure 2.1).

Looking at the "Outcomes" column, we get a general understanding of what is required of a good leader. The "Tools & Inputs" column lists tasks that help define what is in the "Outcomes" column. Tasks such as "Search out challenging opportunities to change, grow, innovate, and improve," along with "Experiment, take risks, and learn from the accompanying mistakes," help define the outcome of "Challenges the Process." Though not shown in Figure 2.1, individual tasks could be listed for each item in the "Tools & Inputs" column. For example, "Search out challenging opportunities to change, grow, innovate, and improve" could be divided into "Take advance classes on management" and "Get involved with large projects."

After all six disciplines are discussed, the book will then cover more about how to define and improve disciplines like leadership. At this point, concentrate not on the data but instead on the structure or process that Kouzes and Posner (1995) used to define leadership. Leadership in the Goal State column will never change, but the five items in the Outcome columns might change. Depending on the type of leader a person wants to be, he or she might add, modify, or delete a few of the defined outcomes. Once that is done, then in the Tools & Inputs columns the action items can be added to accomplish the outcome. If detailed tasks need to be added to achieve these tasks, they can be added to the right of the appropriate Tools and Inputs item. In other words, the left side of the structure contains goals that are intangible, which is to say that they can neither be measured directly nor is there one specific action that is being stated to do for improvement. As the structure keeps moving more to the right, finer details gets added until, finally, in the far right column there are specific action tasks that can be defined, accomplished, and measured. This structure provides a way to trace what is going to occur for improvement in that discipline.

NEGOTIATION

Most upper managers—such as the chief information officer (CIO), the chief financial officer (CFO), the vice presidents, and the system officers— have good negotiating skills because it's dependent on their success. They create ideas, set the company's direction, and make short-term and long-term goals for the entire enterprise. Then they must use negotiation to get others to buy into their ideas and then to execute them.

One person alone cannot create and implement short- and long-term plans. Instead, it takes a group. One person might come up with the idea, but it becomes a reality only through negotiation with others on, for example, funding, resources, priority, and a timeline for what needs to be done. In a large organization, some areas are overstaffed for maintenance and project work; these tend to be those with upper management that have good negotiation skills. Other departments, however, suffer from being understaffed because their upper management is not good in negotiation.

As a person looks down the corporate ladder they will notice that normally closer to the front line manager, the negotiation skill is not very well developed. At the lower levels in an organization, there normally is just maintenance and daily work. If something is broken, it just gets fixed. If something needs to be maintained, it's done as it's always been done. With that type of work, there are few discussions or decisions. There are very few unknowns or opportunities to make a major decision. An exception to this occurs in project work. Many large projects start out mainly as nothing but unknowns. Individuals assigned as team members on a project are able to develop the discipline of negotiation as they address the unknowns.

In negotiation, there are three possible outcomes. The best is a win–win situation. In a win–win, all people involved in the negotiation gets the majority of what they want. It's easy to accomplish this because many times people want similar things and differ only on minor items. Another outcome is a win–lose. One party in a negotiation gets most everything they want, and the other party in the negotiation gives in and gets left out of what they want. This is not the best outcome. The last outcome is a lose–lose situation. In this outcome, neither party is willing to change their point of view. Every party involved takes a stance and is not willing to compromise even a little. Sadly, this occurs far too often. The only way to get a compromise in the lose–lose situation is to elevate the negotiation process up a couple of management levels. Having a different set of people with different roles and responsibilities often generates a different outcome—hopefully a win–win.

There are some general principles to being good at negotiation. First, there needs to be an understanding of the subject matter. It's easy to identify people who don't understand the subject matter being discussed when negotiating. They ask silly questions, are not open to discuss options they don't agree with, and many times are more of a distraction in meetings because the meeting group spends more time teaching them the subject than working toward a solution. Those who understand the subject matter can give quick and accurate responses and are also more likely to compromise from what they originally wanted.

Another principle of good negotiation is to take the time to understand the other party's point of view, no matter how strange it might seem. In business, there is no way to know everyone's experiences or backgrounds. Maybe others have tried a similar idea years back without success. If this is the case, identify the barriers in the previous attempts, and then break them down one at a time. For example, a barrier could be that the person believes it will create more work for his or her area. Time needs to be spent identifying each reason the person believes that and then address why it might not be true now. Only by going through the process of identifying and addressing all the barriers can people agree to a common idea.

A third principle to good negotiation is to be creative. To find the best solution, a couple of alternative options are needed, no matter how strange they might seem. When people start to compare the alternatives, it's easy to see what option is the best.

Most negotiation happens in a meeting. The first rule of the meeting is to make sure make sure everyone understands the goal; this can be accomplished using a process called cornerstones, which explains the reason for the change. There are only two to four cornerstones, and they create a point of reference that can be used to validate the different options and make sure discussions are following a positive direction. People come to a meeting with preconceived ideas; they know what they want and, more importantly, what they don't want. If, for example, during a meeting personal interest seems to have arisen, the group can go back to each cornerstone to make sure the direction that is being discussed meets the needs.

Let's say a certain change is being proposed. The change is being done to reduce cost (cornerstone 1), to decrease delivery time (cornerstone 2), and to reduce defects that are currently happening (cornerstone 3). There are probably 1,001 possible solutions, but only a couple are a perfect fit for all three cornerstones. If you chart the three cornerstones, it would look something like Figure 2.2.

The best solutions are the ones that, when mapped, would appear in the inner section of all three circles. The bad solutions would not interface with all three circles. An example of a bad solution is to hire more staff. With more staff, things can get done faster, so it will meet cornerstone 2, decrease delivery time. Also, with more staff there can be more testing and checking, which would meet cornerstone 3, reduce defects. However, adding more staff does nothing to cornerstone 1, reducing cost, so this solution is not the best one if the goal is to meet all three cornerstones. When the cornerstones or purpose of the change is defined before negotiation begins, it is easy to identify the best solutions.

Cornerstones are easy to define. There must be some business reasons for changing something. The cornerstones are those business reasons defined. Once defined, they need to remain static because key decisions early in the negotiation process will be made from them. Too many times, the best option is not selected because these cornerstones

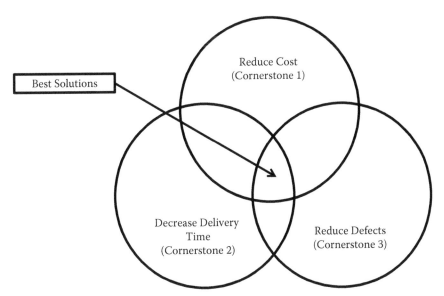

FIGURE 2.2
Cornerstones usage to find the best solution.

are not defined or are incorrect. Remember the three similar projects (see Chapter 1)? The cornerstones the first and second time were quality, doing only what was truly needed to accomplish, and reusability. We knew the first time that there was a possibility of doing it again several times, so design, development, implementation, and even documentation were created around these three cornerstones. The third time the realignment was done, the cornerstone of doing only what was truly needed to accomplish was replaced with following the project methodology approach. Changing the one cornerstone ended up adding on the cost of several hundred of thousands of dollars, decreased quality, and added no value to the project.

A simpler way to understand negotiation is to consider the following statement:

Take 2 numbers, and get the end result of 5 in the most efficient method.

There are three cornerstones in this statement. One is "2 numbers," another is "result of 5," and the third is "most efficient method." There are many possible solutions. You can take the numbers of (2 + 3) or (1 + 4), which give 5. Numbers (1 + 1 + 1 + 1 + 1) or (7 – 2) also result in 5. The first two solutions are fairly simple. They both meet all three cornerstones.

The solution of using (1 + 1 + 1 + 1 + 1) involves adding five numbers, which is not only cumbersome task but also adds the risk of counting wrong because of the amount of numbers being added together. Individuals who suggest this as a solution should be respected enough to be asked why they wanted to use five numbers. Remember, one of the cornerstones was to use "2 numbers." Either they did not understand the cornerstone, or because of their math limitations they are better at adding 5 small numbers together. If this is your end user suggesting this alternative solution, you need to listen. Maybe their skill level does not match the solution. If so, then a learning or training issue must be addressed. I have seen some changes fail because of the complexity it caused the end user. In negotiation you need to understand the other person's point of view, and they should understand yours.

The last solution of (7 − 2) is a good example of a personal interest. Who suggested this either personally likes to do subtraction or is just showing off. The solution of (7 − 2) is more complex because of the subtraction. You could immediately rule out this solution, or you could break down this solution and explain the complexity. If you break it down, then everyone can see the reason it's not the best option: It does not meet the criteria of "most efficient method." Doing this makes it easy for other people to see this is not one of the best solutions.

For a medium to large project, negotiation is a key discipline. Businesses usually have only a vision or idea of what they want, from which there are many different ways to create the final product. Design and details must be defined. All these are done through negotiation. I once had a project that just started out with one statement from the business: "We want to use claims as part of rating processes." From there, information technology (IT) had to come up with the design, business processes, and a system solution to do it. Only through negotiation with our business partners were we able to take the idea and turn the statement into a reality.

Negotiation is a skill that gets developed over time. Those new to management will have little success at first; they can try but will not have the knowledge base yet to be good at it. Managers at lower management levels tend to start out as micromanagers. It's a safe way, with low risk, to do their job. As managers pick up system, business, and people knowledge skills, they tend to get better at the discipline of negotiation. Negotiating is about working with people to reach a common cause.

However, as time passes some managers never develop the skill of negotiation. They remain micromanagers. One reason for this is that they have a trust and control issue. By not negotiating, they feel important because everyone is following their direction. From a micromanager's viewpoint, it's their way or the highway. The direct outcome of not working and negotiating with people is bad morale, low productivity, and bad quality. Since micromanagers never ask for input from their staff, the staff rarely will give 100%. Experienced staff under a micromanager will almost always move to another group so that they can use their knowledge. A company can't tolerate or afford these things because they are all wastes.

PROBLEM SOLVING

Problem solving is not as simple as a person giving an answer; instead, it's about the process around getting the correct information to the problem. The most common type of problem involves something that is broken and in need of being fixed. Another type of problem involves something unknown that needs to become known. An example of the latter is project work: A business has an idea, and the problem is to find and address all the unknowns and issues that are needed to make the idea into a reality. In either type of problem, problem solving covers the processes to ensure that the correct research and best options are indentified to resolve the problem.

Let's say the problem is that a person has a common cold. What do most people do to fix this? They take medicines to stop the cough and the runny nose, to reduce the fever, and to sleep through the night. Taking medicine is a good solution to the problem, except it does not reduce the risk of the person getting a cold again. I don't know where I picked this up, but for decades I have been telling people that for problem solving they need to "fix the disease and not just the symptoms." For example, a lack of sleep, a sedentary lifestyle, and poor eating habits will keep a person's immune system from fighting off infections optimally. If these habits were changed to healthier ones, a person's immune system builds up so that it will better fight off infections and diseases, including colds and the flu. In the short term, taking medicine is the correct solution. For the long term, the better solution would be to change habits.

So how do you know what the best solution for a problem is? Normally, when there is a problem, a quick solution is always presented. Using the 80–20 rule, 80% of the time the first solution is probably going to be right, but 20% of the time the first solution is not the best option. That's a pretty bad failure rate in business. To get the right answer each time, it is necessary to go through the problem-solving process.

First, dig deep enough to identify the problem, gap, or issue. A good process to use for this is a method called the "5 Whys," which Sakichi Toyoda invented and that Toyota leveraged in its manufacturing line to identify the root cause of problems. Today it's still being used in many popular processes improvements concepts. The basic process can be demonstrated as follows:

> Problem: "My car will not start."
> Why 1? Response: The battery is dead.
> Why 2? Response: The alternator is not functioning.
> Why 3? Response: The alternator belt has broken.
> Why 4? Response: The alternator belt was well beyond it useful service life and has never been replaced.
> Why 5? Response: No recommended service schedule has been performed.

By no means do you have to limit it to five. The response to the sixth why might be that there was not enough money to maintain the car properly. Each given response is a valid reason for the car not starting, but as each why is being asked it gets closer to the root cause of the problem.

Often, not enough whys are asked for a problem. The people working on the problem might go down to the second level of whys because that is all that is normally needed to satisfy management. The reason given is accurate, but it does not reveal the root cause of the problem. The problem with not finding the root cause is that the solution employed might not fix the problem permanently. In the previous situation, if we accepted the first response—the battery is dead, so replace it with a new one—then later after driving the car around and using the lights the new battery will also go dead. So we are back to the original problem that the car will not start. Only by digging deep enough to identify the broken alternator belt can things be permanently fixed.

In the business world, this translates into some tough personal questions, because often the cause of the problem can be traced back to one or two people. Some necessary questions are as follows:

> *Did the individuals understand what they were supposed to change and the reason why the changes were being made?* Without a full understanding, these people will not know all the possible effects the chance is supposed to bring.

Were they qualified to make the changes? In other words, did they have the knowledge and skills required to complete the task? Too many defects occur because people are randomly assigned to do a task only because they are available and not because they are qualified to do it.

Were the instructions clear and concise? Today's project process involves many handoffs to bring about change, and with having massive amounts of documentation there are often wrong assumptions put in the documentation or things are stated wrong. It's very easy to interpret something different from what someone wrote or was verbally told to do.

Did the process to make the change get in the way of individuals succeeding in making the change? Large companies have complex processes in place to try to control the development and implementation of change. Many processes are put in place not to help a person developing the change but instead to control and monitor what they are doing. These processes actually decrease these individuals' productivity and limit their quality of work.

All these questions lead to other questions. In this way, the root cause of the problem can be identified and resolved. Frequently, there is not just one reason for failure; it could be a combination of things. So often, though, research stops when one reason is found, and the other contributing factors are never identified and fixed; thus, the problem reoccurs, wasting both time and money.

It's very important to gather all the information accurately around the problem because it is used in the next discipline, decision making, to determine the necessary actions. When a bad decision is made, normally its cause can be traced back to bad (i.e., not enough, assumed) information gathered in the problem-solving phase. I have no idea why some people cannot say, "I don't know the answer to that, but I will find it and get back to you." Instead, they make a statement that is a guess about how things work. Their words are then documented as a requirement in the problem-solving phase, on which decisions, design, development, and implementation are based. There is a chance the assumption could be right, but there is also a chance it could be wrong. These wrong assumptions are not found right away because everyone believes they are true. Most of the time, the project is in the development or testing stage before anyone identifies that the statement was a wrong assumption. At this point in the process, it becomes costly to correct. So as information is being gathered on the problem, make sure the information is accurate and correct. I once heard and firmly believe the statement, "Also validate. Never Assume." It's a very good rule to follow.

Part of the problem-solving process for defects is to identify the cause. This normally ends up being traced back to a single person. It's very difficult to tell someone he or she messed up. This is often handled incorrectly, with it seeming more like pointing fingers than trying to help the person improve. Let's say one of the responses identified was that the person was not qualified to make the change. One plan would be to get the person the knowledge and training so he or she can develop the change correctly the next time. Another plan could be to assign a mentor to watch over this person when he or she does this type of change again. Both are simple solutions and eliminate finger pointing. The person who caused the defect sees that a personal interest is being taken in trying to help him or her improve so the same mistake is not made again. On the next assignment, the person normally will start to ask questions before beginning to make the change, which means they have now started to work in a proactive mode (which is good). The person's quality of work has improved, engagement in work has increased, and loyalty has been built that will last for years to come—all because a manager took the time to identify the root cause of an issue and then came up with a plan to help prevent it from reoccurring.

If the root cause can be identified, it can also lead to the prevention of other possible but not yet identified problems. In the situation of the car not starting, if the decision is to fix everything and then to start regular maintainance, this might reveal that maybe the brakes, tires, transmission, or fluids need to be replaced—all items that might become costly problems in the future if not taken care of. Much is the same in business when solving a problem. In the process of finding the root cause, other items will be found that might not be broken now but have a possibility of breaking. By making enhancements now it will prevent it from breaking and becoming a problem later. Whether you call it foresight or being proactive, finding the true problem and all the effects it had is the first part of the problem solving process.

The second part is to identify the correct solution. For most every problem there should be at least two to three options created to resolve it so a comparison can be made to find the best solution. In the car example, one of the options is to just replace the battery. Another possible option is to fix the alternator belt and replace the battery. Comparing the two quickly reveals that, of the possible options presented, the second option might be the right one to permanently fix the problem.

The best fix, which has not yet been mentioned, is to fix the alternator belt, to replace the battery, and also start regular maintenance. If this had already been in place, regular maintenance would have uncovered the worn-out belt, and it could have been replaced for under $30. This would have saved the cost of purchasing a new battery, plus probably the cost of towing the car to a service shop. So is the best solution always to fix everything and start to have regular maintenance done? It depends. If the car is extremely old, maybe trading it in would be a better option. If the person does not make enough money, maybe regular maintenance is not possible. When looking for possible options to solve the problem, all the variables directly related and indirectly related to the problem need to be accounted for; otherwise, the best option may never be found.

The last item in problem solving is communication to all people affected by the problem. It should include what the problem was, what was affected, and if a decision was made on how it was going to be resolved. Problems dealing with solving unknowns for projects always get documented because of the project methodology requirements. But it's different when solving problems caused by defects. Normally, for a defect, little feedback is given to the customer. Since a problem is a negative, the false belief is that the less information, the better. The truth is that the negativity caused by the defect can be turned into somewhat of a positive. Going back to the customer (whether internally or externally) with good communication shows that the problem was taken seriously. Let's face it: If a problem arose in your area, would you prefer to just get an e-mail simply saying it was fixed or get an e-mail detailing what went wrong, why it went wrong, how it got fixed, and when it got fixed? The latter communicates that the area that caused the problem takes defects very seriously.

Most of the time, when everything is going well nobody pays attention to someone with good problem-solving skills. But when things go wrong, the first people everyone turns to are the ones who can give direction and come up with a good solution to the problem. These people are gathering information by asking the whys. They are also looking for several options to resolve the issue. While most people seem hysterical and demand immediate action, these people remain calm. In each organization I worked in, it's usualy the same people who are called on to solve big problems or issues whenever they crop up.

Following the why process could be used when creating corporate goals. Many corporate goals are created to solve a problem. Most companies at some point have the problem (goal) of reducing expenses. If the why method is used, after exploring several levels of "why", it might be found that certain business modules may be ineffective, inadequate equipment or processes that are causing additional expenses. Only by going through the process is it possible to identify the root causes in need of being changed to run a more efficient organization.

DECISION MAKING

After problem solving, the next step is to make a decision on what action will be taken. How is the best option found? First, the correct research must have been done in the prior step so that the best options have been identified. The option selected needs to take into account both short-term and long-term needs of the company. Even after gathering data that validate the best option, often varying personal interests and different viewpoints will cause disagreement about it being the best choice. Thus, negotiation is needed so that everyone is convinced that the selected option is the best. Just like in problem solving, after a decision is made it needs to be communicated to the affected people, along with why it is the best option.

Several methods are used to help make a correct decision. A common technique is called "Plus–Minus" or "Alpha–Delta." With each option defined, list all the pros and cons of doing that option. On that list should be items such as initial cost, annual maintenance costs after the change has been implemented, short-term results, long-term results, development time, cost, implementation, and complexity being added to the process. Once this list is compiled, compare each option's pros and cons to identify which option meets the needs the best. If the decision is going to have a significant impact, then define two to four cornerstones (see previous Negotiations section) as to the reason for the change to help identify the best option. Included on the list for each option should be how close the solution matches all the cornerstones. This technique will almost always bring to light one option that is superior to the others. Rarely will there be two options with little to no difference between them, though in these instances (as covered in the discussion on negotiation) it does not matter which one is selected. Both will meet the specific needs (i.e., cornerstones) equally as well. Through negotiation there just needs to be an agreement by all parties to one of the two options.

So who makes the final decision? The process is to identify all key stakeholders who will be affected by the decision. If the decision will affect a large part of the company, the decision making can be handed over to members of upper management in the areas affected by the decision. After all, they are accountable for their area. Either they can make the decision, or they can select someone in their area to make it. But beware— most upper managers have been removed from the day-to-day activity and might not fully understand how the decision will affect their area. Therefore, if upper management members make a decision and they have not consulted with their staff, it is a good practice to initiate a discussion with someone on their staff who is a subject matter expert (SME).

Once the correct people have been identified to make the decision, then follows the art of getting the decision actually made. The approval process can be fast and definite, or it can be long and by default. Most people who are in a position to give approval will do so in writing or via e-mail. Of course, there are exceptions to this. Some procrastinate and don't want to give any formal approval, in which case you have to get approval by default. Send a written document or e-mail to the people who can approve the decision. In the communication, give a time frame and specify that if you don't hear back from them within the given time it's assumed that everything is fine and it's okay to proceed. Once that time frame comes and goes, send another written document or e-mail saying that since there were no objections the decision is being approved. This option to get approval by default requires a little documentation, but it's needed. I trust a lot of people, but I also understand the importance of documenting how each decision was arrived at. If a person who is in a position for approval or disapproval cannot (or will not) provide you with a response, you need to take the initiative. If anyone ever questions how the decision was made, you have the necessary documentation to show for it.

I have used the approval by default process many times, and only a few times have there been issues. In these instances, I had documentation on dates, times, and paperwork showing that management was given the opportunity to make the decision but elected to do nothing. After presenting these, there was never any more discussion on the subject.

You might ask how someone could be in upper management who procrastinates on making a decision. It's very simple. One reason deals with accountability. In reality, many managers are good at making small decisions that have little effect. However, when it comes to making major decisions that will have widespread effects, they hesitate because they are afraid they might make the wrong one. Even though they may have research pointing to one best option, until the option is implemented there is no solid evidence. So they worry that if the decision turns out to be bad their name will be associated with it, and they hesitate and procrastinate effecting large changes.

ABILITY TO INFLUENCE THE ORGANIZATION

The leadership discipline involves outcomes such as challenging the process, inspiring a shared vision, enabling others to act, modeling the way, and encouraging the heart (see Figure 2.1). All of these outcomes involve setting a vision and a direction and then allowing people to do their job. They don't entail anything related to actually making things happen. It's like having all the ingredients to make a cake but no mixing bowls or oven to bake it in. The ability to influence the organization is about execution. Individuals can have excellent leadership skills, but without execution skills they will be ineffective in their job. Once the best solution or option has been chosen, the next step is to execute it. From *Execution: The Discipline of Getting Things Done* by Larry Bossidy and Ram Charan:

> Execution is a systematic process of rigorously discussing how's and what's, questioning, tenaciously following through, and ensuring accountability. It includes making assumptions about the business environment, assessing the organization' capabilities, linking strategy to operations and the people who are going to implement the strategy, synchronizing those people and their various disciplines, and linking rewards to outcomes. It also includes mechanisms for changing assumptions as the environment changes and upgrading the company's capabilities to meet the challenges of an ambitious strategy. (page 22)

This is a very wordy way of defining the ability to influence the organization, better known as "execution." From this statement you can get a distinct understanding of what it is versus what leadership is. I have seen many directors, system officers, CIOs, and CEOs make outstanding speeches on upcoming changes. After the meeting, people are doing nothing but talking about the new ideas and proposed changes. But as days turn into weeks or months, nothing ever changes—because nobody executed the idea.

Understanding the infrastructure and workflow is a good start to being able to influence it. Work always flows from one department to another. Learning the flow helps in understanding how changes will potentially affect the enterprise when they are implemented.

Another requirement to be able to influence an organization is by having a social network of internal people. Not just any ordinary network, but one consisting mostly of company performers, or the 20% of the staff that get things done. The performers in an organization can easily be identified. Ask the question: What large projects or changes have been implemented successfully in the last couple of years? Then ask the question: Who were the unofficial and official leaders on those projects? A very small number of people are probably always involved with the large complex tasks. When you identify them, they normally have the knowledge and connections that can be very beneficial in helping to execute change in the company. Think of it this way: If you were playing sports, would you want to play on a losing team or a winning team? On the winning team you would be happier because you are learning the right things that need to be done in order to win. Business is like that. If you hang out with the best, you have a chance to become one of the best.

We have talked about the knowledge that is needed to be able to influence and execute. Sometimes things beyond our control will limit how much can be changed successfully. A good example of this is corporate goals. As soon as upper management states a corporation goal, everyone knows it will be impossible to obtain. Too many barriers or gaps may exist in the company, making it impossible to even come close to meeting the goals. The goals might be excellent—such as "reduce expenses" or "shorten delivery time"—but if a company has an out-of-date distribution system then the delivery time will not change that much no matter what occurs. Or if the company is in a middle of a merger then expenses will actually increase and not decrease until the merger is complete. Another barrier is the workforce itself. If the entire workforce has been in place for decades they are probably not receptive to making major changes in their workflow. Spending time to learn these barriers and thresholds in the company or departments will allow an understanding of the amount of change that can be attempted.

In many cases the company will actually move away from its goal until certain things are in place. If a new distribution system needs to be developed and implemented, costs are not going to be reduced immediately and the delivery time will not improve. If an experienced workforce needs to be retrained, productivity will actually decrease during the transition. Only once the changes are in place and have been running for awhile will the true benefits start to be realized. Being realistic about what can and cannot be accomplished is required to be able to set realistic goals and to make correct decisions. This relates to influencing and being able to execute change because if individuals set mostly unrealistic goals and achieve no success obtaining them, then it only alienates them from everyone else—which translates into nobody taking them seriously anymore. They have then lost the power to influence and to execute change. But those who set realistic goals and accomplish them most of the time tend to be listened to and accepted as influencers.

Many in upper management have lost their jobs because they could not influence the organization after they had set unattainable goals. This is frequently obvious when new management from outside of the company comes in. Immediately they make changes based on their prior company's experience. They make statements such as, "In the prior company we did it this way." In the new company, though, the new changes cause a high level of stress, confusion, and drop in productivity. Do not get me wrong: It's okay to bring in new ideas. But before starting to make changes there needs to be time to identify what needs to truly be fixed first and then to understand the full effects within the infrastructure of the fix. Without doing this, an outside experienced manager is only "guessing" as to what needs to be fixed.

When Deming wrote about this several decades ago, he stated that management mobility was such a major issue that it's one of the top seven diseases plaguing business. He called it "Mobility of management: job hopping." When Japan revolutionized its industry after World War II, one of the reasons for its success was because almost all management positions were filled with staff members from within the company. And Jim Scott's book *Good to Great* mentions research showing that 10 of 11 organizations receiving the distinction of being "great" rarely hired management from outside of the company and instead hired from within.

The majority of members of external management who come into a company are not job-hoppers, but they still are ineffective in the beginning. As for management that are job-hoppers, they exhibit a common pattern and time frame. They stay 2 or 3 years in one job and then hop to the next before the bad results catch up to them. The first year everything is being changed, even the existing benchmarks that are supposed to measure performance. The second year finally there is stability, but again the performance benchmarks are so new that nobody knows if things are better or worse. Around the third year it becomes obvious that the changes are not working because productivity is down and so is engagement. So the job-hoppers either need to find another job or stay and suffer the consequences for not really having any idea what needed to be improved in the company. Most take the easy route and hop to another company or division and start the process all over again.

The effects of job-hoppers' many changes that add no value can be minimized through documentation. Massive amounts of documentation are required when doing projects, but surprisingly there is very little required for making changes in processes, procedures, benchmarks, and goals. Requiring documentation would do the following:

- It would greatly reduce the number of bad ideas that get implemented and end up wasting companies' productivity.
- It would demonstrate that members of management understand what the issues are that they are trying to solve and would show the tentative change plan. Most job-hoppers' ideas are borrowed from other companies in which they have worked, so they do not fully understand all the fine details that made the process work in their prior place of employment.
- It would define such critical items as changes to existing performance benchmarks, plan of execution, and expected results—all critical items to know if the changes are beneficial.
- It would provide a paper trail of what changed and the final results. When a department or team starts to underperform, there is nothing tangible as to why it occurred. If some of the original team members are no longer in the group and the manager has moved to a new company or division, there are only guesses as to what caused the decrease in performance. With detailed documentation there is a roadmap to be able to change back to the old processes to improve the performance again.

To influence the organization, goals must be not only attainable but also clear and concise. We have all been in company meetings in which managers talk about decreasing delivery time by 10% or reducing defects by 25% but that is as far as it goes. These are excellent goals and probably are attainable, but there are no action statements about how to reach them. It appears that managers just randomly thought of some common goals and put percentages around them. Instead of setting a goal to decrease delivery time by 10%, the goal statement could be enhanced by saying, "Through implementing a new distribution network the goal is to reduce the delivery time by 10%." It shows that thought and research has been put into what needs to be done to accomplish the goal. Increasing return on investment (ROI) is another good example that most upper management state every year. For the ROI the very base formula is:

(gain on investment – cost of investment)/cost of investment

There are an infinite number of combinations to reach ROI, however. What are all the factors that go into *cost of investment* and *gain on investment* in which the company is expecting increases? Probably the accountants, who generate the numbers, are the only ones who really know. A good goal statement related to ROI would be, "By reducing travel expenses and getting rid of divisions that are not profitable now and appear they will stay unprofitable in the near or long-term future, the goal is to increase the ROI by 20%." It's clear and concise as to what actions must be taken to reach the goal. It's easy to get buy-in when the goals are concise.

In today's world it has become critical to have clear goals when talking of reduced cost. When *reduce cost* is the only thing mentioned, everyone in the organization immediately relates this to staff reduction. Then for days, weeks, and even months after the announcement, it's all anyone can talk about. Rumors are all over the place, and performance drops drastically. So a goal statement that is not clearly defined actually takes a company further away from attaining its goal of reducing costs.

The ability to influence is just not that you start something and then walk away from it. In one organization I was with, some middle managers said, "We will pay lip service to the CEO's idea until he moves onto another one." Almost every time, they were right. After a short time, the CEO would move on to a new idea and forget about the old one. This is dubbed Management Attention/Deficit Disorder (MADD). Just like a kid opening presents on Christmas day, these CEOs are really excited in the beginning but lost interest after a short time. The CEO in this organization never followed through on their ideas, so nobody else did either.

Management needs to stay involved in the change if they want it to be successful. I am not saying that there needs to be a deep involvement, but just need to be aware of what is happening. Many times members of upper management make a good goal but do little to follow up throughout the company to see if it is being met. They rely instead on status reports or they delegate it to another staff member that reports directly to them. This gives them a very limited view of what is truly happening. The data could be bad, or the people surrounding upper management might not be dealing with reality. Over and over, I have seen status reports that misrepresent the true status of a project.

In a company it's easy to identify the people who are good at influencing the organization. These people push the outer limits and are always involved with large changes that are occurring. They are willing to go out on a limb and advocate for good ideas even though they might not be the most popular. Instead of being complacent, they want to make the company better. Their work ethic usually could be based around the idea of *continuous improvement*. These types of people are good to be in your social network because they can help to get things done.

COMMUNICATION

Most people believe that communication deals only with talking. When 10 people are in the same meeting for an hour, it translates into 10 hours of used labor. For the meeting to be productive, only one person at a time can talk. So, in the meeting there is 1 hour of talking, which leaves 9 hours of listening that occurred among the 10 people. So communication is just not about talking; it's also about listening because that normally is what a person does the most in meetings. Keep this in mind as we cover this discipline.

Most communication happens by having some type of meeting. When in management a person will be required to call (chair) many meetings. It can be as small as a one-on-one conversation or as large as a presentation to the entire corporation. As the chair of the meeting, a person's responsibilities are to decide who attends, what the topic will be, how it will be presented, and what goals and outcomes are expected from the meeting. The success or failure of the meeting is controlled by the chair.

Many meetings end without anything being accomplished, which leads to more meetings to cover the same material again. Signs of a productive meeting include assignment of action items or tasks. At the end of the meeting there is a recap of what was decided and who was assigned what to do. If another meeting is necessary, this recap information will be used as a starting point and also is helpful to any potential new meeting members.

The following steps might seem lengthy but take only a matter of minutes to perform:

1. Define the subject or topic of the meeting.
2. Create a documented high-level agenda, which usually includes random thoughts and ideas.
3. Arrange the ideas and thoughts into a meaningful progression, using, for example:
   a. Bulleted items. Items can be added, modified, or deleted easily.
   b. Sticky notes. On a single note put a single thought or idea that needs to be covered; notes can then easily be arranged to create the agenda.
4. Write down the objectives of the meeting. Is it to only inform people? Is it a meeting that needs approval or buy-in of the subject material? It could be a meeting to explain something to staff members or with the purpose of gathering information from others. Each type of meeting needs a different approach. If the objectives and criteria of the meeting are defined and put into a plan, then the direction of the meeting can be controlled.

Following these steps ensures that the meeting has a purpose to everyone involved instead of seeming to have been called just for the sake of holding a meeting.

Meetings for Informational Purposes

A meeting for informational purpose is based around the type of the information and number of questions that might arise from the information. If the information that needs to be presented is important to the receiver, such as a change in the HR process, then schedule this type of meeting. Or if some information that needs to be sent out is going to generate allot of questions because of the affects it will bring, and then have this type of meeting. If the information does not fit either of these categories, then instead of a formal meeting, send out the information in an email, which is more productive and just as efficient in this situation.

A 1-hour group meeting can become costly in terms of performance. If 10 people are attending, that is 10 hours of productivity used only for the meeting. But in reality it's more. There is the time it takes to get to the meeting along with the fact that a meeting most time does not start until everyone is there. When a 1-hour productive meeting occurs with 10 people, it probably took 15 hours of productivity from the company.

Meetings to Sell an Idea or Get Approval

Some meetings are held to get approval or buy-in, such as an annual review of an employee or a new process that will affect the entire organization. A detailed agenda is required for this type of meeting, primarily to show attendees that you have thought through the change or idea and have a plan. If it's a new process, the agenda will cover how the new process will affect the company across the enterprise as well as the reasons and benefits of the change. The written meeting agenda needs to be distributed before the meeting takes place. Since the purpose is to sell an idea or get approval, attendees need time to review and think about what is going to be discussed. If the agenda is given out at the start of the meeting, odds are most people will be defensive to the changes and ideas. They will feel as if it's being forced upon them.

Part of the agenda needs to include a step for feedback. During this feedback part of the meeting, the chair needs to listen to what is being said, to try to understand other people's points of view and to address barriers that might come up, along with helping to negotiate to get an agreement.

Too many times, in these types of meetings the chair does all the talking, especially in employee reviews. The meeting turns into more of, "This is the way it's going to be," and the attendees have no input. For something that is very personal such as a review, this can be devastating to morale. There are two reasons that this occurs. The first is because the manager is a micromanager and it's their way or the highway. These types are never going to change unless forced to. The other reason is because the manager is insecure with the material being presented. The defensive mechanism is to control the entire meeting by talking. New managers and managers delivering bad news tend to do this. By putting a feedback task in the agenda, it makes sure the other attendees have a chance to give input.

Meetings to Gather Information

The first couple of times a person chairs a meeting to gather information with a large group it can be very intimidating, but after some experience they are the most fun meetings to run. All the attendees have knowledge, and the chair needs to get it out of them. Many times the buzzword for these types of meetings are *discovery sessions, brainstorming,* or *deep dive sessions.* If conducted correctly, a lot of work can be accomplished in a short time. However, these types of meetings also require the most preparation and experience in running them. If run incorrectly, they can end up being a shouting match.

For a discovery session, some preresearch should be done on the attendees. It's a big help if there is knowledge on which individuals are open to change and which are not. It is necessary to understand which people have a strong personality and will try to sell their personal ideas instead of thinking as a team. By no means is it a requirement to know how everyone attending is going to act, but knowing this will help the chair be prepared if one of the attendees starts to resist the change being talked about or tries to control the meeting.

Tools are very important for these types of meetings since information is being gathered from the attendees. Notes are always taken, and they need to be written down on something like a flip chart, where people can rip sheets off and tape them on a bulletin board, white board, or wall. Sometimes in this type of meeting there might be a need to break the invitees into smaller groups, which can go to other locations to brainstorm. It's easy for these small groups to take some flip chart sheets to do their work on. Once done, they can bring them back to the regular meeting and present their material. Another benefit of using a flip chart is that when the meeting is over a person can take all the flip chart sheets back to their desk and slowly put together the meeting notes that will be sent out. White boards are okay, but when it fills up and runs out of room it can impede the knowledge brain dump that is occurring in the meeting. A couple of times I have seen people use a laptop computer with a screen projector. That does not work very well. The meeting went as fast as the one person interpreting what people were saying and then typing it. In other words, it went really slowly. Sometimes the simplest tools such paper and color markers are the best.

Another key tool is a scribe, who is someone who takes the general meeting notes. The chair person never takes the notes. The chair has to stay focused with the task of running the meeting. The scribe doesn't have to know too much about what is being talked about because if needed the attendees can tell the scribe word for word what needs to be written down. Almost anyone can be invited to the meeting to fulfill this role.

When the meeting is ready to begin, the chair must first perform these tasks:

- Introduce the people and their knowledge and responsibilities they represent.
- Review what the purpose of the meeting is and what goals or outcomes are trying to be reached by the end of the meeting.
- Discuss the tools that will be used to gather the information.
- Open the meeting up for discussion, which is where the past experiences come into play.

When the open discussion starts, the chair should not be worried that he or she does not understand everything being said in the meeting but only that everyone else understands. This sounds strange, but the role of the chair involves making sure everyone is participating and voicing their options and that the meeting is going forward with discovery of new information and ideas. When the meeting is over, at a slower pace the chair can review the general meeting notes and flip charts to understand everything. At that time, if any items are unclear the chair can ask individual people for clarification.

Chairs of these meetings must be on the lookout for people who dominate the meeting. If one person is allowed to take over, the other attendees will leave thinking, "Why were we even invited?" Meetings like these turn into one to two people doing all the talking and presenting their own personal views. It's a waste of time for everyone else to be there. The chair needs to make sure that most everyone participates in some form. To guarantee participation, one process that can be used is to place a check mark by each person's name on the attendee list as he or she talks. As the meeting progresses, it gives the chair a quick visual tool to see who has not participated yet. Asking people by name for input can help them to start to participate in meetings.

Attendees many times will present many barriers and obstacles. Chairs need to be prepared to handle these statements that can kill a good brainstorming session. Here are just a few:

- We tried that before.
- It costs too much.
- That's beyond our responsibility.
- It's too radical of a change.
- We don't have time.

- We are too small for it.
- We've never done that before.
- That's not our problem.
- Why change it? It's still working okay.
- We're not ready for that.
- It isn't in the budget.
- Top management will never go for it.
- Let's form a committee.

When these types of statements come up, the chair needs to address them, or else people will repeat them during the duration of the meeting. It's important to address them as soon as they come up so that such statements only get mentioned once. Doing this will keep everyone thinking of the possibilities and the meeting will be a constructive one. The chair could use the question, "Why do you believe that?" in response to these concerns, which should lead to an even better discussion.

In these sessions it is normal to have disagreements; they are good up to a point. They bring excitement, get everyone energized, and make everyone think about who is right and who might be wrong. At times though, it can become disruptive. If a disagreement escalates or does not seem to be working toward a conclusion, then the chair needs to step in quickly and decisively to take back the control of the meeting. It's as simple as speaking up and saying, "I see there are differences. Let's put this in the parking lot and move on." Then ask who wants and needs to be part of this later discussion.

Using a parking lot is another tool or process. It's nothing more than a special visual spot in the meeting room that items can be added to. These items include anything that is a distraction from accomplishing the meeting agenda. This could be disagreements that are not working toward a solution. It could be new topics or subjects that had not been planned on being discussed and because of that people have not had time to prepare or the right people are not in the meeting. It could be a topic that is going into a detailed discussion, which normally affects only a couple of people so the rest of the people in the meeting would be bored and would not participate in the conversation. Items that go into the parking lot are tasks that need to be addressed outside of the current meeting. Having said that, many times as soon as the meeting is over there can be a discussion on an item from the parking lot. That way the people not interested or required for the discussion can leave, while the people that are needed for the discussion are already there.

The parking lot can be put on anything. It can be on a white board or a flip chart sheet. Make a big label that says *parking lot* before the meeting begins. When explaining the purpose and rules of the meeting, also include how the parking lot is going to be used. Each item added to the parking lot should include the names of people that "want" and "need" to be involved with that item's discussion. In the meeting, ask the attendees for these names. Use their knowledge to help identify the best people to resolve the items in the parking lot.

Another skill that has proven invaluable is the ability to read body and language signals. This normally is not a part of companies' mainstream training and can be obtained by searching the Internet for books, seminars, and articles on the topic. Posture can communicate a lot, such as whether a person is thinking about the meeting's subject matter or about the wild weekend he or she had. If the person is slouching and has not been participating, they are probably not interested in what is happening. It is common for disinterested attendees to try to make themselves invisible by positioning their seat behind someone else, hoping the chair does not see them. They reason for hiding is that if the chair cannot see them they probably will not be called on. People who care about the subject will sit attentively and be visible. They might not necessary speak all the time, but by their posture and tone of voice it is evident that they are interested in what is being discussed. A person's response will also tell you if they have been listening. If they answer your question with, "Can you repeat the question?" or maybe answer the question with a question, then they probably have not been paying attention.

With the current technology, more and more people are dialing in remotely to meetings instead of physically attending them. This is good because people from many locations can communicate at once; however, it also introduces more distractions. With emails, internet, cell phone texting, chat sessions, etc. there are more distractions than ever to take a person's mind away during a meeting as they attend it remotely. If you called the meeting, the attendees are charging your department while they are doing these things. Because of the lack of visibility with teleconferencing meetings, it is critical to have a process that can keep track of who has attended the meeting and is participating versus those who do not. When you have 20 people attend a 1-hour meeting and only 5 are participating, that is 15 hours being charged to your department and you are getting nothing in return—which is a lot of waste occurring.

Chairs often make the mistake of believing that since they called the meeting they need to control it. As the chair of the meeting, don't be afraid to give up some control. If someone comes up with an idea, the best person to document it is the person who came up with it. Let the meeting attendees do the writing on the flip charts and white boards if they want to. When you hand the marker over to an attendee, you can see the participation level of the entire meeting increase because the level of ownership has now been raised when people can actually write their own statements and words. Empowerment is very powerful. Sometimes the smallest things that we take for granted can improve the outcome drastically.

Even though it might seem small, another item that can take away from the productivity of a discovery session meeting is where people sit. Normally, people from the same department or area like to sit together because they have the same point of views, interests, or friendship. This tends to lead to small whispering discussions, which are disruptive. The first method to control this noise is to do assigned seating. Even though most people hate this because they cannot sit by their friends, it's the easiest way to break up groups. Look at the attendee list to intermix the people. Split them up based on an area's responsibilities or even titles. A more complicated method involves setting breaks in the room. There will usually be core project team members at these meetings. Don't let all the core project members sit together; have them break up the room by sitting evenly apart instead. By breaking up the room they can help control all the disruptive side conversations that sometimes occurs between other attendees.

For a discovery session, one to two departments are primarily affected by the information being gathered. To get the best input, these people really need to open up. It's important to give them the feeling that they are running the meeting, which is most easily accomplished by where they sit. They need to sit in a position in which they will be facing where the information is going to be written down. Remember, the meeting is not about who runs it but about the content and action plan that comes from the meeting.

An infinite amount of smaller things can be done, but the key thing to remember in these type of sessions is empowerment to others. These people have been asked to freely give information on an idea, problem, or solution that is probably not theirs to begin with. Listen to them. As already stated, the chair should be concerned only with keeping the meeting moving forward and making sure everyone participates. It's like being the referee. If a discussion is going nowhere, put it in the parking lot. If a discussion is getting into fine details, put it in the parking lot. If a person is overparticipating and doing all the talking, cut them short by directing the conversation to someone else. If a person is not participating, find out if they really want to be there or not by simply asking them for their input.

As an example of this working, I was the chairperson a kickoff project meeting that dealt with introducing the new process of capturing additional data to be used in rating an insurance policy. Since it dealt with changing the premium to the insured, there were legal issues. There were also concerns with asking other areas of the company to increase their workload to enter the data. As I put together the list of who needed to attend, I was concerned about one group. The key person from this group had recently seen three other IT projects implemented into his department without being asked about final design or how it would be implemented. With this being the fourth project in less than a year, my expectation was that he would not be open to another IT project forced on him.

To address this concern, a couple of things were done. First, people from my core team were asked to come early to the meeting and were positioned to break up the room. Second, the seats looking at the white board and flip charts were reserved for the department expected to be resistant to the proposed change. In the beginning of the meeting, the department members were defensive as expected. But slowly they started to soften their point of view as the parking lot was used. The final barrier disappeared when they were given the color markers and were asked to put their action item in their own words on the flip chart. This simple act removed all barriers not only for this department but also for everyone else. For the next 3 hours everyone had the chance to add to the white board, flip charts, and parking lot. Very quickly the meeting attendees became a team working together.

As we came across things we didn't understand because we didn't have the correct SMEs present, we put them in the parking lot. Then we would call that person to see if they could come to the meeting immediately. In this open, empowering meeting, the new attendees quickly would open up and give us the information we were looking for. Even though the meeting was originally scheduled to last 3 hours, at the end of that time everyone wanted to continue. So for another 2 hours the meeting continued. At the end of the meeting we had identified all the issues, concerns, and gaps. A communication plan was in place regarding how and when these would be resolved. The high-level design was complete, along with a tentative time-line. So much information and so many decisions had been made in this 5-hour meeting that another large meeting was never needed for the project. The empowerment did not just end after the meeting. As the project progressed for the next 8 months, communication was regularly sent out to everyone, along with continually asking for feedback. The implementation and startup of the new business processes went extremely smoothly. The primary key to the overall success was that in the beginning of the project time was spent on the communication to ensure everyone had a chance to voice their concerns and issues. Very quickly, all people affected by the change became a team that was working toward a common goal.

In conclusion, to be successful in any type of meeting regarding communication there needs to be planning around the processes and methods that will be used. Most people make a big mistake when communicating because the only planning they do is to call the meeting with a topic to cover. They hope the outcome will be a productive meeting. Take the time and think about what needs to be communicated and the best method to do it. Clear, concise, accurate communication is necessary to bring about speedy and accurate change.

IMPROVING MANAGEMENT BEST PRACTICE DISCIPLINES

Understanding the disciplines of management is a very good start to being a good manager, but it's only a start. Nobody is perfect the first time they attempt something, including management skills. In order to get good at it, a person needs to make a continuous, dedicated effort.

All companies attempt to improve their manager skills with seminars and classes. But more could be done. Most companies in the same management level have the same job standards, objectives, and goals in the review process. However, each manager has a different knowledge, experience, system, and even duties. Some work in maintenance and others on projects. Instead of helping to develop managers in their unique environment with their unique management style, the review process is just a rubber stamp process based on how close they are performing to all other managers in the enterprise. Many objectives get ranked as not applicable (NA) or are given a middle of the road rating because the objectives on the review do not match what managers do and how they manage.

Companies could improve management across the entire enterprise using the concept of building blocks or a pyramid (so called because if you rotate an illustration 90 degrees (for example, see Figure 2.1) it looks like building blocks or a pyramid). In a physical structure, the pyramid shape is the sturdiest and most durable structure that exists. Even if a couple of

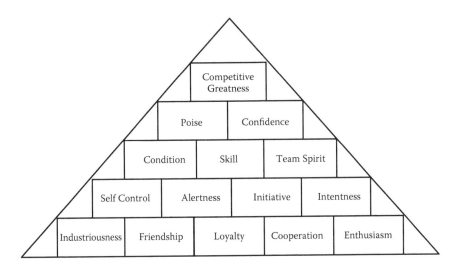

FIGURE 2.3
Pyramid of success.

blocks that make up the pyramid are weak, the structure will still stand. The pyramid concept has been around for decades. For example, consider John Wooden, regarded as the greatest basketball coach who ever lived. In a 12-year span from 1963 to 1975 while at University of California, Los Angeles (UCLA), his team won 10 national championships. His team had four undefeated seasons during that time, with 333 wins compared with 22 losses. Even more amazing is that Wooden never really stressed about winning but instead focused on the principles and fundamentals. In 1948 he developed what he called the Pyramid of Success (Figure 2.3). At the base are simple attributes a player needs. Each layer up the pyramid adds more complexity in terms of attributes. At the very top is competitive greatness, not winning. Wooden believed that the pinnacle was about having the player and team reach maximum personal performance. If that was accomplished, then winning mostly likely would occur. His pyramid challenged players to be the best they could be, no matter the competition. Another person that understood this was Jack Welch. In Chapter 7, when Jack Welch is discussed, one of his leadership points state:

> **"Put values first"**: "Don't focus too much on the numbers. Numbers aren't the vision; they are the products." Numbers come from the outcome of something. If the primary effort is put toward team building, sharing ideas, and improvement, the numbers will end up correct without much attention.

You can see this happening all the time when it comes to engagement scores in a company. All the effort is around the lowest engagement score by doing small things that are supposed to raise only that benchmark. Because of that there is little overall improvement when the engagement survey is given again.

To get away from improvement based on numbers and to work on improvement of values, the values first need to be defined. It's really not that hard to do. Going back to Figure 2.1, we have an example of defining the value of leadership. Defining a value starts out as vague intangible item, or what is called goal state. It's classified as intangible because it can't be measured. Someone told to improve leadership there is no single action statement that goes with it that can be measured. So to define what leadership is, goal state needs to be broken down into what are called outcomes, which identify specific areas that make up leadership. Still, though, they are classified as intangible because they are not specific actions a person can do. Under leadership, if a person is told to encourage the heart, it does not define a specific action a person can do.

It is important to mention at this point that if no specific action is defined then it can't be accurately measured. If someone is asked to measure leadership or encourage the heart, the results would be based on assumptions that certain things would go into those to make up the results. So each person asked to measure the intangible item would use a different set of criteria. If the results are not 100% accurate, then any attempt to improve the item will not be 100% accurate. More importantly, the next time results are asked for there will not be any true correlation between the two measuring times. Using intangible items to measure performance factors outside of a manager's control can have a serious affect on the final measurement. For example, consider a company having to lay off a lot of people because of a bad economy. If the two intangible items of leadership and encouragement are being measured, the performance measurement for every manager in the company is guaranteed to drop drastically. It did not matter that many of the managers probably worked and actually improved many of the action items related to leadership and encouragement.

To get more accurate results, outcomes need to be broken down further into tools and inputs. These are action items that a person can do that are fairly simple. From Figure 2.1, if we look at the two items from "Encourages the Heart," the actions could be "Recognize individual contributions to the success of every project" and "Celebrate team accomplishments regularly." It's easy to put actions around them that a single person can accomplish. Because of this and because the actions can be defined, these are called tangible items at the tools and inputs level. More importantly, they can be measured. For "Celebrate team accomplishments regularly," a report could be created that shows how many times this was done and for what action the team did. In the situation of the company having to lay off workers because of a bad economy, different results are now generated. The measurement is based on the action task of did the manager "celebrate team accomplishment regularly." It no longer has anything to do with the economy, which is outside of the manager's control. So by using tangible items there is a much truer measurement of what is occurring. As you read all 10 of the tools and inputs in Figure 2.1, you can probably think of actions and measurements that can be done around each one of them. If you can define something, then you can measure it. If you can measure it, then you can compare it. If you can compare it, then you can improve it.

For individual improvement, the tools and inputs level is where items are selected that are unique to people's personalities, the department in which they work, and the type of work they do. A company could create a list of 100 items for each outcome in the tools and inputs section. Persons can then select 10 or so items that reflect the type of work they do along with their personality. By having unique tools and inputs that are aligned with the manager's output, then a true measurement can occur of their improvement over time. This also makes management consistent throughout the enterprise. If every manager in a large enterprise has the same goal state and outcomes, they will work better together as a team, which ultimately leads to leadership improvement across the organization. This is a key if a company wants to transform itself into a market leader.

The pyramid concept can be applied for most disciplines that make up management best practices. Your company probably has nothing like this, but to get ahead of everyone else you can easily create one. Start out with each of the six disciplines being a goal state. Then create your own personal outcomes for each goal state. After that, create a personal tools and inputs for each outcome. To help with defining this, you can get input from your manager, along with any peers and subordinates. Once the pyramid is built, the majority of the items should always stay the same throughout your career. The only modifications should be additions to the outcomes and tools and inputs as knowledge and skills increase and different job titles are obtained. Even if you move to a different division or company, your personal management style will probably change only slightly. The tools and inputs item of "celebrate team accomplishment regularly" will be the same no matter what management level or company you are in.

So do you try to improve every tangible tools and inputs item at once? You can, but there would be little improvement over time. When I started in management I was trained to pick only two to three items that are the weakest and need to be improved, then spend the next 6 months trying to improve only those items. If you improve your weakest attribute first, the positive results will be larger. I call it the log chain concept:

> Each link of a log chain except for two can handle 2,000 lbs. One of these two links can handle only 500 lbs., and the other can handle only 1,000 lbs. So the load capacity that can be pulled with the log chain is what the weakest link can handle, or 500 lbs. Even if some of the strongest links that can handle 2,000 lbs. are replaced with ones that can handle 3,000 lbs., the weight capacity of the log chain is still only 500 lbs. But what happens when the link that can handle only 500 lbs. is replaced with a link that can handle 2,000 lbs.? The log chain's capacity increases to the next weakest link, which is 1,000 lbs. This is an increase of 100% by replacing just one link. And if the next weakest link can be identified and replaced, the log chain capacity becomes 2,000 lbs. So by replacing just the two weakest links, the log chain capability has increased fourfold.

Much is the same with skills. Most people don't want to improve on their weaknesses. Instead, they try to hide them by thinking that if they improve their good skills no one will notice the weak ones. In fact, it's just the opposite. If a person is weak in decision making or communication, no matter what other areas they improve other people will see little or no improvement. They will see only that the weakest skill has not changed. We have a tendency to view others not by their strengths but instead by their weaknesses.

A first step in improving performance is to do an honest self-assessment. Again, you need to ask for input from others to do this. As much as we like ourselves, we really need unbiased input. People with whom we have had past experiences can compare what we have done with what they expect from us. Even though it's a frightful task to ask people to be brutally honest, it is required if you are serious about improvement. When asking for feedback, check with people with different reporting levels from you. Someone you report to will have a different point of view from one of your subordinates. You should have input from at least one person above you, one at the same level, and one person at a level below. This is called 360 degree review, which translates into everyone around you.

Identify the two or three weakest traits when all the feedback has come back. The goal is to take the worst weaknesses and make them into the greatest strengths. If you try to do more than this, your effort becomes dilated, and people will see little change. Much like the log chain concept, by working on improving the weakest skills first you will get a greater return. Not only will you see the difference, but so will others. When you improve the weakest items so that they become your strongest skills, then you will probably never have to spent time to fix any of these skills ever again.

Once you have identified a few weaknesses to work on, plan on how to improve each item. This can be done through training, reading books, and behavior changes. Identify simple actions or tasks that can be done on a regular basis to improve the weaknesses. Many times, just being made aware of something and then working on it every possible moment is enough to turn a weak skill into a strong one.

The last step is executing the improvement plan into everyday work and behavior. Visibility and a simple nontechnical technique is a key here. One method is on the side of your computer monitor, list the weaknesses, along with the simple tasks you plan to do to improve them. Or, if you go to a lot of meetings, take a sheet of paper or a label with the items and tasks. If you have a company phone, tape to the back side the task and items. If a weakness is worked on every chance it might come into play in the work day, at some point it will become second nature of always trying to improve it. As time goes by the weakness no longer exists. What has occurred is the behavior pattern gets changed so that without even thinking about it, you will continue to try and improve an early weaknesses, even when they are no longer the weakest items. If it's a complex improvement task that is created or you work only part time on improvement, these efforts do very little to permanently change behavior. What occurs is that you lose interest because of the complexity or because more important things come up that need to be worked on. In a very short time you are back to where you started from, with the same weaknesses.

After working on improving the weaknesses for about 6 months, they need to be reevaluated. Are they still the weakest? If these are no longer your weaknesses, revisit the process to identify the new ones. If a few of the items are still your weakest, then the action steps to improve them did not work. Get more feedback and change the improvement process. Work on the weakness again for 6 months and then reevaluate. Repeat this process, working on your weakest skills. In quality concepts this is called *continuous improvement*. This will be covered in more detail in Chapter 13.

Personal improvement is not a requirement in most companies because the review process works from the top down. Top management sets objectives and improvement items and then passes them down to the next level of managers, who in turn adjust these to fit their situation and then pass them down to the next level of managers and so on until they reach the front-line workers. There is no feedback process in place to go from the bottom to the top. This method allows and actually breeds cave dwellers and fence sitters in that they don't have to make any effort to improve and can still retain their jobs. They know they only have to keep their superior happy. The only feedback process from bottom to top in most companies is the annual engagement survey. These tend to be ineffective because instead of making it a daily effort to improve, cave dwellers and fence sitters only attempt or appear to work on improvement a month before the engagement is given. Once the engagement survey is given, they are allowed to quickly slide back into their old behavior until a month before the next year's engagement survey is given.

To ensure that this does not happen, all subordinates who directly report to a manager should get together as a team and decide one to two objectives they feel their manager needs to work on for the coming year. It is very beneficial if the company has a chart of outcomes and tools and inputs. Think of it as a team being proactive versus reactive. Most reviews are reactive in that they deal with actions that did or did not happen in the prior year. In contrast, this process is proactive, in that it asks for actions to happen in the future. Since the entire team is setting the objectives, no single person who dislikes his or her manager will have much influence over which objectives are selected. This process allows a team's manager supervisor firsthand information on what the team thinks their manager needs to improve upon. At the end of the year, it is recommended that subordinates not comment as to whether their manager improved on the objectives. Because of the reporting structure, a subordinate should never be put into this spot with their manager. Besides, the decision as to whether a manager improved is the sole responsibility of the manager's supervisor.

This simple process puts accountability and traceability into the review process. Favoritism is removed because of visibility. If the manager's subordinates for 2 years in a row requests the same improvement objectives, that would be a visible sign that what the manager is doing is not working or that he or she is not trying. This should trigger the manager's superior to step in and help the manager with improvement. If in the third year subordinates ask for the same improvement objectives from their manager, the issue needs to be escalated even higher, possibly to upper management or human resources, because sometimes the issue is not with the manager but with the manager's supervisor. With traceability and accountability in the review process, the manager's superior has an incentive to make sure their manager is improving. When there are issues the superior would be required to work not only with their manager but also with the manager's subordinates to understand what truly is happening. It's a win–win situation that virtually eliminates the cave dweller managers, along with making the fence sitter managers have to do something to improve.

The process does very little to help performing or good managers. They are probably already using an informal process similar to this. Good managers almost always have open communication with their team. When the team suggests things the manager needs to improve on, they work on it together to make sure some type of improvement happens.

There are no quick fixes for this. The process takes at least a year before a comparison can be done from the prior year's improvement objectives set by the team and what was decided this year's improvement objectives are to be. The process is designed to last a long time, because it is creating a permanent process versus just having another campaign or initiative that fades over time. You can think of this process as a transformation plan to get all members of management in an organization working on personal improvement, which is very similar to what the plans and processes of great leaders like Dr. Deming and Jack Welch did.

BAD MANAGEMENT PRACTICES

This chapter has covered the characteristics of a good manager, so now let's discuss just a few of the many traits of a bad manager. We have all seen the managers who seem to be ineffective or who don't seem to care. Many of these managers firmly believe that since they have a title everyone is supposed to follow what they say word for word. The following are examples of bad management. You have probably already seen some of these personally.

When one person became a manager for the first time, he was asked how he tended to manage. He shared that when he was talking to people not on his team, he was going to portray his staff members' strengths as their weaknesses and their weaknesses as their strengths. He explained that if someone is actually really good at something, such as working with people, outside of the team he would say that this person does not work well with others. If someone was bad at analyzing, the manager would tell people not on his team that this person was the best analyzer on the team. When asked why he would misrepresent his staff members' skills and sabotage their careers, he gave a couple of reasons. The longer the staff stayed, he said, the easier his job became. He could delegate more of his duties and responsibilities to the experienced members on the team. In addition, he said that there were only a certain number of positions above his, and by sabotaging the careers of his staff members who had the potential of advancing up the corporate ladder it gave him a better chance of getting promoted to the next level.

Another manager once explained that when she didn't understand something in a meeting, she made a statement and then defended it. Even though there was no reason or logic behind her statement, she would argue aggressively that her view was the right one. She even used her title as leverage to sell her point of view. Many times people just gave up arguing and went along with what she was saying. By not willing to listen she was causing a major amount of time being spent on an option that was probably not the best one—even it if worked. The best solutions are continuously arrived at by using the knowledge and input from the entire group. The manager was lacking the negotiation discipline.

I have seen some creative ways for managers to waste time. One manager was always on the phone. When I walked by his office, he always had his phone headpiece on, and once in awhile he would say something. One day I noticed that none of the lights on his phone were lit. The manager was pretending to have phone conversations so that his staff members would not bother him. Even if a staff member stood beside his desk waiting for an opening to discuss something important, the manager would never acknowledge them. Naturally, the manager was ineffective at his job, but he somehow lasted almost 3 years in the position before finally leaving to be a manager at another company.

Another manager was better known as the keeper of the defects. Remember that earlier in the chapter I discussed "fixing the disease, not just the symptoms"? Instead of working to permanently fix the defect (disease), this manager wanted to temporarily fix the problem so that the defect would happen over and over. Even though she knew how to permanently fix the problem, she fixed only the symptoms. When asked why, she said that it made it her think she was valuable because she was the SME for fixing the problem each time. She felt powerful in that each time this same error occurred people would come to her to fix the symptoms. Naturally, with this process resources were tied up fixing the symptom of the defect each time. As more and more new defects came up, more and more resources got pulled into maintenance to fix these new defects because few of the old defects were being permanently closed. And where did the additional resources come from? They were moved from the group that was working on the project. On the project side there were never enough resources because of the drain of fixing the symptoms of the defects. This manager's group became known for not being very effective and efficient. Even when additional staff members were added to do the project work not getting done, they quickly got absorbed with fixing the defect.

SUMMARY

At this point we have covered all the disciplines that make up management best practices: leadership, negotiation, problem solving, decision making, ability to influence the organization, and communication. Each discipline has been explained, and the pyramid process was presented to show how a user can define what each discipline means personally.

Improvement begins with a true self-assessment of a person's strengths and weaknesses in terms of these disciplines. Even though it's fun and rewarding to work on improving strengths, it's when the weaknesses improve that performance improves greatly. Just think of the log chain: When the weaker links are replaced, the capability of the overall chain increases drastically. Most companies and people look at improvement as needing to be done only over a certain period of time, such as during periods when there are more defects than normal or when the company is doing poorly. But the truth is that every day through an entire career people need to continue to improve no matter how poorly or great things are going. The process to accomplish this must be simple and can be applied easily every possible chance in everyday work. The goal is to change people's behavior so that subconscious improvement continually happens for the item.

Most companies use only the annual review process for improvement, even though it is not geared for personal development related to persons and the specific type of work they do. Today's workers make the mistake of basing their need for improvement around results from the company's formal review process and training classes they are required to attend. Very few workers take it upon themselves to identify and fix their weaknesses, yet alone take ownership of their own development and improvement plan. Instead they depend solely on the company to do these things. When people do not take the initiative toward self-improvement and the next promotion or job opens up, there is nothing to distinguish them from all the other candidates. People with high potential may never realize what they can do in both career and life because they rely on others to tell them when and what they need to improve upon.

3

Five Disciplines of a Learning Organization

The management best practice disciplines explain what makes up management. Over time, these skills will improve if they are worked on. However, to speed up the learning curve, it is necessary to change how we tend to think. Think of it as another piece of the puzzle that helps us reach the goal faster.

In the early 1990s, I came across an article that left a lasting impression—for almost 20 years I have had a note on my desk explaining the process. Doing research, I was able to find out that the information had come from a book called *The Fifth Discipline* (Senge, 1990). The five disciplines of the learning organization discussed in the article are:

1. Team learning: The ability of group members to suspend their assumption and freely think together. That involves dialogue in the true meaning of the word, as a flow of meaning. It means going beyond personal defensiveness and presenting ideas openly, even when going out on a limb.
2. Building shared vision: If the members of a group truly share their pictures of the future, if they are excited about what they are creating together, then they will act out of inner motivation and will voluntarily go out of their way to contribute.
3. Mental models: The ability to separate the map from the territory. Being able to identify previously hidden models or assumptions. Bringing them out in the open and working with them. Going beyond simply holding onto one's belief is obsolete. Needing to examine which models one is actually operating on.
4. Personal mastery: On a personal basis, working on developing one's vision, one's abilities, one's focus of energy. A spiritual inner drive to pursue mastery, to be the best that one can be.

5. Systems thinking: The ability and practice of consistency examining the whole system, rather than just trying to fix isolated problems. This discipline integrates the other 4 into one coherent effort.

In the business world everyone is part of at least one—and possibly more—group or team. A person could be a member of two projects teams, along with the normal team they report to. Even chief information officers (CIOs) work with several teams to get information and set direction. Because everyone works in a team of some type and they have a dependency on others, for productivity the first rule should be that people need to think of the team first and themselves second. The five disciplines' first two disciplines are team building and building shared vision. The key part of team building is communication and involves not only presenting ideas but also listening to others' ideas, no matter how strange or different. Good business teams use the knowledge and skills of everyone on the team to excel. Teams that perform poorly rarely have open communication within the group. Instead, one or two people dictate to the rest of the team. A by-product of team building and open communication is building a shared vision. Team members slowly start to change their viewpoints to match others. The benefits of doing this will be covered in depth later in Chapter 11 when high-performance teams are covered.

The first two disciplines cover working in a team, and the next two—mental models and personal mastery—cover self-improvement. Individuals must continuously question their knowledge and beliefs because the teams they are involved with are always changing and evolving. Other team members are exposed to learning different things, and new people routinely become part of a team. Individuals' jobs change slowly, day by day, so there is no guarantee that what worked yesterday will work today. People must continuously question their beliefs and viewpoints to see if they match their current working situation. If there is a difference between the two, then modifications need to occur so that they do match. This is where personal mastery comes in. Personal mastery is the drive to be the best. Instead of being complacent, it's about challenging one's own knowledge, beliefs, and viewpoints. Every day we all have the possibility to learn more. Some of us seize this opportunity, whereas others make no effort at all. The latter assume that what they have learned in the past is good enough to carry them into the future. These are the fence sitters and cave dwellers in the organization.

The last discipline deals with system thinking. It's the ability to take a step back and look at the bigger picture instead of focusing solely on the problem, think outside the box. Too many times, people have only tunnel vision when thinking of solutions or problem solving and don't see everything that is being affected, so the best solution for the situation is never found. This encompasses using concepts and practices from the first 4 disciplines. Later in Chapter 15, "Lean Management," the benefits of looking at the whole picture will be covered again.

The five disciplines of system thinking can also be used in real life, away from work. Think of all the individuals and groups you interactive with outside of the workplace, including your family. How do you interact with these people and under what principles? Do you try to think openly, or do you defend your point of view? Do you try to get better in your relationships, or do you just take them for granted? These values or disciplines will help guide you through life.

4

The Effects of Management on Subordinates

POINTS ON HUMAN BEHAVIOR

- The strongest human need is to be acknowledged as a valuable person.
- People make decisions and take action for their reasons, not yours.
- Whatever people believe strongly becomes their reality. People act on their perceptions.
- We have no power to force others to change. Communication effectiveness is a product of our ability to reach out to others, not having them reach out to us.
- Under stress, people revert to using the R-Complex (reptilian) brain: territorial, ritualistic, imitative, deceptive.
- Learning is a holistic process: people need to understand the why before they can pick up the details.

Most managers never think about the effects that they have on their subordinates. In reality a manager affects their subordinates 24 hours a day, 7 days a week, and 52 weeks a year. A manager's actions, or lack of actions, directly influences whether his or her employees go home happy or miserable. Once home, they might either play with their kids and be in a happy mood or have a couple of drinks and do nothing because they had a miserable day. Many managers, however, believe they have no impact on subordinates after the workers leave the office for the day. They don't take into account the personal side of their subordinates away from work. These managers are concerned only about themselves and usually don't realize much success because they earn little respect and loyalty from their staff.

In Chapter 5, the book will cover management duties and responsibilities in the different levels in an organization. For right now, understand that front-line management and workers are the only ones that actually do the execution of work in companies. Because of this, the working relationship between these two must be very strong, probably more than any other two different levels in an organization. When the link between two lower levels is strong, engagement, productivity, and quality are high on these teams.

Because the first level is where the work is executed, formal processes need to be established to help strengthen the link between these two levels. The first way to do this is to strengthen communication between front-line management and the subordinates that report to them. Communication is not just a weekly meeting with the entire group. Managers need to go out on the floor and actually talk to the individuals about their job performance, career, and personal life. The majority of managers don't do this. Instead, many of them talk to someone on their team personally only during the formal semiannual or annual review process. Even though they will say they are meeting weekly or biweekly with their team, a general team meeting is not the place to discuss an individual's personal and career goals.

To encourage good communication, at least once every 2 weeks managers should try to have a conversation with each staff member individually. It could be only 5 minutes and can occur at the staff member's desk. After each conversation, they should write down some quick notes on what was discussed during the conversation, such things as what they accomplished recently, what skills need to be improved, and what actions were requested of them by the manager. These notes can then be categorized into some type of filing system for each team member, which could be as simple as a separate folder for each member. At the end of each week, managers can do a quick check of the personal folders to see if they talked to each team member within the last 2 weeks. By no means is it a requirement to always talk to everyone every 2 weeks. If someone was missed during the 2-week time frame, it should be a priority to touch base with them the following week.

Besides making sure beneficial communication is occurring, this process is extremely valuable for the semiannual and yearly review process. For the annual review, if this process was followed every 2 weeks, there should be 26 different notes that will give an accurate biweekly status of what happened and what was asked of each employee. It contains information for the entire year of all the accomplishments and when good performance was noticed and when bad performance was noted and discussed. Most managers for a review wait until the last second and try to piece together what each employee did for the entire year. Usually, only the latest things the employee did gets reported. Major work accomplishments and excellent behavior that happened 10 months ago seldom get mentioned in the annual review. Therefore, workers will wait until 3–4 months before the review to go above and beyond their normal work performance because they know they will not be recognized for earlier efforts in that year's time frame.

As an employee, would you prefer a review process in which you had no idea what was going to be discussed, with many of your accomplishments missed because they happened early during the annual review period, or one in which you knew everything that would be discussed ahead of time and felt assured that none of your accomplishments over the past year would be missed? Most of us have had the first type of review, with not knowing what was on it and with key accomplishments missing. When this happens, the review becomes meaningless because it is only partially accurate. If management wants continuous improvement though the entire year, then there needs to be a process to routinely check performance of each employee. Annual or semiannual reviews do very little to help continuous improvement occur because 6 months and 12 months is too long of a gap between checkups to see whether improvement is occurring.

It's easy within a company to find areas where managers are not connected with their front-line employees. In these areas, the employees think that their annual review is a just a necessary evil process that occurs once a year that they need to participate in. Unless there is something really bad in the review, these employees will accept what was written (whether it's true or not) just to get it over with. Since these managers only annually or semiannually make an attempt to understand what their employees are doing and their personal needs, the entire review process becomes a rubber stamp process, with no benefits to the employees or to the company.

If we look at the different types of managers (performers, fence sitters and cave dwellers), the performer managers probably already do something routinely outside of the review process to regularly capture what their employees are doing. The other type of managers, however, will resist a process like this. The most common argument managers make against meeting with employees every couple of weeks is that they don't have the time. Broken down, though, 26 meetings that take only about 5 minutes each take a total of 2 hours and 10 minutes a year to capture the information. With all this information available, the actual review can be created in under an hour for each employee. So in just over 3 hours managers can create an accurate, precise review of what their employees did for the entire year. The other process, of managers waiting until the review to start to gathering information on employees, normally takes well over 4 hours. Using the latter process, to find out what their people did for the year managers have to comb through e-mails, status reports, and many other types of documentation, which is all very time consuming. More importantly, the information is seldom 100% indicative of what employees did for the entire year because some things are missing.

With good communication, managers can gain a true understanding of what their employees want out of their job at any given time. Some people at certain times in their life might want to be promoted as fast as possible, whereas others just want to stay in the same job. Both types are required for a successful company. Before technology played a big part in the insurance industry, some employees spent all day long folding the insurance printout into thirds and stuffing it into a window envelope. Many of these employees did this for over 20 years. When we replaced these people with automation, I talked to several and thought they would really be excited that they no longer had to do that simple boring task day in and day out and could be moved to a more challenging position. Every one of them said they would be sad, and many took early retirement instead of moving to another position that would pay more and would challenge them.

Being a young manager, my assumption was that everyone was as eager as I was to move up the corporate ladder. I know some did not want to move very fast, but I never realized that some people do not want to move even one rung up the ladder. Even though these employees who folded the insurance printout had no intention of climbing the corporate ladder, they had the greatest pride in their quality and the speed of work they did. To them it was not about promotions but instead about the satisfaction they got from doing high-quality work day in and day out. Many people would prefer to learn one task and do that for the next 20 years. Because they have done the same thing over and over for years, the quality and speed of their work can never be matched. So what do many managers do many times? Instead of learning what their employees want, which is no change, the managers give these employees more responsibilities and different duties without their input, which results in dissatisfied employees who do not like the company or the manager for whom they work.

Managers might say they don't want people who are not interested in being aggressive and career minded. Then again, who are the first ones who will leave the team on their way up the corporate ladder, and who stays? Now you might say you want only people who don't want to climb the corporate ladder so that everyone stays. But then there is the problem of nobody on the team wanting to be aggressive for new functionality, new processes, and continuous improvement. In this scenario, complacency can easily set in on the entire group. What is needed is a mix of people in terms of career goals: some who want to climb the corporate ladder, and some who don't. Only then can there be stability and freshness in the team. In Chapter 11, "High-Performance Teams," this topic will be covered in detail. For now, just understand that diversity in a team can increase the overall performance of the team.

Another factor that all workers, especially front-line workers, are interested in is their job security. It's not whether they have a job, but instead that the worker knows what they will be working on for the next year. Knowing this they can plan and if needed get training related to the work they will be doing. Not every small task needs to be defined in advance. Everyone knows that future assignments can change over time in line with priorities. But on any given day employees should have a general understanding of what their "possible" work will be for the next 12 months. Earlier it was mentioned about building a working relationship between front line worker and the front-line manager. Longer term planning for a subordinate helps build that relationship.

Some simple tools to display work assignments and priorities for individuals are spreadsheets and white boards. These can be reviewed with the team on a routine basis. In project management it's become standard practice to do this, but in maintenance and small project groups it's still lacking. It should not be a secret what everyone else is going to work on in the future. Team members tend to help one another much more when everyone knows all the work assignments. Many times team members will give advice or just confirm that others are on the right path. Many minds working on something is much better than just one mind. When the work assignments are posted for everyone to see, it becomes a team-building activity and allows the team to work together better with less effort.

When managers try to do team building by taking them out for lunch or drinks after work, this translates into a slight to no increase in overall team performance. How people act at work in their daily job is different from at lunch, and it's definitely different from after a few drinks after work. Better results in team building can be achieved through work-related activities in which the entire team can participate and work together.

Up to this point the discussion has been about processes and procedures that can be used to help build a working relationship between the lower levels in a company. Another factor that strengthens this link is when managers understand how employees work and their capabilities. Everyone does not work the same. Some people perform well at the outset of something, but near the end of the task or project their performance drops. Others routinely need help in getting something started, but once they get going they perform well through the rest of the phases. During these performance drops employees experience stress because they subconsciously know they are not performing as they want to. Even the most knowledgeable staff members do not realize that they routinely perform at different levels depending on the phase or type of tasks they are doing. Giving employees feedback as to why and when their performance is dropping at specific times can help reduce their stress level and can allow them to improve on a specific point.

Another factor is knowing how many tasks employees can handle at one time. Some can comfortably handle working on four or five at a time, while others can only handle one or two. It's important to know how many a person can handle because if more tasks are assigned than what the person believes they can handle, they will get defensive because he believes he cannot get everything done. Normally, the person shifts into a slower mode just to prove it. So a manager needs to first learn from their employees what they believe are their limits on the number of tasks they can work on at once. Then only by talking, coaching, and challenging them with one more task than what they think they can do will managers and employees understand their capabilities.

Managers are by no means expected to do everything listed in this chapter for every employee, but something needs to be done. Instead of managing "tasks" first, managers need to manage "people" first. This can easily be done by taking the time on a regular basis (not semiannually or annually) to understand each employee to rule out the potential for low engagement, late delivery, and bad quality, which all drive up costs. One of the primary keys to building a high-performance team (which will be discussed in Chapter 11) is understanding the beliefs, viewpoints, and capabilities of each team member, which can be done only by getting personal with one another. Without doing this a department or team normally will perform only average or below average, rarely above average.

5

Management Types

So far we have covered the six disciplines that factor into being a successful manager: leadership, negotiation, problem solving, decision making, ability to influence, and commuication. New managers have low skills and knowledge in most of these, but they can still be very successful if they are assigned the right type and level of work. This chapter discusses matching the type of work with managers' knowledge and skills.

As long as the work is simple, all types of managers can consistently be successful with low to average skills in most of the disciplines. Even someone who is a fence sitter, micromanager, or cave dweller type can still be successful. Only managers who are exposed to complex duties, responsibilities, and many unknowns are required to have increased knowledge and skills in all the disciplines. Think of it as a stress test. If managers do not have the proper knowledge for a certain level of job complexity, failure is most likely to occur.

Looking at the different knowledge levels of managers, lowest level is anyone who is in this role for the first time. Only by assigning simple management duties and tasks can first-time managers consistently be successful. Over time, if they are given the opportunity to handle more complex tasks and duties, then they have a chance of increasing their management disciplines skills. An experienced manager, however, who has been assigned only simple tasks for years might never attain high skill levels in all the disciplines. To many times managers are promoted or moved into new complex duties and positions just because they have been in the company for a long time. Often they feel that they deserve better and post for jobs they cannot succeed in because of lack of skill level. This is called rising to a level of incompetency.

If a project starts to fail, the best person to realize it and take corrective actions is a manager with proper skills and experiences for that level of work being done. One company I worked for even delayed starting projects until the right skilled manager was available and could be assigned. The company realized that without someone who could make corrective actions when things started to go bad on a large project the problem could grow to a devastating proportion. In terms directly related to the devastation, there would be additional cost, late delivery, bad quality, and additional resources needing to be added. Expanding on some of the adverse affects:

- When a project goes bad, normally the subject matter experts (SMEs) in the organization are always pulled into the project to get things back on track. Because they are the best, normally they are already working on a high-priority project. Being pulled into another project slows down or even sometimes stops the high-priority projects they have been working on.
- Usually the SMEs will try to keep both projects on their timelines. The only way to do that is to work overtime hours. This leads to burn-out if the process continuously repeats for them, which normally it does.
- If the deadline is missed, then resources have to stay on the project instead of being released to start on the next project. The next projects that have been promised with a delivery date cannot start on time because of lack of resources. So future projects will miss their delivery dates because prior projects are late in releasing resources.
- The customers for whom the changes are being done lose trust because of the cost overruns and failure to deliver on time.

We always plan for what can be called the happy path. In other words, everything fits and works out perfectly. But this rarely happens. What management needs to prepare for is when the sad path happens, or when things go wrong. When assignments are given, management needs to be proactive and ask the question if the correct people and the correct project structure are in place for if and when things start to go wrong. If management does not address this, then the persons who get the assignment needs to. They do not have to turn down the assignment, but they need to ask for a mentor or support system in the beginning. Many front-line managers with the potential to be very good have been fired early in their career because they were assigned to a project that was over their heads.

In the business world there are countless types of managers in the many different levels and types of businesses and departments. Up to this point much of the information covered in this book could apply to most all types of management in any line of business, but the goal from this point on is to concentrate specifically on the different levels of information technology (IT) front-line management. The manager types covered here are a classification of the different front-line IT management and are meant to serve as core types that can be translated to other environments.

MANAGER OF MAINTENANCE WORK

This is a good position for someone just coming into management. A fence sitter could also be successful here. To understand this, we need to look at the work and the people that take up the 360 degree around this position, starting with the most important people first: the subordinates. Unless a team consists of all new employees, the subordinates of this department really don't need too much help when it comes to daily work, maintenance items, and small projects. Most work requests they get assigned are simple changes that they have probably done many times before. Just the manager communicating the changes to the subordinates and having them interpret, develop, and implement the changes is the best way to ensure success. Doing this builds trust between the manager and the team, allows people to feel wanted and empowered, and keeps the manager from becoming classified as a micromanager. For this level of work, it's very easy to overmanage people. Trust your people. One of the management points from chief executive officer of General Electric Jack Welch in Chapter 7 is "Managers muddle things; leaders inspire." Thus, "managing less is managing better."

First-time managers need to spend time learning their new human resource duties, which involve not just giving semiannual reviews but also understanding employees' needs in their current job as well as in their career and their life. If time is spent doing this, the payback is huge in terms of loyalty and dedication from their subordinates for years to come.

First-time managers who come from within the organization already know the company's culture and probably already have a social network of people in place. But when they move up one level in the organization, the viewpoint, culture, duties, and responsibilities change slightly. Understanding the company's culture and expanding the social network at this new level are key essentials to how successful they will be. The old network of people still needs to stay in place even in the new position.

These types of managers have the most dramatic change in duties. When they were front-line workers they were concerned only about their small area of duties and responsibilities to execute the work. As managers they are now responsible for others who carry out the work. Most first-time managers have issues separating their old duties, which were very hands-on and task oriented, from their new manager role, which is mostly hands-off and involves trusting others to do the work needed to execute change. These managers need to move from managing the task to managing the people who do the task. The managers who develop quickly are the ones who learn to trust their people and take a hands-off approach.

Human nature is for people to take the safe road. Most people learn enough to do a good job and then try to get work assigned that is safe to do with their knowledge. Because of this, a manager needs to always be looking to expand their subordinates' capabilities and knowledge. By no means are subordinates thrown into the deep end of the pool, which translates into giving them a task that they cannot complete with their current knowledge. Instead, subordinates need to slowly evolve. They need to be given challenging work that slowly expands their skills. Most people—even those who say they would prefer to do the same thing for the rest of their careers—don't mind once in awhile trying to expand their capabilities. But they need to have some type of support system in place in case there are problems. In a swimming pool, with a lifeguard on duty novice swimmers are willing to take chances. They jump off the diving board and play in the deep end knowing that if they get into trouble the lifeguard will help them. Subordinates need such a feeling of safety and security.

Managers of maintenance also need to interact with other front-line managers at the same level. The new managers can go to other managers when dealing with unfamiliar processes and procedures within the organization. They can also learn a lot by observing other team's outcomes. If they see another team consistently has turnover, they should then take the time to understand why. One team I know of still performed very well, but few people stayed over 2 years in the group. Their manager was very good at training new people, but the training never stopped. Because of trust issues, the manager never really let anyone do anything on their own without looking over their shoulder. So people would transfer out of this group after so long because they wanted to work in an environment of trust. Another manager rarely had any turnover. But when he did it seemed as though he would go through two or three different new people before someone would end up staying. The manager trusted everyone but did little training. From day one, the new people learned by themselves via on-the-job training (OJT) with almost no support. If in the first couple of years they did not make a major mistake to get fired and they took the initiative to learn the job by going to others on the team, then they tended to not leave the group. Some common pitfalls can be avoided and a lot can be learned by talking and watching other managers and their teams.

The only expectation upper management has for front-line managers responsible for maintenance is that they generate the necessary reports and perform their human resources duties on time. The daily work is small, and there is little expectation to make major changes that will save the company millions of dollars. Instead, the attitude is: Don't break anything; if something is broken, fix it really fast.

If we take a look at the level of competency in each of the six disciplines of management best practices (see Chapter 2), new managers could actually be marked low or average in many of the disciplines and still be successful. Certainly, being good at several of the disciplines would make their job easier, but it's not a requirement for the team to perform successful consistently. These managers actually have little influence in what is occurring. Their primary job is to keep things going, which can easily be accomplished if they trust their people and allow them to do their work.

TECHNICAL MANAGER

These managers are primarily responsible for quality and continuity of the changes going into the system. They must have both system and company knowledge because they will need to negotiate what changes are best for the system and company in both the short term and the long term. Instead of dealing with the items the company has defined in detail, technical managers work at the other end of the spectrum, taking a business vision or idea involving mostly unknowns and making it into a reality. Most of their work involves using the project structure of design, approval, resource allocation, development, training, testing, and implementation. With working with mostly unknowns at the start of the project there is larger risk of failure. Bad requirements, bad design, wrong resources assigned to work on the project, and impossible timelines are just a few of the items that can cause a project to fail. Technical managers must manage these obstacles so that the project can succeed.

Another thing to be managed is the continuous training throughout the project phases. The knowledge and skills needed for the analyzing phase are different from what is needed for the design phase and the development phase. People's roles and responsibilities change from project phase to phase. In a linear project process, many project members come on board for a few phases and then leave before the project finishes.

Looking at the entire project process, business partners are the primary source of input in the first project phases of initiate and analyzing. In the later project phases of design, development, and implementation, the technical staff members are the key resources. For most projects, business partners requesting the change start the project and then leave. They help set the vision, direction, or goal, and that is all that is required from them. It's up to others to execute the project. To help analyze and define the fine details around the change, on the business side there are business analysts, and on the technical side there are system analysts, technical leads, developers, and maybe an IT architect. When the project gets ready to start development is when the developers take over to build the change. Besides these people, another person is normally solely responsible for running the project, which is different from leading it. A technical manager leads the project; a project manager (covered in the next section) is responsible for running it.

With so many people coming and going, someone who understands the systems and company needs to manage and monitor the continuous training—especially when the technical staff start to come on board for the project in later phases. The best person to manage and, often, give this training is someone technical and with management experience. If a new person just assigned is not grasping the work that needs to be done or does not have the skill level to do it, these managers normally can see these deficiencies early and know how to take action steps to fix these deficiencies. They really are the only ones that can do it since they have the system knowledge, people knowledge, and title.

Technical managers are also the central persons handling the intangible items on a large project. They understand the processes involved to get things done. Their knowledge and contacts are primary keys in addressing issues, negotiating, and getting decisions made. As mentioned earlier, technical managers' primary concern is the integrity of the systems and processes being changed, not how the project is run.

To be a good technical manager it takes a social network of people, which consists of upper management, management at the same level, and many subject matter experts (SMEs). Being successful is hard to obtain without this network of people in place. People who report directly to this position for a project need to be willing to learn, listen, and follow instructions. They can learn a lot by following the technical manager. The managers in turn need to understand how to communicate effectively with their staff. They need to be proactive at the slightest sign of a resource having problems. If they don't, a small issue can become a big issue in a very small amount of time when dealing with projects.

Relationships with other management at the same level are all about sharing concepts, ideas, and knowledge. Watch and ask questions as to how others handle such things as running meetings. What is the process to get a decision made? How do other technical managers handle each phase of the projects? Do they do anything special with their direct reports that get positive results? Are they doing anything (or not doing) that is creating negative results? Look specifically at the six management best practice disciplines and see how each manager displays or doesn't display them. Try to identify why some managers are always successful on projects and why others always struggle on the projects. Again, many pitfalls can easily be avoided by understanding the mistakes others have made.

For reporting to upper management, the relationship is very close. Often, two people in upper management have both accepted the challenge of the project and have approved it: one is a business stakeholder, who came up with need for the change; and the other is from technical upper management, who would be responsible for ensuring the change occurs. These people thus have taken on personal ownership and are responsible for the success or failure of the project. The larger the project, the more involved upper management will want to be. Normally, weekly status reports are given to upper management on the status of the project. The report shows what phase the project is in, what percentage of that phase is complete, milestones or commitments made by certain dates, how much money has already been spent on the project, as well as the project's next steps. In addition, high-priority projects normally also require regular face-to-face meetings with upper management who authorized the project.

Project managers who are on the project have the responsibility of creating the reports. They normally have little to no system knowledge or development skills and are at the mercy of whatever people tell them. Thus, there is no way for them to know if a developer or business analyst gives an inaccurate status. Most of the time, it's not that they are purposefully not telling the truth; it's just that they really have not thought of all the things left to do and don't have a realistic view of how long things are going to take. Because of their company and system knowledge, technical managers can work with everyone to make sure the true status is reported so that the reports are accurate.

At this point we need to make a few statements regarding status reports. The status reporting must be 100% truthful. It is tempting to hide or omit the fact that a milestone date was missed. The hope is that things will get caught up before the next status check. Most times things do not get caught up and instead get further behind. What starts to occur is a domino effect in that when one milestone is missed it causes the next one to be missed, until the project is in serious trouble. At some point the truth will come out as to the true status. Communication to upper management must include every possible issue and concern. This builds trust and keeps management aware of small issues that could become potentially larger issues in the future. Upper management members are not naïve; they know that large projects always have issues, delays, and surprises. If the weekly reports say that everything is fine and there are no problems, they know that either something is being hidden or that the people running the project are not in touch with reality.

A technical manager position is not always needed. Only when the work is classified as medium to complex is there a need for a technical manager to be involved. The purpose of this person is to fill the knowledge and skills gap necessary to address the many unknowns and to manage the large amount of resources being used. Even though the title is technical manager, it refers to someone with good to excellent skills in the six disciplines—leadership, negotiation, problem solving, decision making, ability to influence, and communication.

Often, people are put into the role of leading the technical side of a large project without much experience or skills to complete it. Instead, there is a hope that these people can step up and do the things that are required so that the project is successful. Matching the skills and knowledge of the person to the complexity of the work eliminates one more risk when dealing with complex work. As more risks that get reduced or eliminated, the odds increase on the probability of success.

PROJECT MANAGER

Project managers run the projects. Their role differs from that of technical managers, whose primary responsibility is maintaining the integrity of the systems. I first learned about the project manager position in the early 1990s when a large corporation was implementing project management. Several years later I was also privileged to be in another large corporation when project management was implemented for the first time. Surprisingly, both companies had major setbacks on large projects when the project manager position was first implemented.

These managers have taken classes, read books, or attended seminars specifically dealing with the concepts of running a project. From this training they have learned the different parts of a project and how to put together a project plan to execute it. They also understand tangible items such as critical paths, variances, scope creep, estimating, documentation, acquiring resources, setting up funding, budgeting, financial reporting, controlling when the project enters and ends a phase, communication plans, procurement, reporting project progress, and status. Unlike technical managers, who are required to bring system, resource, and company knowledge, project managers are required to have knowledge only on how to run the project.

Each project a project manager runs will require different resources with different skills and knowledge because each project is unique. Resources are only assigned temporary to the project because they will only work on it for a short time. This means that project managers are not responsible for staff development. To staff a project, these managers send a resource request to the area affected by the change. Who gets assigned and when the resource is available to work on the project are controlled not by the project managers but by the managers to whom the subordinates officially report. Project managers just take the resource names given to them and assign them to a task in the project plan.

Project managers' responsibility to upper management is to report the project status. Project managers gather the status information by talking to other project team members and checking the project plan. From the project plan they can report the financial part of the project along with the completion percentage of the project. They also report and ask for help from upper management for any problems that are outside the control of the project. The most common issue is lack of available resources to do a project. Departments that own the resources might decide that currently there are more important tasks for their staff than to work a project. Upper management needs to step in and help negotiate a solution. One solution could be that the department needs to release some resources to work on the project because it is a high priority. Another option is for upper management to give project managers approval to bring in outside contractors to do the project work.

Both companies I mentioned earlier first tested the project manager position with small to medium-sized projects, most of which were successful with this structure. But on large projects when just a project manager was the only management assigned, the projects normally failed to meet all three success criteria—delivery date, cost, and quality. Remember that people placed in this position have little knowledge on systems, might have some knowledge on the company, and have little control over the resources assigned. Without this knowledge and control, project managers are heavily dependent on the assigned resources to handle intangible items such as ability to influence, decision making, negotiation, problem solving, correct human resource assignment, and knowledge of the true status of the project. Plus, on large projects the daily workload of project managers deals mostly with administering the project. With potentially more than 50 people on the project, a project manager can be overwhelmed by the daily duties to create or control all the tangible items such as critical paths, variances, scope creep, estimating, documentation, acquiring resources, setting up funding, budgets, phase control, communication plans, procurement, reporting project progress, and statuses.

Stepping back to high generic level, a project can fail for only two reasons: Either the tangible items are not being managed correctly, and/or the intangible items are not being managed correctly. Note that the former are the responsibility of the project manager, and the latter is the responsibility of others on the project team, such as the technical manager.

SYSTEM RESOURCE MANAGER

Large systems are normally broken down into subsystems with a different manager assigned to each subsystem. However, many of the changes requested affect the entire system and not just one subsystem. This structure of several managers in the same system causes issues related to receiving work requests, resource assignments, and setting priorities on what work needs to be done first.

Work requests can come from anyone or anyplace. The request for change can come from any internal department, upper management including the president of the company, routine maintenance, or even government regulations. A work request can come in the form of a formal request document, e-mail, phone call, or even a hallway conversation.

Because of the different type of inputs and the different possible formats, it's almost a requirement that all work requests go to a central person, a system resource manager.

The duty of system resource managers is to gather all work requests and present them to the other managers. The other managers will set the priority of the work, along with assigning the work to a specific person. The system resource managers then controls, document, and monitor all the work that is being done. A single point person gives quality to the project and provides control over knowing who is working on what and when someone is done with their work so that they can be assigned something else. Once work is assigned by the resource manager, even if a manager wants to use their own team member for something else, the manager must get approval from the system resource manager. The system resource manager has the final say on resource allocation once they are assigned.

Without a central point for work requests, it greatly decreases efficiency and adds confusion in the department, and the most important work does not get done first. When a work request comes in, a manager's response might not be what requestor wants. The requestor normally subsequently changes the request slightly and sends this similar request to another manager in the group. The second manager most likely will give a different answer. And if the requestor still does not like that answer, it will contact another manager in that system trying to get one of them to give them the answer they want to hear. What ends up is there are several different answers on the same work they are requesting to be done. You cannot blame the requestor for taking this approach. The change they are requesting might be the most important change that needs to be done in their area. But in terms of the enterprise and other business requests, it could be a very low priority.

In one company, a process was in place so that each manager would receive the work requests. The only centralization was that each week they got together to discuss the new work requests and to find available resources to be assigned to each request. The issue was that one of the managers never seemed to have staff available to help share in the work requests that came in through the formal process. Digging further into what was occurring, a business area had a personal connection with the manager. When that business area wanted something done, they just called that manager and told him what work they wanted. Most of the time, the manager would assign his staff to help that business area. In return the business area would recognize the effort and reward him and

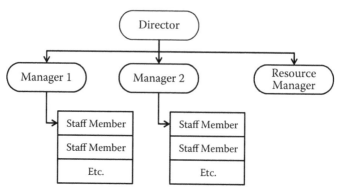

FIGURE 5.1
Organization chart with resource manager.

his team with things such as cookies. This seems harmless, but most of the work the business area was requesting and getting done was of low priority. Resource time could have been spent better on more important work requests from other areas. Even though there was a formal process in place to submit work requests, the business area had found a way to go around the process by just calling this specific manager. Just like everything else in the world, business partners will follow the path of least resistance.

Figure 5.1 shows how the organization chart would look with a system resource manager in place. This system resource manager has no staff members who officially report to him. His or her duties are to manage the work coming in and then to assign resources to get those tasks done. Once again, the system resource manager has no responsibility in resource development, problem solving, negotiations, influencing, or decision making. Those duties fall back on the regular manager to whom the resource officially reports.

There are many other types of managers besides the ones covered here. The purpose of this discussion is to classify a few of the different types and make you aware of the factors associated with those positions. Success depends on starting with the correct people with the correct knowledge and skills for the type of work that is being done. Notice I did not say *title*. The biggest cause of waste in business today is that work gets assigned based on a title and not the knowledge and skills. Large projects require project managers, so they are just assigned because that is their title. It doesn't matter that these people may have experience only on small to medium-size projects. They are available, so they get assigned to run large projects. The same thing happen with a technical lead and technical manager. There is a need to have one on a project, so a person who might have worked only in maintenance now suddenly finds himself leading the technical effort on a large project. He or she got the assignment only because he or she was available. The project methodology defines that people fill these positions, but it says nothing about the skill level they must possess.

Some interesting statistics are available from several different sources on project failures. At the start of Chapter 26, it covers some of those findings. One is that on all project work being done, companies are averaging overall less than a 33% chance of meeting all three criteria's of meeting the original projected deadline, cost, and quality. With companies trying to reduce expenses, a 67% or more failure rate is not very good in today's world. It's a very costly rate in terms of money and resources. A way to increase that success ratio is by assigning the right people with the right skills to the right type of work.

6

Crisis Management

Murphy's Law states that if anything can go wrong, it will. This is never truer than in the business world. I was once told by upper management that a person holds a title and not a position. Thus, at any given time the company can move a person into a different area or situations it wants to if it believes there will be better overall results. Especially good managers that have a tendency to be put into bad situations that they did not create but are responsible for fixing. Managers do not even have to be moved into a new position for a crisis to happen. A new responsibility may be thrust upon them that they are not ready for, or resourcing needs might suddenly change, and suddenly everyone on the team is turning to them to fix things.

Most managers at some time will end up in a bad situation where the normal processes and procedures seem to not work. When this happens in the projects and teams there is mass confusion, low performance, low morale, and high stress. There appears to be little leadership and no direction. Crisis management is needed to fix these situations, which may involve temporarily breaking some of the rules and goals to get things back on track.

The best way to explain this is to cover one of the situations I have been put in. A new system had been implemented for over a year and was still having problems. During the day when users were adding data the system would routinely break. At night multiple jobs ran to process the data that had been entered during the day. These jobs were also breaking every night. The first year there was not one night that at least one of the nightly jobs did not break. Each nightly breakage required a developer to resolve it. This was before technology was available to be able to work from home. So to fix the issue the developers had to get dressed and drive into the office. In addition, these nightly jobs ran anywhere from 2:00 to 4:00 a.m.

Between the nightly problems of being called at 2:00 a.m. and the daily problems, morale was very low in the team. The first week I was the manager over the group, every team member approached me and asked for a transfer.

I first talked to the team and told them that for the next 6 months there would be no transfers. That really did not go over too well, but I asked them to give me a chance to improve what was happening. The first thing we did as a team was to look at the work priorities. In the past the team's primary goal every day was to fix the data to get them through the system each night. So much time and energy was spent doing that that very little was left to fix the true issues causing the systems to break.

Our company's golden rule—that customer service came first—was challenged first. Upper management members were presented with an option that for a time span customer service would suffer while the systems were being fixed. The downside was that for a short time our customers would hate us, but over time they would hopefully forget about the bad times and welcome the new, stable systems. When dealing with upper management, always present at least a couple of options; this shows that you don't have tunnel vision. Presenting only one option makes it seem like you are threatening upper management: Either they execute your idea, or the issue will continue. We presented the alternate option of adding staff members to the group to work on the system fixes. Naturally, management went with the first option of changing the rule that customer service did not come first because it did not cost them any money.

After management members gave approval to allow customer service to suffer, the next step in the process was, as a team, to identify the best people to work on the fixes. A team that has been working together for awhile already knows the best ones to do it and, more importantly, the ones who still care about making things better. Good people can get worn down and just give up. Even new management cannot change their attitude. The members the team selected to work on the system fixes were then isolated. Our business partners could no longer have direct contact with them, and other team members also had limited access. As many distractions as possible were removed so that they could work full time on the fixes.

The next task was to create a list of all the problems that had occurred since the systems had gone to production. With each problem was the estimated amount of time it had cost the company up to that point. There was a high-level estimate on what it would take to resolve the problem permanently. Once the list was created, approximately 75 individual reoc-curring problems were identified.

At this point the items on the list were reviewed, and the quick fixes were identified. Even though these quick fixes were not causing the major issues, they were still a distraction. In the past, the team members worked on the large items first, but they could never finish fixing the large issues because so many small issues kept occurring that needed immediate attention. With this new approach, when most of the small issues got fixed there were far fewer distractions occurring, so now there was time to work on fixing the larger issues.

When most of the simple problems where fixed, as a team we talked about the best way to fix the rest of the issues. The new plan was to group problems together related to the part of the system in which they were occurring. If there were five to six different problems with print, these were all put together as one fix. Development and testing on the fixes that were grouped together were all done at the same time to save resources and get it done quickly.

Of course, as more and more fixes got implemented, the systems became more stable. In turn, there were less nightly and daily calls. Compensation hours were given to developers for every hour they had to come and fix things after normal business hours. The year after I took over the group, only 44 hours of compensation time were given versus the year before, when 400 hours of compensation time were given. Team morale improved as well. After the 6-month no-transfer period was up, no one asked to be transferred. They were now proud of the systems and want to stay and help improve the system even further.

It does not take being moved into a new group for crisis management to happen. The workload could greatly increase for a manager, with more incoming tasks and requests than what can be addressed. When this hap-pens, a backlog of tasks and requests develops that needs to be addressed at some point. In this situation, the first step is to list all the outstanding items. New ones will keep coming in daily, so the tool being used to document the open items needs to be flexible enough to be updated every day. Each item on the list needs two values: (1) its importance or priority; and (2) its complexity. The complexity many times will be related to the amount of time it will take to address the item.

Frequently, people try to accomplish everything at once and end up accomplishing nothing at all. Every day, pick out only three items that have a high importance, and make sure at least one of them is complex.

Then work at resolving these three items for that day. If there is still time in the day after resolving the three items, then work on some smaller simpler items that can be addressed quickly. If all three items are not addressed in the day's time, then the next day the items left open are worked on again as the highest priority.

This process puts the work in order of importance. Work follows the 80–20 rule: 20% of all work requests are important, and the other 80% are not. People tend to greatly overreact. What may seem really important today may not be all that important tomorrow after they have had time to think through it. If managers react to every new request that comes in then they could be wasting their time on items that might not be the highest importance compared with what is on the backlog. By no means are lower-priority items totally ignored. Instead, only the most important ones are worked on first. For the older items on the list that have a low priority, at some point follow up with the person that reported the issue so see if it still exists. It's surprising how many of these low priority issues are from people that just overreacted and there really were no issues. Over a short time, fewer items will be high priority and high complexity, in which case there is more time to do the normal daily work.

One last thought on setting the priority: If the priority happens to be set too low, the person who initiated the request will let the manager know. They will continuously check with the manager on when the item will be addressed. Even though the item appears to have low importance, it's the best usage of time to give it a high priority and address the item. Time gets wasted in follow-ups, plus it does not build a good working relationship if the person keeps being put off.

I have used crisis management several times in my career. Mostly, it's when projects are going so badly and the key leaders of the core project team have left. In each situation I used the following steps to get out of the confusion and get things back on track:

Step 1: Get organized about what is happening. Look at what the true problem is. As mentioned before, don't just fix the symptoms; fix the disease. In the first situation of the system being unstable, the original management priority was first to fix the symptoms (bad data) and second to fix the disease (bad code). Since fixing the bad data was taking up most of the entire day, there was never any time to fix the code to stop it from happening.

Step 2: Set priorities. When setting priorities, look to see if breaking a barrier or rule will get to the end results faster. In the previous situation, the company's primary objective of customer service being first was temporarily waived for the group. Once the priorities were changed, there was communication not only to the team but also to all of upper management and all the customers. This communication included priority changes and the plan to fix the systems. Often, simple is best. The plan we communicated was that the smaller, quick fixes would be performed first so that there were fewer distractions when working on the larger, more complex issues. Routinely progress communication was sent out to everyone on items that were fixed and the items still left open. Everyone understood what the goal was, the plan, and priority to get things done.

Step 3: Isolate the correct resources to work on the fixes. When in crisis mode, it's not about training. It's about getting current and back on track as fast as possible with the best quality. Identify the best people to resolve the issues. Once these resources are identified, isolate them from distractions. In the past I have taken away phones and e-mail capability and have even asked resources to put an out-of-office or in-quarantine sign in these people's cubicles just so that they would not be disturbed. A small team dedicated to one thing can obtain great accomplishments in a short time.

This process works because it's based on core principles. When individuals, groups, and project team are in a crisis mode, they are used to nothing but confusion and failure. When we talked as a group after things turned around, everyone said the biggest issue before was never seeing any improvement no matter what happened. Turning around a team never occurs overnight; it takes time and starts with small successes. Working on the smaller quick-fixes first leads to small, quick successes, which gives a small sense of hope and a sense of direction to the team. These small successes then feed the process that leads to successes on larger items, which in turn gives more hope and more sense of direction to the team.

The team also said what helped a lot was that by pulling all the issues together into one document they could visually see what was causing all the failures, which follows the core principle of identifying the complete problem. In management best practices, this is the discipline or *problem solving* (see Chapter 2). In the previously presented situation, most of the team thought that hundreds of different defects were causing all the problems, instead of only 75 individual reoccuring issues. The process follows the core principle of building a visual roadmap or a project plan to resolve not just the problems but also the crisis. This was accomplished only by using the management disciplines of *negotiation, decision making,* and *ability to influence the organization.* The last core principle is using the management discipline of open *communication.* All through the process, from the beginning to the end, a team effort was required. This involves communication during the processes while creating the list, setting the priorities, and even selecting the specific people to work the issues. This instilled ownership and pride into the team members.

I have also applied this process in an academic setting with success. In 1997, a college at which I worked was behind the times in terms of technology. The few personal computers (PCs) on the college campus did not have software or hardware that would work in 2000. Most of the software on campus was only a DOS version and not Windows. The college structure varies slightly from a business structure. Universities are composed of many different departments. Because of how the federal government grants money, each department is almost a separate company or kingdom that many times cannot share funding. For example, if the Department of Natural Sciences gets a government grant, the grant money may be restricted to use only for specific things related to the Department of Natural Sciences. The money cannot be used for the music department even if it is broke. But IT needed to support the entire campus, and we had limited resources to work with because of limited funding. We followed this process:

Step 1: Get organized as to what is happening. With approval from the president and vice presidents, we asked each department to fill out individual requests on every item it thought it needed. Some departments filled out more than five requests. The role of IT was to help identify the cost in terms of purchasing, labor to install and support. Departments supplied the business justification reasons for the request.

Step 2: Set priorities. Once all the requests were handed in, a campus meeting was held with all the directors, deans, vice presidents, and president. Each request was presented to the group by the originator of the request. The purpose was that the department who asked for the change would be the best ones to sell the change. After all the requests were presented, they were put up on a wall. Then each person in the meeting was given three color-coded stickers. Each color represented a priority. The attendees were then were asked to put their stickers on projects based not on their own department needs but on campus-wide needs. Naturally, the group was told that there was the possibility of an override rule by the president and vice presidents since they were ultimately responsible for the entire campus. The outcome was a list of around 47 items identified that needed to be done on campus in terms of technology. Some were as simple as installing a new computer and software for a new chemistry instructor to the more complex task of upgrading databases, servers, and operating systems for software that does the registration, financial aid, reporting grades, and human resources duties for the entire campus. A project plan was put together on how and when things would be completed.

Step 3: Isolate the correct resources to work on the fixes. To free up resources we first looked at getting additional temporary work studies to help with the daily support issues. Work studies is mostly federally funded, so it was inexpensive for more of them to workout. In the past to save costs the process on campus was to buy the individual parts that make up the computer and then build the PC ourselves. To save time for the core team, we went back to a vendor that supplied many of the PC parts for the university and asked it to build the PCs for a short time. Even though this would cut into its short-term profit, in return it would get a very large order immediately. There would be a long-term profit from needing to order a larger number of spare replacement parts to have in inventory for when parts failed. Also because of demands of new software, when PCs were required to be upgraded in a department, the orders for those parts would be larger because of more PCs on campus. This was especially common in the late 1990s when new software on the market was requiring more memory, larger hard drives, and faster video to operate correctly.

We also changed who we serviced. Two points of servicing we provided did not fit the direct campus goals. One was a college-related site 4 miles away from the main campus. This site provided computer classes related to business needs of companies in the area. The other was a YMCA on the campus that in the past had been supported. Servicing to both of these locations was changed because it took away from the primary goal of supporting the students, faculty, and administration on the main college campus. A company was found to handle support for these locations and we trained them on our configurations on the licensed software we used on the main campus. Again, the rules were changed to better serve the primary purpose, which was to support only the students, faculty, and administration on the main college campus.

The accomplishments in 18 months were pretty great. During this time the campus went from 175 computers with very few connected to a network of over 500 PCs on campus all connected to the network with e-mail and internet capability. Besides availability for students, all faculty and administration staff had PC availability. All software used in the classrooms was the most current Windows applications. Of the 47 original items identified as needed for the college, there were only five items left to do after 18 months.

One last comment on crisis management: It's not fun and games. Things do not change overnight. It takes time to understand the issues and get others to understand them also. People just don't flock to the new person who is assigned to turn things around. Instead, because of being buried in work and not seeing an end in sight for a long time, they are much more defensive when a new person comes in. By no means does that mean they are bad workers. It just means it takes longer and more effort to come together as a team working toward a common cause of getting out of the crisis. In the beginning it can become very frustrating because things are not progressing fast enough, not only for yourself but for your team, upper management, and your business partners who requested the change. But with a plan, resources, and priorities, things will always improve slowly at first and faster later on.

7

Jack Welch and Management

We have covered several components and their examples of management best practices. To help understand what has been covered up to this point, we should look at what others have done in the business world. Jack Welch, chief executive officer (CEO) of General Electric (GE) and one of the most influential businesspersons in the last several decades, is a perfect example. Jack Welch, chief executive officer (CEO) of General Electric (GE) and one of the most influential businesspersons in the last several decades, is a perfect example. Some people think he is a great business leader, while others question his methods and outcomes. Welch took a good company and made it great—GE is admired by all companies in terms of growth and profit. In 1980, the year before he became CEO, GE's revenues were $26.8 billion. In 2000, twenty years after he took over, the revenue had increased to $130 billion. The company went from a market value of $14 billion to one of more than $410 billion at the time of his retirement. For this growth to happen, he had to do a transformation of management (see http://www.ge.com/company/history/bios/john_welch.html).

In the 1980s, Welch worked to streamline GE. He pushed managers to handle more responsibility and be productive. If inefficiencies were found within the organization, he either removed or changed them. If a GE division was doing badly, it was sold off. If a certain management area was doing badly, then management was replaced in that area. His point of view was that a company needs to plan on being #1 or #2 in their line of business.

In the beginning of the book it was discussed of 20% of the people are *performers,* 60% are *fence sitters,* and 20% are *cave dwellers.* Those percentages are based around the 80–20 rule. Out of 100 managers, 20 are performers, and out of those same 100, 20 are cave dwellers, leaving 60 in the middle. Welch used the same concept, only different percentages. He still had 20% as top performers, but the middle group consisted of 70%, with the last group which was classified as poor performers was 10%. Jack answer to how he learned about percentages was on the playground as a kid when baseball teams were formed. The best players were picked first and put in key positions. The middle group of players that had average skills filled out the easy positions that few balls got hit to like second base or right field. The kids with poor skills end up on the bench. Based on this early childhood observation he came up with 20–70–10 ratio. One last observation Jack had was that the kids on the bench never really took the time to get better and, usually in a short time, found other pursuits that they could enjoy and excel at. Out of this concept was borne the concept that the bottom 10% of managers should be fired from the company each year. This gets rid of the worst managers and at the same time brings in new managers with new ideas. I agree with the concept of getting rid of weak managers but not with percentage methodology. The flaw is that if a team of managers are all very good, the lower 10% still need to be fired. An example is a couple of years ago, I came across a company that had implemented this plan at several layers of management. In one department, all the managers were top performers, but because of the company's directive each manager had to be "ranked" and then the lower 10% removed if possible without being sued. Normally, this was attempted by creating a bad review that was mostly untrue and then giving the person a below average performance rating. The company guidelines stipulated that only 20% could be ranked as high performers; 60% were ranked as average and 20% as below average. Thus, the performance review had nothing to do with performance but was all about ranking the people and then creating a review to match the ranking.

If a manager left and was replaced with a new person, it opened up an issue at the next ranking and review time. Since all the existing management team members were top performers, where would the new person be ranked? If the ranking was truthful, the new person should be ranked as the lowest because she could not outperform the existing management and did not even come close to the knowledge all the other managers had. To avoid new management being ranked the lowest, an existing manager was picked and ranked the lowest. To validate the ranking again, an untrue review was created.

The director had no flexibility in or control over the process because at that level the 10% directive was also in place. If the director, who had spent the time to train and build a high-performance team of managers, did not meet the company's directive of trying to get rid of the bottom 10% of his managers, then he could be put into the bottom 10% at his level and could possibly lose his job. The company's management started to self-destruct because instead of the emphasis being on working toward making the company better, it was around ranking. The management team members no longer worked together because they were afraid someone they helped might end up being ranked ahead of them.

Welch is known for removing many of General Electric's management layers. He shifted empowerment to the lower management levels, which in turn allowed a reduction in the number of management levels needed in a company. Welch's 25 viewpoints on management leadership are outlined as follows to help us better understand Welch.

JACK WELCH'S 25 LESSONS IN LEADERSHIP

"Lead": "Managers muddle; leaders inspire. Leaders are people who inspire with clear vision of how things can be done better." Leaders at every level need to energize, excite, and inspire rather than exhaust, depress, and control.

"Manage less": It is amazing how much people will do when they are not told what to do by management. In the new knowledge-driven economy, people should make their own decisions. Managing less is managing better. Close supervision, control, and bureaucracy kills the competitive spirit of an individual or a company if done on a larger scale.

"Articulate your vision": Leaders inspire people with clear visions of how things can be done better. The best "leaders do not provide a step-by-step instruction manual for their teams" but instead come up with new idea and articulate a vision that inspires others to act.

"Simplify": Keeping things simple is one of the keys to business. "Simple messages travel faster, simpler designs reach the market faster, and eliminating clutter allows for faster decision making."

"Get less formal": It is "so important to maintain the kind of corporate informality that encourages a training class to comfortably challenge the boss's pet ideas." Nobody knows everything, even management. Only by being able to be openly challenge ideas can there be validation that the idea will add value to the company.

"Energize others": "Genuine leadership comes from the quality of the vision and the ability to spark others to extraordinary performance. Getting employees excited about their work is the key to being a great business leader." Managers can accomplish this with challenging, empowering, exciting, and rewarding their employees.

"Face reality": "Face reality, and then act decisively. Most mistakes leaders make arise from not being willing to face reality and then to acting on it." Most of the time the reality is not a pretty picture and facing it often means saying and doing things that are not popular to get things on the right track.

"See change as an opportunity": "Change is a big part of the reality in business." The willingness to change and adapting are strengths. Wanting to cling to the status quo and being complacent are weaknesses.

"Get good ideas from everywhere": New ideas are the lifeblood of business. "The operative assumption today is that someone, somewhere, has a better idea; the operative compulsion is to find out who has that better idea, learn it, and put it into action"—fast.

"Follow up": "Follow up on everything. Follow-up is one key measure of success for a business." If follow-up does not happen, then an assumption is made, which could be right or wrong. Doing this validates that things are progressing correctly as well as showing a continuous interest.

"Get rid of bureaucracy": The way to harness the power of your people is "to turn them loose and get the management layers off their backs, the bureaucratic shackles off their feet, and the functional barriers out of their way."

"Eliminate boundaries": "To make sure that people are free to reach for the impossible, you must remove anything that gets in their way." Boundaries prevent the flow of ideas and add handoffs across the company. With boundaries also comes territory. All these items get in the way of people trying to reach for the impossible.

"Put values first": "Don't focus too much on the numbers. Numbers aren't the vision; they are the products." Numbers come from the outcome of something. If the primary effort is put toward team building, sharing ideas, and improvement, the numbers will end up correct without much attention.

"Cultivate leaders": Cultivate leaders who have the four Es of leadership—"energy, energize, edge, and execution." Great leaders tend to grow other great leaders within the company.

"Create a learning culture": "The desire and the ability of an organization to continuously learn from any source, anywhere—and to rapidly convert this learning into action—is its ultimate competitive advantage." Leaders turn their companies into a learning organization that is increasing their knowledge.

"Involve everyone": "Business is all about capturing intellect from every person. The way to engender enthusiasm is to allow employees far more freedom and far more responsibility."

"Make everybody a team player": "Managers should learn to become team players," and take action against those who won't comply. Managers who are not team players tend to be complacent.

"Stretch": "Stretch targets energize. We have found that by reaching for what appears to be the impossible, we often actually do the impossible; and even when we don't quite make it, we inevitably wind up doing much better than we would have done."

"Instill confidence": "Self-confident people are open to good ideas regardless of their source and are willing to share them." Confidence is equated with speed and quality in a team.

"Have fun": "Fun must be a big element in your business strategy." The actual work that needs to be done is very boring most of the time. Leaders can add fun things around the work, which will help people wake up each day energized and excited about tackling a new set of challenges.

"Be number 1 or number 2": "When you're number 4 or 5 in a market, when number 1 sneezes, you get pneumonia. When you're number 1, you control your destiny." Companies that are not number 1 or 2 need to strive toward that goal. Accepting being number 4 or lower means that leadership is not aspiring to be the best.

"Live quality": Companies should aspire to "change the competitive landscape not just by being better than their competitors but also by taking quality to a whole new level." Not only will this will greatly reduce the waste that goes with low quality, but excellent quality also sets companies apart from the competition.

"Constantly focus on innovation": There must be constant focus on innovation. "You've got to constantly produce more for less through intellectual capital. Shun the incremental, and look for the quantum leap."

"Live speed": "Speed is everything. It is the indispensable ingredient of competitiveness." The slower a company reacts to market changes, the better chance the competition has to take the company's market share.

"Behave like a small company": Small companies have huge competitive advantages. They "are uncluttered, simple, informal. They thrive on passion and ridicule bureaucracy. Small companies grow on good ideas—regardless of their source. They need everyone, involve everyone, and reward or remove people based on their contribution to winning. Small companies dream big dreams and set the bar high; increments and fractions don't interest them."

Most of these points are simple. They deal with empowerment and accountability. For an organization to be great, everyone needs to participate. And maybe that is more what these points are all about: A company cannot have managers in a position who are not willing to listen and take action. But in companies there normally are many managers that are content with their position and have become complacent. Even when a good idea comes about, they take no action because it would cause them to have to take part in it. This would change their normal routine and job security. It's much safer to do nothing and stay unnoticed versus trying to make the company better.

In a small company, management complacency does not happen as often. With fewer managers, the company depends on each manager to perform at an average or above average level. If just one manager and his or her area become complacent, it could seriously affect other areas through which the work flows. In a large company, management complacency is more common and actually breeds itself. Many departments have five or more managers, and if most of them are in the complacency mode the few that want to be proactive in the department and bring about beneficial change are looked upon as troublemakers and outcasts. Over time, rarely will the managers that are complacent change their mode. Instead, the managers who want to be proactive and bring change about get frustrated and worn down by the complacent managers. They become part of the problem when they accept the complacent mode of the other managers in their department.

In closing, carefully reread Welch's points. Many of the points could go into the outcome column of the process discussed back in the Improving

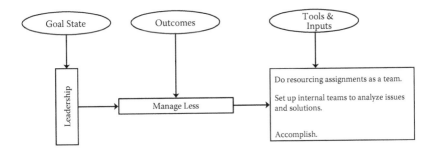

FIGURE 7.1
Improvement process—goal state, outcomes, tools & inputs.

Management Best Practice Disciplines section of Chapter 2. Each of the outcomes could then be expanded by creating action tasks for the tools and inputs of those outcomes. Figure 7.1 is an example of how to expand Welch's second point, "manage less."

8

Robert Greenleaf and Servant Leadership

When the word *management* is used, we think of people out in front, leading everyone. When I first got into management in the mid-1980s, I was told that managers needed to be in charge of their people, to control them and make them respect me and my title. That concept never settled with me, and I took a slightly different approach: by trying to earn people's respect. In the early 1990s, I came across a philosophy called servant leadership, which put a label on many of the things I had already been doing.

Servant leadership originated with Robert K. Greenleaf in the essay "The Servant as Leader" (Greenleaf, 1970). Greenleaf spent most of his organizational life in the field of management research, development, and education at AT&T. I was first exposed to it in the early 1990s but learned it better in the late 1990s when I attended a year-long session with monthly meetings of the "Leadership Institute—Leadership for the 21st Century."

Greenleaf asks the question: What makes someone a great versus average leader? He defines a servant leader as someone who naturally feels motivated to serve but ends up becoming a leader. The opposite of servant leadership is a person who puts leadership first before everyone and everything. Many managers fall into the latter category; they assume that a title will make them into a leader. They normally do not work with their team but instead tend to set goals and objectives with no input. Then they try to push their staff to meet these goals and objectives. This type of manager is at the opposite end of the spectrum from a servant leader. To determine what type of management style a manager has, he can draw a line with "servant leader" on one end and "leader first" on the other and put a tick mark on the line where he thinks his management style falls. Then each member on his team can make a mark on the line as to what they believe his style is. This serves as a reality check of how the manager believes he is managing versus how he is actually doing.

A servant is often thought of as someone who waits hand and foot on others. By no means is that the type of servant that is being talked about. Being a serve-first manager means making sure that other people's highest-priority needs—such things as having room to grow, feeling needed, empowerment, having the proper training and tools, and getting rid of barriers to job performance—are being met. Most of these things deal with employee development, for which management is responsible.

So why should a manager look at servant leadership? We can answer this by considering why we might follow someone. The answer is because we believe the person will take care of us. If we know someone is going to set us up for failure or suddenly disappear when things get tough or start to go wrong, we definitely would not follow the person too long. Those who are interested only in themselves will never have loyal followers because they are not concerned about others' well-being. Several decades ago it was much easier to get workers to follow blindly. The expectation was that once a company hired a person, there was a very good chance that person would retire from it. In today's world of company downsizing, layoffs, outsourcing, and job-hoppers, workers are much more leary of companies. The worker in today's world has the mindset of "what are you going to do for me before I will follow you?" Managers who believe in leading first cannot answer this question except to threaten job security or entice with money. In contrast, this question is not asked of serve-first managers since workers are well aware of what their manager has already done for them. This is how trust and loyalty are built.

A characteristic of lead-first managers is to make statements first and not to listen very much. They tend to push through issues instead of stopping and understanding how to resolve the issues. Servant leaders listen first and spend the time to gather as much information as possible to make an accurate decision. They make sure the right people are brought into the conversation who are or will be affected. Within reason, they listen to everyone with insight. Again, who would you follow: the lead-first or the serve-first manager?

Greenleaf also defines the characteristics of a great leader, one of which is knowing the unknowable. Since servant leaders are in tune with their workers and their environment, they have the ability to pull in past and current information and experiences to come up with an educated guess as to what is going to happen in the future. They can foresee barriers or issues before they become actual problems and can make practical decisions to avoid them. This is the art of being proactive, and most great leaders have this ability.

All great leaders must continue to be proactive; otherwise, they end up reacting to events. It is common for leaders in management to be great at being proactive only in certain positions or situations. For example, a manager may generate outstanding results in a certain position but then gets moved to another position and suddenly disappears within the organization. You never hear the person's name mentioned again. This manager may possess all the skills and knowledge from the prior position but in the new situation doesn't have the foresight or proactive attribute. Hence, the person loses most of the ability to lead. So how do you keep foresight? It circles back to listening and serving first. It is necessary to understand everything that is happening around you and the needs of everyone who works around you.

9

Management Wrap-Up

Over the years I have watched many people become managers for the first time and then fail. It's not that they did not have the talent to be a good manager but that they did not know what a good manager does or how to become one. One week their only responsibility was themselves, and the next week they were responsible for 10 people. It's a drastic jump.

A new manager in a small company has a good chance to grow and succeed. With being more visible to everyone in the company, most everyone will try to help with the development of the new manager. This mentoring helps build a consistent management style throughout the entire enterprise. Part of the reason small companies succeed is because all members of management pretty much think and manage alike. In a large company, this does not happen. There is seldom a standardization of what and how to manage. This disconnect among managers is a barrier that hampers a large company's performance.

The tolerance for poor management is much greater in a large company versus a small company. I have worked about an equal amount of time in large and small companies. In the amount of time I have spent working in a small company I have seen four managers removed from their positions for not getting results. However, in the large companies, which probably have 50 times more managers, I have seen this occur only twice. In a large company most managers who realize they are doing a bad job just move to another manager position in a different department. Poor performing managers will keep moving to new lateral positions every couple of years. They never stay in one position long enough to be held accountable, so there is never a need to try to improve. A poor performing manager in a small company does not have the number of opportunities to move laterally because there are far fewer positions in the same management level. There is more of a need for a poor performing manager to continuously work on improvement, because there is no place to hide in a small company.

A large company needs to become more like a small company in terms of management. First, define in fine detail what management means in the company. Whether it's the six disciplines of management best practices or something else such as Jack Welch's 25 points, some process needs to be built to help management be consistent across an organization. Without this definition, existing managers can manage any way they want to. Also, new managers coming in after the initial company training need some type of roadmap to help them development their management skills and knowledge. Without this, the overall company performance is hindered because of the lack of consistency among managers.

One of Jack Welch's points (see Chapter 7) sums up what large companies need to try to accomplish to get better and compete against smaller companies:

> **"Behave like a small company"**: Small companies have huge competitive advantages. They "are uncluttered, simple, informal. They thrive on passion and ridicule bureaucracy. Small companies grow on good ideas—regardless of their source. They need everyone, involve everyone, and reward or remove people based on their contribution to winning. Small companies dream big dreams and set the bar high; increments and fractions don't interest them."

10

Business Model

In management there various levels and titles: managers, directors, system officers, vice presidents, associate vice presidents, chief information officers (CIOs), chief executive officers (CEOs), and probably a 100 others among the different organizations around the world. For operational efficiency, companies organize management titles according to a hierarchy tree for reporting, which creates levels. I have worked in a company with only four levels and others with seven or more. Much of the information in this book is primarily centered on the management near the front lines because that is where the waste and inefficiencies occur. At these lower levels, the front line management team directly affect the front-line workers, plus this is where all the actual work occurs.

To better understand how the business levels work, we need to understand how our current business structure came about. When Henry Ford invented the automobile assembly line in the early 1900s, his company became very successful. Ford had only one type of car. Every car off the assembly line had the same engine, same color, and same features. He used to say, "The customer can have any color so long as it's black." Materials, manufacturing, inventory, sales, profits, and loss were consistent across the Ford enterprise because it built the same car over and over again in every assembly line and plant it had. Hence, Ford could have a flat business structure and still be operationally efficient, and this made it easy to calculate whether the company was profitable or losing money.

General Motors (GM), on the other hand, started out with only Buick, but very quickly purchased another 20 companies including Pontiac, Oldsmobile, Chevrolet, and Cadillac. Its philosophy was that the customer should have a variety of car options, which made it a more complex company compared with Ford, which in turn led to operational deficiencies across the enterprise because of the business structures in place at the time.

In 1923, Alfred Sloan became GM's CEO. Along with Ford and Jack Welch, Sloan is one of the greatest corporate leaders of the past 100 years. The pyramid business structure and processes he created are still being used today in almost every enterprise throughout the world. Sloan's pyramid business model made the primary key money and not the product. He introduced the ratio of return on investment (ROI) as a measurement of a company's success. The implication of this is that at the very top level of the enterprise all the money is in one pot or bucket, which then gets divided and distributed to each division. Then it's each division's responsibility to divide the money even further into each of the division's departments to pay for expenses. The money keeps getting divided until finally the expenses of the front-line worker and equipment are covered. Figure 10.1 reflects this funding process.

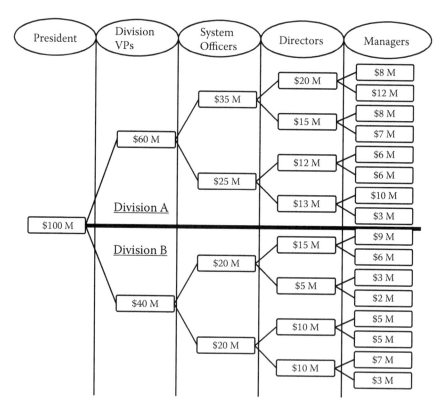

FIGURE 10.1
Corporation funding.

Sloan's business model allowed senior upper management team members to control the enterprise through budgets without having much of a hand in daily operations. Most of the daily decision making and direction for departments was pushed down to middle management or lower. As long as divisions or operations met the estimated ROI senior upper management expected, there were no issues.

But Sloan's pyramid business model, based on money, created an issue. Managers at most all levels were held accountable primarily based on their accounting practices and not the product. If a manager was given $1 million and her area was expected to create $2 million of profit, it's about financial numbers and not the product. To meet the goal the manager could use cheaper material, cheaper labor, or shortcuts. How the results were obtained did not matter as long as the ROI ratio was met. Since the process centered on money, a manager with no product knowledge but good accounting knowledge achieved more success than a manager with no accounting knowledge but with product knowledge. Even though managers might know the product better and understand how to reduce defects and make the product better, it did not matter if they didn't know how to stay within budget.

In the 1970s the positive results that Japan was getting by concentrating on the quality of the project started to make businesses change their thinking. Managers' primary responsibility shifted back to the product and its quality. Technology and automation also have helped with this change in thinking. Creating financials are no longer labor intensive and are easy to create. There are financial software packages, defect tracking software, project tracking software, and time reporting systems that can generate numerous reports on up-to-the-minute costs as well as exactly how much money has been spent thus far. (This assumes, of course, that users keep their time up to date.) Instead of managers having to enter the data financial spreadsheets, the front-line workers now enter their time directly into these various systems. The manager need only make sure everyone enters his or her time correctly in order to create accurate financials. This frees up more time for managers to spend on both staff and product improvement.

Every process and procedure has strengths and weaknesses, and Sloan's business model is no exception. One weakness is that the company's financial goals rarely mesh with the needs of front-line managers or workers. The more work a company can get out of an employee, the more revenue that person will generate. This is seen when ccompanies downsize the number of workers. Usually, there is still the same amount of work to be done, but just now with fewer employees. The retained workers then need to increase their productivity in an attempt to stay current. Another weakness is that quality is not a primary objective. For example, a company moved two assembly lines to Mexico, and the defect ratio increased 10–15% over what was happening before. Everyone talked about how the two lines would be moved back because of the increase in defects, but that never happened. Because the labor was so much cheaper in Mexico, the company could afford to sacrifice quality. Even though fewer products were reaching the market because the amount of defects increased, the labor cost had been reduced so that now the ROI ratio and profit had gone up.

Everyone needs to understand the economics of this. In the simplistic form, if originally, before moving the assembly lines, the company gain on investment was $21 million and the cost of investment was $12 million, the profit is $9 million. In terms of ROI factor it would be 75% (21 minus 12 divided by 12). If the cost of investment (cost of labor) can be reduced by 50% to $6 million, and the company still wants to maintain $9 million in profit, it can afford a gain on investment to drop to $15 million, or a decrease of $6 million. If this happened, then the ROI ratio has gone up to 150% (15 minus 6 divided by 6). On the surface profit appears to have stayed at $9 million, and ROI has gone from 75% to 150%. Looking at just the financials, it appears there is a large improvement. But in reality, more defects are occurring, which gives the company a bad reputation, along with the fact that revenue has dropped, both of which the competition will leverage to take customers.

Another weakness is that with the many levels and senior upper management needing to understand only financials and not the product, there is a major disconnect between senior upper management and what is truly happening with front-line management and the front-line workers. This is especially true when upper management is not home-grown but instead comes from other companies.

Without Sloan's business model, it would have been almost impossible to have a large diversified company. Using Figure 10.2, what Sloan's business model does is, starting at the director position on up the chart, defines management responsibilities as setting direction, goals, controls, reports, and budgets. None of the day-to-day work that generates revenue is done at the director level and higher. All the execution of work, plans, and ideas, which generate most of the revenue, is done at the manager level and front line worker, which are the bottom two levels.

FIGURE 10.2
Management layers—duties and responsibilities.

A company-wide engagement survey is a valuable tool to help recognize if all the levels from the top to the bottom of an organization are working together. If they are not, the engagement scores will be high for the top levels and dramatically lower for the lower levels. In Figure 10.2, the drastic drop would occur between the director, manager, and front-line worker level if there was a disconnect between the goals and direction set by upper management and the ability to execute them.

There is one more piece of information on the business model that is important to understand. Using Figure 10.2 as the template, if for each person in a level there are five subordinates reporting to them and at the top there is only one president, this adds up to 156 people in levels 1 thru 4; in levels 5 and 6, there are 3,750 people. This means 96% of all employees work in the bottom two levels: front-line managers and front-line workers. Having 96% of the workforce disengaged from the corporate vision and goals is not healthy for the company. Upper management needs to make sure company goals and direction is communicated to and understood by the lower levels.

11

High-Performance Teams

Success and failure do not just happen. Many factors influence an outcome. Management style is one of those factors. Another piece of the puzzle deals with the team itself. It has been proven that the outcome of something can be affected by resource attributes or behaviors. As you read this chapter, think of teams you have been involved with in the past and the behavior characteristics associated within them.

DEFINING HIGH-PERFORMANCE TEAMS

In professional sports where teams are built through trades and drafts, a person is on the team because of both skill level and how the athlete fits into the team's chemistry. Every week we hear of gifted athletes being traded because they don't fit into the team or the coaches don't use them because they have other skilled players in the same role. A certain variety of roles and behaviors on each team must be filled. The teams that come together and understand one another's skills and roles normally finish at the top by the end of the playing season. Teams that have too many leaders or no leaders at all finish at the bottom.

Once in awhile a project team excels in its task. Maybe the team was given an impossible task and delivered the project on time and within budget. Or maybe a project team delivers the project 25% cheaper and 25% earlier than was originally expected. Maybe you have seen two different teams doing similar work. One team completes projects consistently under budget and earlier than expected, while the other team is always over budget and can never meet timelines. If you know what you are looking for you can understand the reasons one team tends to succeed and another fails.

One of the buzzwords in the business environment is *high-performance team* (HPT). Few seem to understand the characteristics of an HPT or, better yet, how to build one. Commonly HPTs can take a dream or vision and turn it into reality quickly and accurately. HPTs use *stretch goals* versus *descoping*. I have participated on several HPTs and have also built and run some of them. Each HPT consisted of the same characteristics and went through the same phases during team building. While the majority of large projects in the organization were not meeting their original requirements and deadlines, the projects with the HPTs tended to succeed.

It should be noted that HPT concepts do not apply to a company's cabinet or a special executive team. At this level, a person might have one behavior in a board meeting but another behavior in department meetings. Plus, it's already been mentioned that the actual work done within a company is done only on the first (workers) and second (managers) level. From the third level on up, it's about giving direction, goals, control, and status reports. It's tough to build an HPT when there is no actual work. So think of an HPT as consisting of only front-line workers and front-line managers.

HPT MEMBER CLASSIFICATION

Have you ever heard the saying, "If everyone was a general, there would be no wars." There is a lot of merit in this saying. Generals might propose war and plan attacks, but if there are no soldiers to actually fight the war, it's not going to happen. Projects work the same.

Besides not following the project process, correct staffing of a project is probably the second biggest reason for a project's failure, especially in large companies where people are assigned to a project not based on skills and experience but instead because they are available. Every time people are just randomly assigned to a large project, failure is not too far behind. Think of it as a coach of a basketball team where players are just randomly selected to be on the court for the game. Odds are they will not win too many games. You need the right resources in the right roles on the project to increase the odds of success.

On the other end of the spectrum, I have seen failure occur when all the best people (high performers) are assigned to a top-priority project. A project with the best people on it would seem to be completed quickly and with very good quality. But this is not always true. Many of these projects with high performers end up in the "challenged" or "failure" category by the end. Why? A project team needs to have a variety of behavior characteristics to provide checks and balances for both the team and the project.

Information on behavior patterns and the effects on teams has been around for decades. The mid '80s was the first time I came across information on it. At that time the material covered some of the minor reasons such as that it leads to fighting and that nobody can agree on things. Over time I was exposed to this concept several different times. Each time the concept of using behavior characteristics for a team seemed to be maturing. Instead of the primary information focusing on why projects fail, the information turned to increasing performance with the right behavior characteristics on a project team. The maturity of this subject is parallel with the maturity of project methodology. This makes sense since every project methodology applies a team concept.

When I began building and working with my own teams, I started to apply the knowledge of behavior characteristics and the results were pretty good. I wondered why more companies had not caught onto this concept. Not until the servant leadership class did I learn that many of the local companies and even some medical organizations had already been using behavior characteristics to staff their departments and projects. If on a project it's proven that a diverse group of people will improve the outcome and performance of the project, it would also lead to the assumption that it would also work in a department structure where people have to work together on a daily basis. The concept had been out there but not well published.

The behavior concept starts with the fact that each person can be classified in one of four behavior classifications. The goal is to have someone in each of the four behavior classifications for optimum team performance for the project team. Even though everyone posseses behaviors from all four classifications, normally one classification is dominant in a person. Most people will always retain this one dominant behavior. Various tests are available to evaluate employees' behavior.

The first behavior classification is drivers. These people take decisive actions and make decisive decisions. They like control, prefer freedom to work, work quickly and independently, and have very good administrative skills. Mostly these people become managers. But don't get confused. Many managers do not have the driver behavior. It's one thing to be able to lead in getting maintenance and small projects done, but when it comes to leading a major complex project that will change how the company does business, a manager without a driver behavior will have no idea on how or what to do.

Up until the mid-1990s the only career path for a driver personality person was into management. There were no other job avenues to reward these people. But when they went into management they ended up feeling unsatisfied and frustrated in their jobs. The clerical duties of status reports, paperwork, human resource duties, and endless meetings did not allow these driver personalities to do what they were good at. Many of them failed because they could not do the simple routine daily tasks of a manager.

In the mid-1990s, companies started to create positions for the driver types other than in management—such as information technology (IT) architects, development consultants, and solution analysts. In these roles the driver personalities were satisfied because they could do what they liked and were good at, which was to lead in bringing about change. And their pay was matching manager position pay. No longer did the driver personality have to get into management just to make more money.

The second behavior classification is influencers. These are the visionaries and dreamers. When the project is going through a tough time, they remind everyone of the purpose and benefits of the project. They can go out and get resources and funding immediately. They also tend to think outside the box and challenge things. These people will say, "What if we did this?" or "Can we do that?" Caution should be used because a person and team can easily get caught up with their dreams and stray from what was originally promised. Cost, deadlines, and barriers don't exist for them.

The third behavior classification is steadiest. These people would best be defined as the slow movers. If there is a need for fast action or results, these people are not it. They like to understand everything that is supposed to be changed before anything happens. Then it's a slow process to make the change. They don't adapt to sudden changes. They like belonging to a team but want to stay mostly hidden. They can easily be persuaded to follow the group.

The last behavior classification is conventionalist. These people are not risk takers. They ask many questions and want all the answers before any actual work is done. They don't do anything unless they have tons of data to verify that changes need to be done. They tend not to think of solutions outside the box. These people are always asking, "Why do we have to do it?"

There are probably many other similar versions of the behavior concept. I once attended a seminar in which the four behaviors were labeled

TABLE 11.1

Behavioral Personal Actions

INFLUENCER	DRIVER
Makes spontaneous actions and decisions	Makes decisive action and decisions
Likes involvement	Likes control
Dislikes being alone	Dislikes inaction
Tends to dream and get others caught up in their dreams	Prefers freedom to manage self and others
Have good persuasive skills	Low tolerance for feelings, attitude, and advice of others
Exaggerates and generalizes	Works quickly and impressively alone
Jumps from one activity to another	Very good administrative skills
Seeks esteem and acknowledgment	

STEADIEST	CONVENTIONALIST
Deliberates when taking action and making decisions	Not risk takers
Likes close personal relationships	Very careful about taking action and decisions
Dislikes interpersonal conflict	Asks many questions about specific details
Supports and actively listens to others	Likes structure and organization
Not eager to change goals or direction	Always wants to be right
Works methodically and cohesively with others	Can be overly reliant on data
Enjoys belonging to groups	Prefers objective, task-oriented, intellectual work environment
	Works precisely and often has good analytical skills

as controlling, supporting, promoting, and analyzing. This concept is out there but is just not well defined or publicized.

Tables 11.1 and 11.2 provide more details about each behavior classification. As stated already, a person normally has one dominant behavior classification. I have met and worked with a few people who actually have a different behavior pattern based on the project needs. They slide into a behavior role that is missing without understanding why. You probably know people who can do this. If the meeting is going smoothly you never know they are in the meeting, but if the meeting is going badly these people get things back on track. If someone jumps to a quick decision, these people question whether it's the best solution and prompt more discussion. Or if nobody is making a decision, they recommend one just to get something out in the open so that a discussion can occur. The people who can adjust their behavior type are noticeable because things tend to go smoother when they are present on team assignments.

TABLE 11.2

Behavioral Personal Attributes

INFLUENCER		DRIVER	
Prefers involvement with people		**Prefers to be in control**	
Charismatic	Inspiring	Demanding	Commanding
Demonstrative	Enthusiastic	Unconquerable	Contentious
Persuasive	Convincing	Aggressive	Pioneering
Encouraging	Animated	Brave	Forceful
Outgoing	Trusting	Competitive	Goal-oriented
Warm	Friendly	Decisive	Assertive
Compassionate	Sociable	Enterprising	Determined
Charming		Direct	Responsible
STEADIEST		**CONVENTIONALIST**	
Prefers predictable structure		**Prefers procedure and order**	
Adaptable	Systematic	Painstaking	Meticulous
Deliberate	Methodical	Precise	Perfectionist
Unhurried	Habitual	Systematic	Accurate
Consistent	Patient	Prudent	Cautious
Possessive	Steady	Compliant	Agreeable
Stable	Unruffled	Orderly	Neat
Calm	Composed	Conservative	Diplomatic
Relaxed	Loyal	Conventional	

HPT CHARACTERISTICS

The layout pattern of the boxes are important. As mentioned already, checks and balances must occur when there are four behavior types on a team. This occurs because the attributes that make up a driver personality are the opposite of the steadiest personality. The attributes of an influencer are direct opposites of the conventionalist personality. The layout of Table 11.1 is important because it is designed so that the opposites are diagonal for checks and balances. A steadiest is the primary check on the driver and vice versa. There is also a secondary check on the driver with the conventionalist. The diagonal behaviors are the first balance point, and the top to bottom is the secondary balance point. It's a simple formula that greatly increases the potential for a group of people to become an HPT. This ensures that one behavior does not overpower any of the others on a team.

Teams and projects fail many times because the team does not have this behavior diversification to handle all the situations. If everyone on the team is an influencer, then nobody in the group can make a decision because there are no drivers. If members on the team are all drivers and influencers, then there is nobody to ask the question, "Why are we doing this?" So many times the best solutions are not found. If everyone on the team happens to have the driver personality, then there tends to be little discussion and quick actions without much validation as to what is being changed—that is, if a decision can be made amid the fighting. When two or more drivers, who are strong personalities, get together on a project, it can be very explosive. Both want to drive and control the project their way.

To illustrate this, a project once had nothing but influencer personalities on it. The business expectation was that the project would be completed in two years, but the final product was a really sophisticated solution that took 3 years to develop and 4 years of implementation across the organization. If a conventionalist and steadiest personality had been on the project, there would have been more questions about the complexity. The true cost and the overall length of time of full implementation of the project probably would have been discussed and documented. From that there would have probably been a request to come up with another solution, which could have been far less complicated, developed much faster than 3 years, and implemented in a fraction of the time. But since there was no one to ask questions, the influencer group picked the most complicated one without realizing the total effects and consequences.

Another large project started out with one driver personality. The project was progressing on schedule. One of the additions to the project in the early phases was another person with a driver personality. Suddenly, the project team started to have issues, ranging from not getting decisions made to the format of the documentation. Things became very territorial. At one point, one driver personality put a password on all documentation and did not give it to the other driver personality. The one driver personality realized what was happening after a month and was able to change their behavior to be more in the influencer category. After that change, the team went back to being an HPT and was able to generate quality results in a short time.

Some common rules should be followed when building an HPT based on behavior characteristics:

- There can only be one strong driver, better known as an alpha driver. Other drivers can be on the team, but they cannot be very strong in this behavior. Otherwise, there will be conflict on what needs to be done and when.

- There can be one or two influencers on the team. Any more than that and it's a waste of time and just adds confusion to the team. It's tough when there are more than two influencers on the team because many times each has a different vision of what needs to be done. It takes additional time to analyze each different vision. Then there is the time needed to explain and negotiate why one vision is better than another's. There is nothing worse than telling several influencers that their dreams, ideas, or visions are not the best ones. The response often is not acceptance of the vision approved but instead is modifications to their vision. You will hear them say such things as, "What if we changed this?"
- There can be several conventionalists on the team. They tend to ask a similar question over and over: "Why are we doing this?" It is a good to question to ask, but at some point this becomes a distraction. We would like to think that everyone assigned to the project believes that the change is needed, but that is not true. In the conventionalist category there are at least two types of people. One type is the cautious people, and the other type is the people who are against doing any type of changes at all. For the conventionalists against the change, they hope to be able to stop the changes by questioning everything. To keep things going and address the questions, there needs to be a strong influencer or driver on the team. They can answer each question and still keep the group moving forward. If the person continues with all the adverse questions, then the person needs to be talked to. If the person has not bought into the change or maybe even the team concept, then it's best to replace the person on the team.
- There can be several steadiest personalities on the team. It's best to have at least one that is a subject matter expert (SME) of what is being changed, and the rest of the people in this category can be fairly new. This group of people operates as the glue to the project. When a large issue comes up, the driver personality demands that immediate action needs to be taken. The influencers are presenting many new ideas and visions to get around the issue. While the conventionalists are telling everyone that the changes never should have happened in the first place and they need data to resolve the problem. The steadiest, on the other hand, just go about at the same pace as if nothing has happened. They address and fix the issue and then move on. It almost seems as if they just don't care, but they do.

- The team chemistry must periodically be reviewed. A behavior pattern might be missing because a resource was expected to fill that need, but in the team environment they are not displaying it. If the behavior pattern the person is showing does not fit into the team, then replace him or her. For that one team it just did not work for that person. Explain to the person that this happens all the time in professional sports. Teams trade top-performing players just so that the team has better team chemistry to accomplish the task of winning. It's nothing against the person; it's just that they did not fit into "that" team and task. On the next team that is built there is no reason they will not be selected.

Putting together a team that has a balance of behaviors is a much better start then just randomly pulling names out of a hat to fill a resource need. Using balanced behaviors does not guarantee that a HPT will evolve and generate large results, but it does greatly increase the odds of this happening. Once again, it's about increasing the odd of success to reduce the chance of failure from happening.

HIGH-PERFORMANCE TEAM LIFE CYCLE

Putting a group of people together to form a team and having them immediately start to work on proposed change does very little to get them to an HPT level. It takes a certain amount of time to build up to that level. Over time, some team-building phases must occur before the team starts to perform as an HPT:

Forming: This is when the team is first put together. Team members need to learn about one another. They need to understand other team members' points of view, skills, knowledge, experience, strengths, and even weaknesses. It's also the phase in which the team can see what skills and knowledge might be missing for the project. It's a scary time for many people that are on an HPT for the first time. Most people on the front line never have had a chance to give input. Or if they have given input it's fallen on deaf ears and nothing became of it. First timers on an HPT tend to be cautious with their manner and communication in the beginning. To get people to open up quickly, there normally is a person who plays the role of facilitator on the project team whose primary purpose to use some team-building exercises that will get the individual team members to start to think, communicate, and work as one team. Very little work gets done in this phase since most of the effort is learning to work together as a team.

Norming: This is a common phase that occurs multiple times during an HPT life cycle. It's a calm phase where individuals have time to comprehend and analyze what is occurring in the group setting and how they fit in. In this phase they decide to change their viewpoint toward the team and the work that needs to be done. In terms of work, people with similar views start to join together so performance increases during this phase.

Storming: This phase is where everyone's views are challenged. The purpose of doing this is to get the entire team working and thinking as one. Let's say that a new project team is built with 10 members. On the first day there is a good possibility that the 10 members each have their own viewpoints of what is supposed to happen. As they go through the HPT building process they start to merge with other team members that have similar viewpoints. The merging happens because there is safety in numbers. A single person voicing his or her own personal viewpoint will always lose to a group that has a similar viewpoint. Sometimes the storming stage can escalate into some loud discussions. People tend to defend their viewpoints instead of trying to think from a team concept. This phase will also show the behavior types of the team members. The driver types will want to jump into development; the influencers are dreaming; the conventionalists don't want to change anything; and the steadiest want to talk about it more. At times it might seem like the group might be going backward. Normally, this is a short time period. It's strongly recommended that a facilitator, who is neutral to the team, be part of the team through this team-building experience. They can referee and coach the team through this. A good facilitator will know when to change the team's activities so that instead of doing activities that are challenging viewpoints the activities do just the opposite. During these storming phases performance often decreases. Not everyone needs to verbally participate in the storming phase. People with a shy demeanor will participate very little in this phase no matter what the facilitator does. What they will be doing is listening closely to the different viewpoints, so that later they can make a decision as to the viewpoint they want to support and follow.

Norming: This is the same as the first norming phase. The goal after the first storming phase is that the 10 individuals merge into four or fewer groups. This can visually be seen as in-group meetings, with people start to sit together. It can also be heard because members will start to support each other's viewpoints when there is a discussion on them. Again, performance increases during this phase.

Storming: Repeat this phase because not everyone arrives at the same viewpoint overnight. If after the first storming phase there are four or fewer groups with the team, then after the second storming phase there probably will only be one or two different groups. Most of the time it takes two or three times to go through the storming stage before the entire team starts to think on the same wavelength. It can visually be seen that the team building is working because at the end of each storming phase there will be fewer different viewpoints because team members are starting to think alike. The storming sessions are no longer needed when everyone is thinking together and agreeing on things.

Norming: Repeat this phase so that team members have time to analyze and comprehend what is occurring within the team.

Performing: This is the phase the team needs to get to. This phase is where most of the work is done. At this point the entire team is working together. Strengths and weaknesses of each team member have shown themselves by this time. Team members understand their roles in the project and how to work and depend on other team members to get things done. Because of the speed and quality of things getting accomplished, in this phase the team can be classified as a high-performance team.

Figure 11.1 shows what the process looks like with only two storming phases. Table 11.3 shows the different phases along with typical behaviors that are shown during that phase and the important skills for that phase.

The last phase of the HPT cycle has nothing to do with performance so it's not in any of the diagrams. It's called adjournment and occurs at the end when the project is over and the team is being disbanded. The first part of adjournment deals with reward. The more successful the team was,

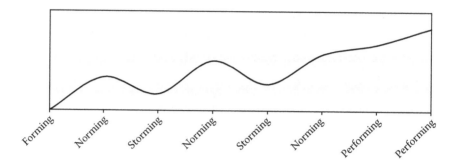

FIGURE 11.1
HPT—Performance chart.

TABLE 11.3

Team Behavioral Pattern of Each HTP Phase

Stage	Typical Behavior	Group Focus	Important Skills
Forming	Polite Impersonal Hesitant	Define Purpose (cornerstones) Mission Common Goals	Goal Setting Organization Facilitating
Storming	Conflicts Panic Confrontation	Role Identity Belonging Grouping	Effective Listening Assertiveness Conflict Management
Norming	Resistance Fades Confidence Gains Developing	Process and Procedures Support Team Thinking	Communication Affirmation Objective Setting
Performing	Effective and Efficient Task Focused High Performing Team	Results Relationships Recognition	Evaluation Reviewing Continuous Improvement

the bigger the reward should be. It does not necessarily always needs to be monetary, but money does help pay the bills. Rewards can be in the form of upper management broadcasting the accomplishments of the team through the organization. It can be that upper management personally talks to each team member and thanks them for their dedication. Another reward is for the wrap-up meeting or lessons learned meeting to be held off site. Make it a team lunch or supper and, depending on the complexity and length of the project, maybe invite the families of the team members. Even though there might have been a lot of stress and very hard work through the project, people tend to always remember how the project was closed. The purpose is to keep the team members happy so that they will want to be part of another HPT in the future.

It can take 1 to 2 months to get a team to the HPT level. They will still be productive shortly after the team is formed, just not at a high level. Normally, the additional effort to build an HPT is done for projects only with a span of 6 months or more. Some might think that once a team is built, retain that team forever and just give them a new project once the old one is done. It's possible but not really recommended. An HPT works because everyone is working toward a common goal on a single project. If the project and goal changes, then the team is back to square one in that each person will probably have a different viewpoint of the next goal and how to accomplish it. You can use the same team for another project, but the team has to go through all the phases of forming, storming, and norming before beginning to perform at a high level again. It will not take as long as the first time to get to the performing stage because the team already knows one another's strengths and weaknesses.

Another reason not to assign another project immediately to the same team is because the level of performance cannot be sustained indefinitely. Besides burnout, promotions and turnover will change the team dynamics. You can delay a promotion or give additional pay for the person to stay until the project is done. But at some point there needs to be a definite end so that people can move into other things. Also, if people can never see the end of something, they are less likely to work as hard. It's best that the entire team is disbanded once the project is done. You will be surprised that most of them will want to work together again on the next project, which is okay for them to do that. It should be voluntary and not mandatory.

On projects, a couple of things must be watched for during the HPT cycle:

- Rules must be set up early on how to listen to others and use proper constructive communication. Arguing in the team is valid because it shows the conviction and passion someone has. But it must be done in a constructive manner and with no personal verbal attacks. Calling someone stupid or incompetent on a project team, which I have seen done, does nothing for team building. A facilitator can help the team members create these communication rules as the first task for the newly formed team. Once created, the rules need to be posted so that all team members can see them all the time. In one

HPT we had a stuffed animal rule. Someone had brought in a small stuffed animal. The rule was that during a heavy and loud storming session, a person could talk only while holding the stuffed animal. There was also a 2-minute time limit. The logic behind the rule was that only one person could talk at a time. The 2-minute rule logic was so that a person had to think about what they wanted to say before they said it. With only 2 minutes they needed to make sure to get their point across before getting cut off. As a group we decided upon 2 minutes because we figured any longer and the person would end up ad-libbing and repeating things to make their viewpoint stronger than what it really was. The stuffed animal would be passed back and forth during the discussions. Many times it was just between two people loudly discussing, every 2 minutes. The rule also allowed the most timid team member to voice their option without being interrupted. During one of the heated discussions that had gone back and forth several times between two people, a timid person requested the stuffed animal. For the next 2 minutes the timid person constructively told the other two that they needed to grow up. Everyone was so shocked by this timid person finally speaking up that after talking most everyone gave the timid person a thumbs-up and smiles. That ended the heated discussion immediately between the two people. Many times humiliation works wonders to fix conflict.

- If there are more than two storming phases, then the facilitator might need to look at replacing a person from the team and bringing someone else in. Sometimes people just don't want to be part of a specific team or a team never comes together. If after two storming sessions an individual is still promoting his or her own viewpoint and nobody else is supporting it, then the facilitator needs to talk to the person one on one to find out what is occurring. And if the person is not open to becoming part of the group in thought and viewpoints, then he or she probably needs to be removed from the team. No matter how much team building occurs, the person will probably never come around to the team concept of everyone thinking as one.

- If a new member comes on the team because of replacement, or it was found a specific skill was required, the team might go back into a storming phase until the new person is oriented into the team. If that does happen the team normally gets back to the high-performing level quickly since it's only one person being introduced into the team. The new person almost always will have to change their viewpoint to the team's. The team had already gone through the team-building process and members are thinking and acting as one unit. A single person will have only a slight influence over the group.

- An HPT doing projects does not last forever. Performing at a high level for a long time on project work is draining. Team members need to be monitored for their energy level. At some point the team needs to be dissolved. A good limit would be 36 months in the performing phase.

An HPT is not strictly for projects. It can also be used in any department environment where there is a group of people working together. I have seen it used in a dentist's office. In a manufacturing line it will not work because most the jobs are single tasks with very little interaction with other people. But in a general office setting it works perfectly. In these team settings there needs to be diverse attributes to handle all the different situations. But what normally happens in the everyday world is that the manager hires only people that are very similar in looks and behaviors to themselves. Each team member is almost a cookie cutter of the other members. When talking to teams like this and looking at their performances, most always they don't perform as well as teams that have diverse behaviors. Diversification is good; similarity is not.

If you are not familiar with an HPT, you might be asking why there is such a big deal about them. Remember one of Jack Welch's lessons in leadership (see Chapter 7):

> **"Stretch":** "Stretch targets energize. We have found that by reaching for what appears to be the impossible, we often actually do the impossible; and even when we don't quite make it, we inevitably wind up doing much better than we would have done."

How is this done? If the resources fail to reach for the impossible every time, pretty soon the resources start to accept that the impossible can never be reached. An HPT actually breaks the barrier of impossibility many times. Many projects are delivered months before the original effective dates and hundreds of thousands under initial forecasted budgets. Even the probability of success increases for a project if the HTP concept is applied versus doing nothing at all.

The core method of forming, norming, storming, and performing has been around since 1965. Psychologist Bruce Tuckman used the phases to describe the path a team must follow for high performance. With the introduction of project methodologies, which involves a dedicated team to do the project, Bruce Tuckman's concept is a key method to obtain high performance from these teams.

12

Quality

INTRODUCTION TO DEFINITION OF QUALITY

Have you ever heard management say, "We need to improve quality"? Everyone talks about it, but few seem to understand it. Efforts to achieve quality normally start in upper management because of goals, issues, or problems that are occurring within the organization. But as the directive is passed down through the levels of management, nobody really understands how to accomplish this. This was probably one of the hardest things for me to understand. It took several years of reading books, attending seminars, and analyzing personal experiences before I began to grasp the concept of quality and to understand enough to make changes to improve the process.

First, quality is an outcome of something that was done. We can say we are going to add quality to the project team, but that creates no results. However, if, for the project team, a formal test plan will be used and a system subject matter expert (SME) will be assigned to the project, then these steps will improve the project quality. The tangible factors of using a formal test plan and adding an SME bring about the intangible factor of quality.

Quality goes hand in hand with advancement in our culture. Think about it: Nobody wants to purchase and use a product that is not both efficient and cost-effective. The automotive industry serves as just one example of how quality has affected our culture and will be covered shortly. But first let's start at the beginning.

GENERALIST VERSUS SPECIALIST

In 1776, economist and philosopher Adam Smith published *The Wealth of Nations.* Most of today's companies, no matter the type, can trace their structure and workflows to the concept of a pin factory that Smith describes in this book. To create a pin, there are 18 distinct operations, including drawing out the wire, straightening the wire, cutting the wire, grinding one end to a point, grinding the other end so that a head can be attached, attaching the head, painting the head white, and attaching each individual pin to a sheet of paper so that a group of pins can easily be marketed.

Smith's theory was that if a single person was assigned to perform only a single pin task, it would produce far more pins and with better quality than having each individual do all the tasks necessary to create the pin. Naturally, to create a single pin, an assembly line was needed to pass it to the 18 different people who would do each task separately. Smith classified individuals workers assigned to do single tasks as *specialists.* These individuals don't have to worry about anything else in the entire process except their one task. They might not see the end product or even care about it. Workers who created the entire pin by themselves were referred to by Smith as *generalists.* The issue with generalists is that some workers might be good at cutting and straightening the wire but bad at sharpening the point and attaching the head at the other end. Other workers' skill levels will be much different for these same tasks. Thus, the quality of the pin depended on generalists' skill level for all 18 tasks.

If specialists were used in the pin factory, 18 people could probably produce over 20,000 *consistent* pins a day. In contrast, if generalists were used to create each entire pin by themselves, 18 people may not even produce 1,000 consistent pins in a day. Sure, they might be able to create 20,000 pins like the first group, but with all the 18 different tasks that come into play, there might be only 1,000 pins that are similar at the end of the day because each person has his own view as they make the pin of such things as the length, the size of the pin head, and how sharp the point should be. Another factor that reduces production is the time it takes to go from one step to another in the process of creating the pin. If one step is to cut the wire with scissors and the next is to straighten the wire with a hammer, the worker has a performance loss because he or she needs to lay down the scissors and pick up a hammer. The group of generalists therefore will have lower output than the group of specialists. You might think these numbers are wrong, but it will become clearer as you keep reading.

Even though the concepts of the generalist and specialist originated in 1776, it was not until over 100 years later, in the late nineteenth century, that these concepts took hold in business—specifically in the automotive industry. For about the first 10 years after automobiles were invented, they were assembled by a team of workers. Each team would build its own automobile. Parts for the automobile were normally separated and stored in a central location for each team to access. In today's business world the team concept gets promoted as the best way to increase performance and increase quality. So at first you might say that since it's a team building the automobile, it must be a quality process. But that would be a wrong assumption.

Let's break down the process of building some of the first automobiles. Several teams in the company created the same type of automobile. The resource process that builds the automobile ensures poor quality because of the differences in skills, experience, and work ethics of each team. Even if it was possible to originally create teams that were close in terms of knowledge, experience, and skill, as the teams evolved they would become different, which would create different results. One team might like to play poker. They start to play not only once on the weekend but once on a weekday night. The games might go very late, and there is drinking each time. So on days after the poker games the team's performance would be low, and the quality of the work would suffer. As another team evolves, they might turn to a weekday night of sporting activities. Because they are exercising they are in better shape to lift and work faster than the team that plays poker. Not only do they perform better, but their quality of work also is better.

Another process that originally added poor quality and reduced performance was in how material and parts got to the automobile for assembly. Originally as fast as the parts could be made they would be moved to a central storage location for all teams to access. When a team went to gather parts, let's say two front fenders, there was no way to get two matching ones made the same day. One fender might have been made that day and the other one several weeks ago. As time went by, everything changed ever so slightly, especially in the early twentieth century. Machines making the car parts would slowly wear out over time, so the output they created kept changing. We notice when things change suddenly, but if changes occur slowly over a long span of time, nobody notices—until, for example, two fenders on an automobile are trying to be matched. The team had a couple of options when the fenders did not fit. One option was to make the two different fenders work by forcing or modifying them to fit, which follows the concept that if it does not fit, get a bigger hammer to force it to fit.

Another option was to go back to the bin and try to find two fenders that closely matched. All these options wasted time and reduced quality.

For over a decade after the automobile was invented it didn't quite catch on. The initial time to build the automobile was long because of all the rework that had to be done to get things to fit and the inefficient process. All this increased the cost and also increased unreliability. In the beginning, automobiles were novelty items that only the rich could afford. The rich might plan on going someplace with their automobile, but there was an excellent chance that they would get home either by walking or having a horse pull the automobile.

Henry Ford invented the assembly line for automobiles. He got the idea, from all places, from a meat-packing company in Chicago. Each person in the meat-cutting line was responsible to cut only one type of meat from the animal. Instead of the disassembling process of the meat-cutting line, Ford reverse engineered the process to assemble the automobile. Just as in the meat-cutting line each person had a specific task, in the automotive assembly line each person had a specific task. Doing this changed the auto worker from a generalist on the team to a specialist of a single task on the assembly line. When the movable assembly line was fully implemented, the time to assemble an automobile went from just under 13 hours to an estimated 1.5 hours. Hence, the moving assembly line as we know it today works because the workers are specialists to specific tasks.

The movable assembly line also made the delivery of parts more efficient. Each part had its own assembly line from conveyer belts feeding into a specific point in the main assembly line. No longer was time wasted having to go get a part. Also with this process parts were used in the order they were created. Over time things change slightly, even though it might not be noticeable. Since the part is on the assembly line, routine checks will quickly notice when the part dimensions start to change. Trending can also be done to forecast when the part will probably no longer fit. Well before that happens changes can be made so that the dimensions are accurate again. The result is that the part off the assembly line will always fit so there is no time wasted in re-work or wasted in material. In today's inventory process this is called first in, first out (FIFO).

There were several beneficial outcomes of the automobile assembly line:

- Because workers became specialists to a task, countless more cars could be built in a given time frame versus the old method of a team of generalists building a car—more than eight times faster.

- Specialists workers needed to know how to do only one single task. So an unskilled worker could very quickly learn the task and not affect the production output. In the generalist process production was slowed from the very beginning with a new, unskilled worker. Until the new worker learned all the tasks, production output was lowered for the whole team.
- Because of the number of cars that could be created and the consistency among them, their reliability increased while the purchase cost decreased.

Automobiles went from a novelty item that only the rich could afford to a machine that the general public could afford and depend on.

On a larger scale, Ford applied Smith's concept of a pin factory to the automotive industry. Looking at the changes in how automobiles were created, the difference was that quality was added to the process by using an assembly line.

TASKS GROUPING AND QUALITY

At first glance the concept of quality appears to break everything down into very small tasks so that people can become a specialist to a specific task. This is partially right but also partially wrong. Three times I have seen new upper information technology (IT) management come in and immediately apply that concept and break down an area's responsibilities into very small pieces. Then they assign a very small group to that specific function or task. All three times the end results were negative.

Each time the tasks were broken down too far. When a tire is put on a car, seven tasks are required after the car has been jacked up and the old tire taken off. The first is lifting the new tire and putting it on the car. The six other tasks are putting on the six lug nuts to keep the tire on. It's not very efficient to have one person put on the wheel and then six other people put on one lug nut per person. People would end up interfering with one another in trying to do their job with so many in one small area. There would be a lot of wasted time as people would be waiting for others to finish their task before they could do theirs. Labor expense would be greatly increased because of this waste.

What the new management was doing was not looking at the overall process. Even though the work covered a wide range of tasks (data entry, data storage, and printing), it did not require a different person per task. When the work assignments were broken down too far it resulted in delays. People were waiting until others were done to do their development, testing, and implementation. It's a good process to break down processes into individual steps or tasks for understanding. In Lean management, this process of breaking things down is called value stream mapping (VSM). But many tasks and steps need to be merged together at times to obtain maximum output and excellent quality. This concept of being able to do multiple tasks in a process deals with another knowledge area called processing engineering, which will be covered in the next section. It looks at processes and procedures to find the bottlenecks that cause workers to be robbed of reaching their full working potential.

Unless some of the tasks require a skill or knowledge that the common worker does not have, it's best to group tasks together and have one person do them. This is where knowledgeable management comes in. They should understand the processes that would allow workers to reach their potential at the same time of not overworking them. An example of a task that should be broken out would be when a change needs to be done for web development and also mainframe development. The skills and knowledge to do web development are very different from the skills used to make changes on the mainframe. Good web developers have taken years to learn this type of development. In this situation it would be recommended that the changes made to the web application be done by a web developer (specialist) who understands that development environment and that another developer who understands the mainframe be assigned to that environment.

REPORTING QUALITY AND PERFORMANCE

When new management comes in and implements changes that end up making things worse, have you ever officially heard that they messed up? I never have. Instead, the statistical numbers and reports that they generate always appear that they brought about beneficial changes. They create what are called SWAG (silly wild-ass guess) numbers on new reports. Or another common trend is to change how data are reported on existing reports. The purpose is to mislead everyone about what truly is happening.

It is well known that small organizations can adapt faster, have better quality, and can deliver products faster than a large company. Why? One of the primary factors is because they normally are consistent year in and year out. Small companies usually retain their upper management longer. Hence, the same vision, goals, concepts, and processes are in place longer. Because of everything being the same for a long time, data that are gathered routinely can be compared with past data measurements to accurately measure performance and quality to see if they are improving or getting worse. If a company is consistently changing processes and the guidelines on what and how to measure performance and quality, there is no relevance then between the historical data and the new data captured for performance and quality. So it's really unknown if the changes are making things better or worse.

Many times when new management comes and makes sudden changes there is a common pattern as to what happens. At first poor results are tolerated because these are new processes with new management. But very shortly, the tolerance wears off. The new management knows that so they change how performance is reported as well as the rules on how benchmark data are reported. Some of the ways to change the rules are as follows:

- Minor defects that were reported by the old management now start to slide under the radar and never get reported.
- The severity of the defect is downplayed. What used to be reported as severe defects are now reported as medium or low defects.
- The causes of defects start to be blamed on others. Major effort is put into trying to find another area that caused the defect so that the defect gets counted against another group.

To prevent management from changing how things get reported to fit their own personal needs, detailed documentation is needed for the criteria of measuring quality and performance. Reports that document quality, defects, and performance must have strict requirements that can be changed only with the approval of upper management.

Job-hoppers, covered in Chapter 2, are notorious for making changes to how things get reported. This is why Deming talks about job hopping as being one of the seven deadly diseases in business in his book *Out of the Crisis*.

A company will always need to look for outside management at some point to bring in new knowledge and ideas. Detailed documentation on the benchmarks of quality and performance need to be put in place to limit the amount of damage a new person can do, along with the length of time they remain in the company before it becomes measurable that their changes are not working. With this in place, all new management can be held accountable to the standards that the prior management used. After the first year there would be a way to see whether the new management's ideas are making things better or worse.

I talk about new management deliberately changing the rules on how things get measured and reported, but many times this happens by accident. Without any mentoring or documentation from the prior management, new management has to figure most things out by themselves. New management can talk to their staff to understand what was done in the past to help figure out some of it, but without formal detailed documentation around data used for benchmarking there is little new management can do but to guess why past management reported something the way they did.

If detailed requirements on benchmarks are in place, then they need to be periodically reviewed to make sure defects, quality, and performance are still being measured and reported as to how the enterprise wants it. If something does need to be changed and there is approval from upper management to make changes, it would be best to do it during a time of stability when very little change is occurring. That way it can be documented what effect the changes had on the results. If benchmarking measurements are changed during a time of massive changes in the department or division, there is no way to validate whether the changes to the environment caused the results to change, or whether the results from the new way things are being reported caused them. Without this, there cannot be correlation between the new results and the historic reports and data.

There are thousands of ways to make bad data look good. The first step to prevent this is having detailed requirements around the factors and criteria on how performance is reported. Only this way can a team, department, or division know if they are improving or getting worse.

MEASURING QUALITY AND PERFORMANCE

In the IT world we don't create tangible items. We create or change lines of code, which in turn will create a tangible result for business. So measurement of performance is tough. Some companies try to count lines of code that are changed monthly, but it's very misleading. One developer might take 1,000 lines of code to accomplish something, but another highly skilled developer might take only 100 lines of code to do the same thing. If part of the review process for a developer was based on the number of code lines and defects, the first developer could have up to 10 defects and still match or better the review rating if the skilled developer had only 1 defect. Also, there is the factor that code logic can run from simple to highly complex. Creating complex logic naturally increases the risk of creating more defects. The point here is that most of the time it's very hard to find good quality benchmarks for IT performance measurement.

To measure performance, most of the time more controls are put around a process. In the IT world where it's very hard to measure output, we see this logic applied all the time. There are complex processes and controls for project management, release management, and testing. But the controls actually add to the reduction in productivity by having to do new steps or tasks that are taking time away from the worker. Let's say that in the past a regular change took 10 days and produced five defects. With how quality is measured it would be reported that a defect is being produced every 2 days. But when the controls were put in place it took longer to make the changes. Instead of 10 days it now takes 15 days to do it. There are still five defects created over the 15 days, but now it appears there is only a defect every 3 days with this new control process in place. On the report to upper management it appears quality has been improved by 50% with the new process because it went from one defect every 2 days to one defect every 3 days. But in the real world, quality has stayed the same and the only thing the control did was reduce performance by 50%.

By no means do the new processes and procedures make it that obvious that production is dropping 50%. Instead, the waste creeps in. Maybe the new process requires the developer to attend a new 1-hour meeting before they can release their changes. Or there is a new form that needs to be filled out that takes 15 minutes no matter if the change is small or large. Or maybe the approval process has been changed and now upper management must approve specific changes. Because upper management is not always available, there is wasted time in tracking them down to get their approval. Even if they are available, it takes additional time to explain everything to them.

If we are talking about performance and quality, then outsourcing needs to be mentioned. I have never heard of a company using outsourcing to reduce defects or to increase performance. Instead, the primary reason for outsourcing is to reduce labor costs. But because the outsource staff does not have company or system knowledge, it might actually take 50% longer to do the work and there is going to be a much large number of defects. On paper it appears that labor costs are being reduced, but in reality it might be costing the same because of lower output and more defects. So cost is being just moved around with reducing it in one area but increasing it in two others. So what truly is the overall cost savings? To understand the full effects of a change and costs, the correct measurements for performance and quality need to be in place to measure it. Regarding Lean management, which is discussed in Chapter 15, there is the concept that many times what appears to be a benefit in one area, when actually measured with all factors and applied across the enterprise, will actually decrease company value.

Getting back to measurements, a good example of using the wrong measurements for quality is Taco Bell. In 1983, Taco Bell was faltering when John Martin took over. Just like its competitors, Taco Bell had created many controls and complex processes under the impression of adding quality. The assistant manager could disassemble and reassemble the 12 parts of the deep fryer with a blindfold on. There was such a large focus on themselves and their processes that they forgot to ask the question: What does the customer think of all of this? The answer was, Nothing! The customer's expectation was to get their needs met as simply and quickly as possible in a clean environment. To survive, Taco Bell had to first understand its customer's needs and then redesign its processes and measurements so that the customer was the primary point of quality.

Companies that can put their work into a unit of work don't have such a problem measuring quality and performance. They have defined all the labor costs and performance measurements involved with creating the unit. Included in this calculation is the cost of defects. For a defect, think of it this way. Initially a company pays to create, test, and implement the change. Then because the change did not work as intended, it has to pay again to fix the change, retest, and reimplement. In IT many companies have defect cost reported outside of the normal costs of the initial development. In the total budget they reserve just 10% to fix defects. When a defect comes in there is no effort to trace it back and assign the cost to the development area that caused it. Without doing that there is no way to define the cost of a unit of work. And without doing that there is no way to understand the true cost of changes to process and procedures as well as such things as outsourcing.

By no means am I against change or even outsourcing. If we went back to the four different high-performance team attributes (see Chapter 11), when it comes to change I would be classified as a conventionalist. I'm very critical of actions and decisions. I'm reliant on data that are accurate and complete to understand if the changes are good or bad. Without data that are accurate and complete, there is no possible way to measure the outcome of a change. So it's only a guess or an assumption the changes are beneficial.

When specific items are being looked at to become benchmark points they need to be easily measured and easy to be defined. The process to capture the data should not decrease performance. Measuring the correct things and making sure there are accurate and consistent measurements over a long term are the most valuable tools to understand if changes are beneficial and the company is on the right path. Without that it's only a guess. Measurements are also important for trending. By looking at past measurements, future outcomes can be predicted. This is valuable information for a company so that it can set attainable goals.

The concept of quality will be discussed throughout the remainder of the book. The goal of this chapter was to provide readers with a high-level understanding of what quality is by explaining such things as specialist versus generalist for a task. In addition, the chapter discussed how important it is to have consistent accurate measurements for tracking performance and quality.

13

W. Edwards Deming, Father of Quality

We have talked about Adam Smith defining the criteria for quality and Henry Ford implementing it on a large scale with the movable assembly line. The person who refined the concept of quality was Dr. W. Edwards Deming. He is known as the father of total quality management (TQM).

To understand Deming, it helps to understand something of his background. In 1917 he entered the University of Wyoming and graduated in 1921 from there with a Bachelor of Science (B.S.) in electrical engineering. In 1925 from the University of Colorado he received a Master of Science (M.S.) and in 1928, a Doctor of Philosophy (Ph.D.) from Yale University. Both graduate degrees were in mathematics and mathematical physics (taken from http://deming.org). In the early 1940s Deming introduced the idea of statistical quality control. At the time he was working for the U.S. Census Bureau. In 1946 he started his own company teaching his concepts to various industries.

After the war with Japan, Deming served as a U.S. advisor to Japan in its rebuilding process. They say timing is everything. It's possible that we might never have heard of Deming, if it were not for the fact that Japan's industry was devastated by the war and the prewar industry culture in Japan was not based around quality. Deming was able to apply and get validation that his concepts and philosophies worked based on the results from Japan. What Deming did was to give a set of directives to Japan management. His directives were fairly small and simple. Instead of having an instruction book of 1,000 pages, he came up with only primary 14 directives or points. These 14 points were not tangible statements but instead were philosophies or principles for executive, management, and quality engineers to follow. His influential work in instructing management on quality was one of the driving forces behind Japan's turnaround. In just a few years after the war, there were noticeable signs of economic growth, mostly because his points changed Japan's philosophy of management. In today's world, Japan's technology excellence in many products such as electronics and automobiles can be traced back directly to Deming's work that started in the early 1950s.

You might think that turning Japan's industry around was not a big deal, but it was. After the war, Japan had a negative net worth. After losing its territories, the only asset left was the island of Japan itself. The island is devoid of natural resources such as oil, coal, iron ore, copper, manganese, and even wood. To feed the entire Japanese population, most food had to be imported. In addition, before the war Japan had a reputation of producing shoddy work, but quality was not an issue before the war because it could leverage resources from its acquired territories. After the war, Japan's survivability depended on instilling quality into every aspect of life. It could not afford to waste anything, since it had nothing left. So the fact that Japan turned into a world leader in a very short time is an amazing feat considering where it started from.

Deming believes that instead of companies setting goals and direction based on lenders, stockholders, and price and earnings ratio and dividends, they need to set direction based on a consistent purpose. It can be as simple as having two directives. The first might be improving quality, which translates into costs decrease by less rework, fewer mistakes, and better use of resources and equipment. The second directive might be to capture the market with better quality and lower price. If these two directives are followed, then earnings, stockholders, and lenders will be taken care of. It will also ensure staying in business and providing job security for employees.

By now this concept should sound familiar—it's the third time it's been mentioned. It was one of Jack Welch's points (see Chapter 7):

> **"Put values first":** "Don't focus too much on the numbers. Numbers aren't the vision; they are the products." Numbers come from the outcome of something. If the primary effort is put toward team building, sharing ideas, and improvement, the numbers will end up correct without much attention.

This concept was also mentioned related to management best practices, where managers need to manage the people and not the tasks that create the performance and quality numbers.

Deming's 14 points are intangible statements. Depending on the company, level of management, and knowledge, each point has a different meaning in how it would be applied. Let's take a look at the 14 points as Deming stated them in his book, *Out of the Crisis* and then my interpretation in the IT world.

1. Create constancy of purpose for improvement of product and service, with the aim of becoming competitive, staying in business, and providing jobs.

For management this is very important. At all times the organization must look for ways to improve and evolve. It cannot just be an annual campaign that gets marketed one day of the year throughout the organization. It must be an everyday process and communication to the organization. Just maintaining status quo is not acceptable.

Enterprises struggle with this because of barriers, one of which is the many management changes. With each change in management there are new visions, new processes, and a different definition of *improvement*. With all these variables and changes at work, it's impossible to create and maintain a consistent purpose for improvement. By the time the front-line workers understand and become familiar with the new benchmark measurements, a new management team comes in with new changes. Companies need to identify barriers and then create a plan that will ensure consistency.

2. Adopt the new philosophy. We are in a new economic age. Western management must awaken to the challenge, must learn their responsibilities, and take on leadership for change.

Most companies, until 2000, did not have such things as change management, release management, project methodologies, quality, downsizing, contactors, outsourcing, and best practices. Managers today need to have more knowledge and skills to lead their teams and control their environment because of these factors. Managers who don't make the effort to improve normally end up being complacent. When that happens they rarely take leadership roles to bring about beneficial changes.

3. Cease dependence on mass inspection. Eliminate the need for inspection on a mass basis by building quality into the product in the first place.

The current trend is to stray away from this. Instead of creating processes that require fewer inspections, companies are creating complex processes that have many controls, checkpoints, and inspections. With many more checkpoints and different people involved with the complex processes, nobody truly understands the big picture. Work has become more segmented with these complex processes. Instead of increasing quality, just the opposite is occurring. Quality is decreasing because of the many checkpoints and handoffs. There is also a higher cost in the administration of a complex process versus a simple one.

Simple processes with few handoffs are needed. Usually this can be done by moving accountability and responsibility to the front lines. Complexity and waste occur when there are several handoffs and when approvals are far away from where the actual work is being done. Just recently a Senior VP I was talking with summed it up a way that I had not thought of before. Complex processes are much easier to create then a simple process. It takes knowledge and thought to create a simple process that is effective, whereas a complex process most times is built around multiple inspections and checkpoints that are easily put into the process without very much knowledge. This will be covered more in Chapters 14 and 15.

> 4. End the practice of awarding business on the basis of price tag. Instead, minimize total cost. Move toward a single supplier for any one time, based on a long-term relationship of loyalty and trust.

This is a big issue in today's companies, in which primary work stems from return on investment (ROI). Outsourcing is employed to reduce cost, which increases ROI and leads to more profitability. However, outsourcing also results in more defects and more time to get things done. Companies are saying that cost is their number one concern; someplace at a lower level are quality and customer satisfaction. Consumers, though, have a primary concern of good quality, reliability and good service when needed. Especially for high price ticket items customers are willing to pay a little more for these factors. Nothing will lose customers' loyalty and trust faster than producing a defective product or offering insufficient product support. As companies become more global, something as simple as a language barrier can cause customers to leave permanently.

In Deming's statement there is the phrase "minimize total cost." Without knowing the true cost of a unit of work it's very hard to understand a change's effects. Many changes that are implemented will decrease the cost in one specific area or type of work, but it will increase costs in other areas in the form of lower productivity and more defects. Accurate and complete measurements need to be in place to measure the total cost.

> 5. Improve constantly and forever the system of production and service, to improve quality and productivity, and thus constantly decrease costs.

This is also called continuous quality improvement. It deals with always looking to improve what is in place. By consistently improving, the company will get to a point of being one of the market leaders in its line of business. Profitability will increase because ways will be found to reduce costs and defects and to increase productivity. Deming created a process called Plan-Do-Check-Act (PDCA) that can help accomplish this.

6. Institute on-the-job training.

Not only does training help employees do their job, but time and money spent on their improvement makes them feel as though they are wanted and are a part of the company. A well-trained staff member will want to give input on enhancements and is always looking for ways improve the company.

7. Institute leadership. The aim of supervision should be to help people, machines, and gadgets to do a better job. Supervision of management is in need of overall as well as supervision of production workers.

Once again the question is, "What is leadership?" In order to institute leadership, one must first acquire it. And to acquire it, it must be defined. In the beginning of the book it was covered that companies need to create tools such as Figure 2.1, to help staff members with this development. Even those with excellent management skills should still be looking to improve their skills even further, as part of continuous improvement. In the tool should be action tasks that managers could do in order to help their people, machines and gadgets do a better job, which is what is mentioned as the aim of supervision. Everyone in an organization needs to institute leadership. The only way to do that is to create a process that can give un-biased feedback, such as having subordinates being able to set a couple of HR objectives for their manager. Only then can the last statement be achieved of needing to overhaul how supervision is being done.

8. Drive out fear, so that everyone may work effectively for the company.

Probably the biggest reason people fear failure is the consequences that go with it. One person I know would take someone's failure and promote it to everyone just to make themselves look better. Most managers don't go to that extreme but are willing to push or deflect the blame immediately to the lowest levels or other areas.

When a defect or a negative trend starts to occur, instead of immediately blaming a single person or department, do a root cause analysis (RCA) to find the real reason. A good series of questions to always ask are as follows:

- Was the person/department given correct instructions? Probably the largest cause of a defect is miscommunication. Never assume anything, always validate (NAAAV).
- Did the person/department have the correct knowledge/support to do the task?

Fear can easily be removed through positive communication. Even in a defect situation, try to make it a positive experience by finding out truly why it happened. In my career, I have never met one person who deliberately caused a defect, so defects must occur for other reasons.

9. Break down barriers between departments. People in research, design, sales, and production must work as a team to foresee problems of production and in use that may be encountered with the product or service.

Organizations are going backward in this. As was discussed in point 3, they create complex processes, checkpoints, and handoffs with the assumption that quality is being added to the process. With these changes, what is occurring is barriers between departments are being built. Instead of thinking of what it takes to do the task and bringing all the people together to accomplish it as a team with few barriers, companies are breaking the task down so that it fits into each department. As mentioned before, controls, delays, and handoffs decrease quality and productivity.

10. Eliminate slogans, exhortations, and targets for the work force asking for zero defects and new levels of productivity. Such exhortations only create adversarial relationships, as the bulk of the causes of low quality and low productivity belong to the system and thus lie beyond the power of the work force.

I have seen very few slogans that had any effect on the outcome of what the company manufactured or the services it offered. Instead, people, processes, and procedures primarily affect the outcomes. The only slogan I have witnessed that did have any influence was in the first company

I worked for, which was an insurance company. The slogan placed throughout the enterprise, even over the entry and exit doors to the cafeteria, was, "Our Agents Pay Our Salaries, Let's Serve Them Well." It identified who we had made the primary customer in the organization (the agent) and why (they pay our salary). It's nice to have slogans once in awhile, but don't put a lot of time, money, or emphasis on them. To the workers, it's just some more words upper management came up with that don't help them do their jobs.

11a. Eliminate work standards (quotas) on the factory floor. Substitute leadership.

11b. Eliminate management by objective. Eliminate management by numbers, that is, numerical goals. Substitute leadership.

We are talking about quotas, service-level agreements (SLAs), and deadlines. True capability of performance is never met with numeric goals. On the manufacturing side, if a person has a quota to make 100 items a day and has control over the entire process, they probably will only make 100 each day. Some days they might work fast in the morning and create 75 items and then in the afternoon make only 25 items to meet the quota. Another day they might create 25 in the morning and then create 75 items in the afternoon. So what is the true capability of the worker? Is it 100 items per day, or much more?

In project work, buffered estimates are given to set deadlines for tasks. Even with a buffered estimate the task is seldom completed early. Give a person 10 days to do a task that takes only 2 days, and most every time on the 10th day is when the task will be completed.

Leadership is a key here in that managers need to stress not quotas and deadlines but instead continuous work and worker improvement. It goes back to Deming's point 7 in that they need to help people to do a better job.

12. Remove barriers that rob hourly workers of their right to pride of workmanship. The responsibility of supervisors must be changed from sheer numbers to quality.

Numbers, measurements, and quotas do nothing for the front-line worker. It's a good way to measure things, but if we revisit Alfred Sloan's concepts of business hierarchy (Figure 10.2), these are only things that management are interested in. The only thing the front-line worker is interested in and has control over is completing the assigned work on time and with good quality.

One last thought that follows high-performance teams and Jack Welch's point of eliminating boundaries is that if a person wants to try to attempt the impossible, it becomes harder to do with barriers, deadlines, quotas, and management by numbers. All these things get in the way of trying to reach the impossible.

> 13. Institute a vigorous program of education and self-improvement.

Several decades ago a company's philosophy was to have workers work as hard as they could every day. The thinking, decision making, negotiating, and so forth were supposed to be done only by upper management. In the last couple of decades this has changed. Companies have realized that their workers probably know just as much as management of the product they create. It's no longer about endurance and strength but more about using what the worker knows to help improve the company. And the only way to make people start to think of ways to do their job better is through education and self-improvement practices.

> 14. Put everybody in the company to work to accomplish the transformation. The transformation is everybody's work.

This is hard in large companies with 20% of the staff being performers, 60% being fence sitters, and 20% being cave dwellers, but it's not impossible. Process and procedures need to be built that will require improvement from everyone continuously. It cannot just be something that is required only annually or semiannually. These processes and procedures must also create some type of consistency across the enterprise to help everyone understand and work together toward a common goal.

Most companies miss the mark in getting few of the 14 points accomplished. Normally the president, chief financial officer (CFO), or chief information officer (CIO) sends an e-mail or holds a teleconference to announce a new transformation. The transformation plan is first announced to all the upper and middle management. Middle management then goes back to their areas and explains the plan and reason for the plan to their lower manager. Then in turn these lower management people explain the plan and the reason for the plan to their people. This process continues until it gets down to the front-line workers. The formal process is called *train the trainer.* At each level the plan and reason for the plan gets changed slightly because of the interpretation of what a person hears from upper management, then how he presents to his subordinate. By the time the front-line people get the plan and reason, it has changed drastically from what was originally announced.

For example, a large company has eight levels from the very top to the front-line workers. In the first two levels, the transformation message is understood 100%. It is expected that the single CIO or chief executive officer (CEO) and the vice presidents know what the transformation message is. But starting at the third level on down, the transformation message starts to lose 10% at each level. The reason for the loss is new managers, incompetent managers, or managers who are more interested in job hopping and politics than in the betterment of the company.

Because of the 10% loss at each level, everyone reporting underneath that manager does not get the chance to hear the correct plan. At level 3 if there are only 10 managers, then 9 understand and passed the transformation plan down to their people. The one manager who did not understand the plan will be not be able to pass this information correctly to the people underneath them in their reporting structure.

Let's assume in level 4 there are 10 people for person from level 3. If 9 managers from level 3 did understand the plan then 90 subordinate managers will get the correct transformation instructions. But again there is 10% loss. This translates that out of the 90 that did get the correct information, there will be 9 managers in that group that will not understanding the information, nor will they pass the correct information on the transformation to anyone who reports directly or indirectly to them.

Continuing down through level 6, 35% of the staff at the level is getting the correct transformation plan. Two thirds of the company at level 6 is trying to transform according to plan, and the other third at that level is not following the proposed plan. At the lowest level 8 there are almost as many people that got the correct transformation plan as those that did not get it. Hence nothing truly changes because of the confusion caused by inconsistent communication.

Here is a chart showing across the company what is occurring at each level:

- At level 3: 90% are getting the correct message and 10% are not.
- At level 4: 81% are getting the correct message and 19% are not.
- At level 5: 72% are getting the correct message and 28% are not.

- At level 6: 65% are getting the correct message and 35% are not.
- At level 7: 59% are getting the correct message and 39% are not.
- At level 8: 53% are getting the correct message and 47% are not.

A better method to execute a transformation plan for a company is to create a team (or specialist) that understands the plan and the reason for the plan. The team then goes through the enterprise and spreads the information to everyone with meetings and e-mails. There are many reasons for doing this:

- Consistency throughout the enterprise of explaining the plan and the reason for the plan to all levels.
- Using this second method of a team going throughout the enterprise, even though there will still be 10% at each level, it's not a 100% loss of subordinates under a manager that does not get it. Just because the manager does not get the message or want to get it, all the subordinates under that manager do get the opportunity to hear the correct plan and message.
- If a manager does not understand the transformation or does not interpret it correctly, since the subordinates were in the same meeting they can help explain it to them, and more important how the transformation affects their specific area.
- If a manager is incompetent or disagrees with the message, since the subordinates understand what is suppose to be happening the manager has only two options. One is to get on board with the transformation, or second is do nothing and become an isolated island. If all the subordinates understand what is supposed to happen and their manager is not following the plan, odds are very shortly the subordinates will go over the head of their manager to tell the upper management that their manager might not be following the transformation plan. It's important to remember that with bad management odds are most of their staff is not too happy to begin with so someone on the team will be more than willing to tell upper management.
- Several weak management links will not be the primary reason the transformation did not occur since the transformation plan was communicated to everyone with a consistent message from the transformation team.
- If the transformation plan needs to be modified, the team implementing the plan across the enterprise can easily make the modifications.

Since they are the only ones implementing it they know what areas have already been informed. They can go back to those areas and explain what the changes are and why. Communication will be clear and concise on the execution and expectations of the transformation.

- Over time the team implementing the transformation can go back to each area and see if the transformation plan is meeting the objectives.

In closing this section, if a company wants to execute a transformation plan, it needs as much support as possible. It needs to stack the odds in its favor. The 10% communication loss at each level will always occur because people resist change or don't understand it. But the process can be changed to make sure that only 10% is lost, by making sure everyone receives the transformation information directly at each level, and not through the trainer process. A company that is trying to implement change cannot have at level 8 only 53% of the employees understanding what needs to be done while 47% have no idea what it means. With those percentages, there is almost no chance of any type of beneficial change occurring.

CONTINUOUS QUALITY IMPROVEMENT

Most companies have a one-time effort for improvement. They create a project for a limited time to work on it. Once the time is up, improvement efforts pretty much stop. Most of the one-time efforts are looking only at the changes that will save millions of dollars. Small changes that can be beneficial are normally not looked at. Continuous improvement is just the opposite. It deals with working on improvement year round, and most changes occur in small increments that yield small to medium returns.

So how do we do continuous quality improvement, but naturally through a proven process? Deming's process dealt with a statistical method to visually see quality improvement. The original concept came from Walter A. Shewhart. Because of its circular process, it has been referred to as either the Deming wheel or sometimes as the Shewhart wheel:

1. "Plan" the product. Design or revise a business process to improve results. What is the goal or objective of the changes, and how do you plan on doing the change?
2. "Do" it. In other words, implement the changes.

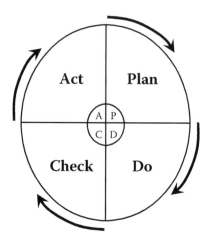

FIGURE 13.1
Deming Wheel: Plan-Do-Check-Act.

3. "Study" the results. Analyze the changes that occurred, and see if they match the expected results from step 1.
4. "Act" on the results. Review all the prior steps and modify the process to improve on it.

After step 4 is completed, then repeat the process starting with step 1. Continue to cycle through the steps until there is little improvement between cycles. It's a simple process that instills continuous improvement. It has also been called Plan-Do-Check-Act (PDCA) or Plan-Do-Study-Act (PDSA) (Figure 13.1).

A better way to understand this is to think that the goal of a project is to improve seed corn in a dry climate. In the plan, we document what we want to improve and then come up with a plan to do it. No matter how much research and analyzing is done, only by changing the seed corn, planting it, and then harvesting will we know for sure whether the changes are good or bad. After planting the corn and waiting for it to grow, then we check for the results. Much like a unit of work, all the benchmarks involved with the process of growing the seed corn need to checked. Last, we act on the results. Was the seed corn improved or made worse based on the goal? What conclusions can be made from the results, and what changes could be tried next? Then the entire process is repeated with new changes to see if the seed corn can be improved even more.

Whether the second results are better or worse really does not matter. What matters is that statistical benchmark data will point to the direction of improvement. If the results are worse on the second attempt, there is justification to go back to the first plan and take a different direction from what was taken in the second plan. Only by going through these iterations can there be statistical validation that the seed corn has been improved for a dry climate.

Companies can use this concept when dealing with reducing defects or creating speed-to-market processes. Document what is in place for a process, and then gather benchmark data involved in the process. Go through the iteration several times, each time checking to see if the changes made the process better or worse. Based on the results from the prior iteration, make adjustments for the next iteration.

To reduce risk and to better understand the full effects of the changes, test them in a small pilot project that has limited consequences within the organization. After it proves that the changes are beneficial, then test them on a larger scale within the organization, again using the PDCA process. It's necessary to test on a large scale since many times when a change or process is put under stress the results that come back are different from when testing on a small scale. This will create accurate data so that better decisions can be made.

Continuous improvement is about taking small steps over and over again to reach a state of high performance. As each step is taken, there is validation that the changes being made truly are beneficial. But what companies normally do is try to fix everything at once. There is no iteration process, so all possible fixes and enhancements need to be done at one time. There is also no trial and error process to make sure the changes are going to be beneficial. With the process of having to do all improvements at once, rarely will the solution allow peak performance after they are in production. Because of the everyday changes in the environment and business world, by the time they get changes developed and implemented they do not necessarily match 100% of what is needed for peak performance. Only by continuing to make small changes and adjustments can processes and procedures continue to match the current needs of a company.

THEORY OF CONSTRAINTS

The theory of constraints (TOC) is similar to Deming's wheel and the continuous improvement PDCA process. It's based on the premise that the achievement of a goal is limited by at least one constraining process. Only by increasing the possible throughput in the bottleneck process can the goal be obtained. Does this sound like the log chain concept again? By increasing the weakest link, the overall capability of the log chain can be increased drastically. TOC can be applied to almost every type of business from manufacturing, project management, and marketing to sales.

There are five basic focusing points to TOC:

1. Identify the constraint (the resource/policy that prevents the organization from obtaining more of the goal).
2. Decide how to exploit the constraint (create a plan on how the resource/process can be improved for peak performance).
3. Subordinate all other processes to the previous decision (align the whole system/organization to support the decision).
4. Elevate the constraint (if it's still the major constraint after changes have been implemented, make more changes in order to get rid of the performance barrier).
5. If, as a result of these steps, the constraint has moved, return to Step 1. Don't let inertia become the constraint.

TOC is just another of the many versatile tools for continuous improvement.

14

Process Engineering

Quality is an intangible outcome from efficient and effective processes. To create these beneficial processes there is a knowledge area called process engineering. Process engineering is rarely about throwing away the entire old process. Instead it's about fixing or changing parts of the process that are limiting performance of the overall process and creating bottleneck.

Let's revisit the log chain concept. There are two weak links of 500 lbs. and 1,000 lbs., respectively, and all the other links can handle 2,000 lbs. each. With these weak links in the chain, the chain can handle the capacity of only the weakest link, which is 500 lbs. Do we throw away the entire chain, or do we find the two weak links and replace them? Normally we spend the time to find the weak links and replace them because it's cheaper.

Much is the same in business processes. There are certain points (links) in a process that might be causing a bottleneck. These need to be identified and changed so that they no longer are the weakest link in the process. In the log chain if we remove the two weak links then the overall capacity of it becomes 2,000 lbs. But the capacity of 2,000 lbs is based on the situation of one end of the chain being attached to the item that is doing the pulling and the other end to the item that is being pulled. If the situation is changed the capacity can be increased further. Folding the log chain in half so as to make it appear there are two chains, and then connecting each line of chain separately to the puller and pullee objects so that there are two separate chains between them, increases the capacity to 4,000 lbs. By doubling up the log chain the pulling capability of the log chain has become 4,000 lbs even though each link can still handle only 2,000 lbs. Believe it or not, business processes, with their many hand-offs and steps, are very similar to a log chain. One weak step can decrease the entire performance drastically. Process reengineering finds these weak steps and the potential for performance improvements, then produces a solution that provides optimum results for the entire process and person by getting rid of the waste effort that is occurring.

Consider the following example, which covers the difference between quality and process engineering. It starts out with a process that is wasteful to create a widget. Changes are made to the process to incorporate the worker as a specialist. Then process engineering is used to change the process even further for optimum performance. The following steps are used to make the widget:

1. The size of the paper is 6" × 6", but the size of the widget is 4" × 4", so the paper needs to be cut to the correct size (requires paper and scissors).
2. Put a five-sided star in the upper right corner of the paper (requires a pen).
3. Fold the paper in half. Then fold it half again with the star on the outside.
4. Put a five-sided star on the opposite side of the star that is already there (requires a pen).
5. Punch a hole into a corner of the widget (requires hole punch).
6. Hang the final widget on a peg (requires a peg).

Applying the concept of generalist to build the widget would mean that each individual person would have to do all six steps. If we have five people individually building each entire widget, then the following steps need to happen before the process can even begin:

- Paper split into five parts (so that each individual has their own stack to work from)
- Five scissors
- Minimum of five pens (but probably should have a spare for each person for backup so 10 pens are needed)
- Five hole punches
- Five pegs

Looking at the final product, many things have a chance of not being consistent. The first is the size of the paper that was cut. Without rulers or templates each person has their own vision of what 4" × 4" is. When a person cuts a 4" × 4" square, when actually measured it might only be

3.5" × 3.5". Another person will end up with some other size. Another chance of inconsistency is the format of the star and the size to make it. The punched holes will not be consistent because some will have holes punched on the corners of where the last fold was made, and others will punch holes on the other two corners away from the fold.

Let's add quality to the process by changing the process to use the concept of specialist to build the widget. This would mean that each person would be responsible for doing one task. So the process would be as follows:

1. Person 1: Cuts paper to 4" × 4" (need paper and scissors).
2. Person 2: Draw five-sided star in the upper right corner of the paper (need pen).
3. Person 3: Fold the paper in half, and then fold it half again with the star on the outside.
4. Person 4: Draw a five-sided star on the opposite side of the star that is already there (need pen).
5. Person 5: Punch a hole into a corner of the last fold (need hole punch).
6. Person 5: Hang the final widget on a peg (need a peg).

With this approach then the immediate cost savings are as follows:

- One pair of scissors and one for backup (savings of three pairs of scissors).
- Have minimum of two pens for each person who draws the star. Steps 2 and 4 (savings of six pens).
- One hole punch and one for backup (savings of three hole punches).
- One peg (savings of four pegs; not a mechanical item so no backup needed).

This is a good example of playing with data to make things appear what they truly are not. There really is no savings on equipment. There are only so many stars a pen can write before it runs out of ink. There are only so many sheets of paper that can be cut before the scissors need to be sharpened or replaced. Same with the hole punch. It appears that there would be large savings, but there are no savings except that there would not be a need to carry as much inventory on hand. Then again, if some of the equipment in the process cost millions of dollars, this might free up some money.

Getting back to the widget process, the differences between the generalist approach and the specialist approach would be greatly noticeable. With one person cutting all the paper in the specialist process, the size of the cut paper would be more consistent for all widgets. In the specialist approach there are only two people drawing stars (steps 2 and 4) instead of each of the five people having to do it in the original process. Because of this the stars would be more consistent. With one specialist punching all the holes, naturally it will produce more consistent results. Quality has been added to the process because the workers were given simple single tasks that made them specialists versus having to do all the tasks to build the entire widget (i.e., generalists).

Let's look at applying process engineering concepts to improve the process even further. If you ever get a chance, bet a group that this widget process with the specialist approach can be changed to reduce staff by 40% while at the same time quality will be maintained (if not improved) and productivity in terms of the number of widgets created per hour will remain the same.

Looking at the first step, cutting the paper, scissors have the capability of cutting more than one piece of paper at a time. So in step 1 let's change it to cutting 10 sheets of paper each time. We have increased that step by a factor of 10. This concept can also be applied to the hole puncher. It might not be able to handle 10 widgets, but probably three of them can be punched at the same time. The obvious benefit of doing more at once is speed and consistency, which translates into better quality. Cutting 10 pieces of paper at once means 10 identical pieces. The same applies to punching holes into three widgets at the same time.

Step 2 involves drawing a star on one side of the paper. The next step in the process is to fold the paper twice and make sure the first star ends up on the outside (step 3). And step 4 is to draw another star on the opposite side. The issue here is that a skill level is needed to make sure the first star is folded to the outside each time. At some point the star will get folded into the inside no matter how careful the folders are. When this occurs, a defect is introduced. W. Edwards Deming calls these in-system defects because the process itself is designed for it to happen sooner or later. This will cause the widgets to either be reworked or thrown away, which reduces production. A better process would be to fold the paper before any stars are put on. It would guarantee that the stars would be on the outside every time. Instead of adding resources to check for errors and having to rework defective widgets, change the process so the error can never occur. This follows the second part of Deming's point #3: "Cease dependence on inspection to achieve quality. Eliminate the need for inspection on a mass basis by building quality into the product in the first place."

With the changes the process now is as follows:

1. Cut 10 sheets of paper at a time down to 4" × 4".
2. Fold the paper in half. Then fold it in half again.
3. Put a five-sided star in the middle of the paper.
4. Flip the folded paper over, and put another five-side star in the middle of the paper.
5. Punch a hole into a corner of three widgets at the same time.
6. Hang the widgets on a peg.

Earlier it was promised a 40% (two-people) reduction in staff while still maintaining the same number of output and quality. Some steps have increased capacity so much that in a very short time the output will start to be stockpiled waiting for the next step to process it. The order of some of the steps has been changed to pick up performance and eliminate the possibility of an error. So now an adjustment can be done on resources:

Step 1: The person doing the cutting of 10 pieces at once is going to get way ahead of everyone else, since the time to do this task was reduced by 90%. After enough cut paper is stockpiled, this person can be assigned to do other tasks.

Step 2: Folding the paper is still a full-time job. We have not picked any time up here. But now there is the possibility of the person from step 1 helping with this step.

Steps 3 and 4: Putting the stars on both sides has become more efficient. Because the paper is now folded before the first star is drawn, the two steps involving putting a star on both sides of the paper follow one another. One person can do both stars. Even though it's double work to put both stars on, the work is in front of the worker. They only need to flip over the widget to draw the other star. In the original process the first person putting the star on had to reach for the next widget, draw the star, and then pass the widget onto the next step. The step for the second star was the same. The new process takes half of the time it took for delivery of the widget to the work spot, along with half of the amount of time it took to pass it onto the next step. To do both steps of drawing stars on both sides probably takes

1.5 times longer than if only 1 star was drawn. But in comparing the old process with the more hand-offs, time has probably been reduced by 25% to put both stars on each side of the widget. When Lean is covered in Chapter 15, this is classified as waste that occurs because of the transportation of work from one area to another. In terms of quality, there will be more consistency because now the same person is putting the star on both sides.

Step 5: Punching holes in three widgets at once reduces the amount to do this task by 66%.

Step 6: In the original process using the generalist process, there ended up being widgets on five different pegs. With the specialist concept there is an assembly line, so all the widgets ended up at the same location. So some efficiency was gained there.

It was said earlier that staff would be reduced by 40% and still produce the same amount of widgets in an hour. The person cutting the paper can also take over the task of punching the hole and putting the widgets on the peg. With a 90% savings on cutting the paper and another 66% punching the holes and putting them on the peg, there is still time left over for this person to go help with putting stars on both sides or maybe help folding the paper.

So the final process looks like this:

1. Person 1: Cut 10 sheets of paper at a time down to 4" × 4". Once there is a sufficient stockpile of paper, this person moves to steps 4 and 5.
2. Person 2: Fold the paper in half, and then fold it in half again.
   a. Person 1 will come and help at some point.
3. Person 3: Put a five-sided star in the middle of the paper, and then flip it over and put another star on the other side.
   a. Person 1 will come and help at some point.
4. Person 1: Punch a hole into a corner of three widgets.
   a. Person 1's primary duty is to make sure there is enough cut paper from step 1. After that they float between drawing stars and punching holes and hanging the widgets.
5. Person 1: Hang three widgets at a time on the peg.

Before changing the process there were five people involved. Now only three can produce the same amount of widgets and quality, thus achieving a 40% reduction in staff. Other things can be done to improve quality and increase performance even further. For example, the very first time the paper is cut, take the top sheet and save it as a template. Place this template each time on top of the stack of 10 that is going to be cut. The template will ensure that each time the cutting occurs the size will almost be the same. With the cost savings of two people being reduced in the process, different equipment could be purchased that has more capacity to speed up the process. An industrial paper cutter and industrial hole puncher would allow even more consistency and more product output to occur in each of those steps. Instead of manually drawing stars, stamps could be made that would increase quality and productivity. All of this is about removing waste in the process so that labor is freed up to help in other steps.

15

Lean Management

One of the concepts that is gaining popularity is called Lean management or Lean performance. It's based on the principles from Toyota's production system (TPS). These concepts helped take Toyota from a small car company to one of the market leaders in the automotive industry in terms of quality and efficiency. The primary goal is to get rid of waste that occurs in the product process. Toyota even came up with three types of wastes called *muda, muri,* and *mura.* But for most Lean efforts everything is based around the *muda* waste. *Muda* translates into any activity that is wasteful, meaning it does not add any value or is unproductive. Seven activities fall into this category:

- Transportation: Work is moved from one department to another for no reason. A process can be set up to go through many different departments and people that is more about control instead of adding value.
- Inventory: Normally people think of this as the material or final product that needs to be stored until it's sold. The goal is to keep the minimal inventory on hand to meet the demand. But this also deals with resources. Until the final product is completed resources are stored or held captive. The goal is to keep the minimal resources on hand to meet the demand.
- Motion: More work is being done than what is required to create the product. Tasks and processes are involved that do very little, if anything, to help in the creation of the product.
- Waiting: The process is based on stops and starts as it goes from one department to another or through different phases.
- Overproduction: Production is done ahead of demand. Things are not done just in time (JIT). An example is a linear project process, where tons of documentation is created and maintained early in the

project process but never used in the later phases. It occurs because early in the process it's unsure what is needed and what is not. So on the safe side, documentation is overproduced.

- Overprocessing: This deals with purchasing very expensive equipment when something much cheaper could create the same results. In processes and procedures it deals with creating very complex solutions for something that could get the same results with a simple process.
- Defects: The effort put into inspecting and fixing defects.

As this topic is covered you will realize that Lean is similar to the other topics already covered. Process engineering and continuous improvement, deal mostly with making changes to reduce or eliminate waste. The Deming wheel makes small changes to remove wastes so that optimum performance is met.

Lean at a high level is about doing more with less, which could be time, resources, money, processes, or even inventory. It deals with looking at the entire process that exists from the start to the end in a company. It encompasses going across departments and even divisions if that is the path of the product being created. The concept is to use the big picture to make large performance increases instead of using individual items at a department level that will end up optimizing only certain parts of the process.

This is different from what happens most of the time in companies. Normally when there is an improvement initiative it's left up to each department to make its own improvement efforts. Usually, only a couple of departments end up making major improvement changes in their part of the process, with many other departments doing little or nothing to improve their process as the product processes through. The end result is that there is little change in the end result. Just because one or two bottlenecks are removed in one department, the work will still encounter the many other bottlenecks in other departments; thus, large performance increases in the process do not happen.

Another factor is that as a product is passed down through the different departments there are dependencies and handoffs. Instead of the product having a continuous flow there are stops and delays before the product goes from one department to another. The ability to make changes to the procedures around the exchange points from one department to another is normally out of the control of a single department. It takes the collaboration of two departments for changes to occur. But many times a new process will increase performance in one department but for the other department will increase the workload. Because of this there is resistance to implementing the beneficial change from the department that will have to do additional work. The only way to get around the territorial issue and to obtain large performance increases is to look at the entire product process at a company level and not just at a department level. With the Lean initiative, at the enterprise level the team can address and overcome those issues and barriers to create the most efficient and effective process, no matter how much work the changes will make in a department.

Normally, Lean is thought of as being applied to manufacturing where a tangible item is created. But it can be used in a variety of situations, including in the project process. As a project goes through the different phases, many handoffs occur, along with many different people from different departments involved with each phase. So in the project situation a large amount of waste (*muda*) occurs.

Lean works only if there is buy-in from all of upper management. Many of the improvement changes will happen across several departments. Whether Lean or something else, the most common reason for all improvement effort failures deals with upper management who did not buy into the improvement initiative and are not open to making changes. Without upper levels trying to improve, it becomes a barrier for the lower levels to execute the improvement changes.

To begin the Lean process, an organization should select the person who best understands the entire product process from the start to the end. This person should be assigned to lead the Lean improvement effort for that product. Besides the company and product knowledge, they should also be very knowledgeable in all six best practice disciplines: leadership, communication, ability to influence, negotiating, problem solving, and decision making. This person will report to the top person responsible for the product. Besides showing everyone involved in the product process that the improvement initiative is being taken seriously, this also gives a direct reporting relationship so that barriers such as territorial issues or challenging the direction of another upper management person can be addressed quickly and concisely. The Lean lead duties include leading the implementation of the changes along with monitoring their effects. The Lean lead needs to be a hands-on person who drives for results.

The second task in Lean is to understand the current environment the product passes through. The lead person must perform value stream mapping (VSM) on the product, wherein its process from start to end is documented. On the surface this might seem simple, but each product process can have several different flows for the same product. The most obvious flow is the tangible product that is being passed from department to department, but additional flows deal with information and people processes. All of these flows are affected when a change occurs, and all must be defined and measured to see if improvement occurred.

To create these flows, the Lean lead and their team need to go out to the different departments to gather the necessary information from the front-line workers associated with their product. There are many ways to do this. One creative way is to video the path of the product. For example, in the early 1990s I was on a team that reengineered the business personal lines of two insurance companies into one company. Part of this VSM was done by video recording the product process. To be able to issue and support an insurance policy was our product for the project. The product process for one flow began the minute a piece of mail came into the company. From that point, the filming started. As each department did a task to the piece of mail, it was filmed. This gave a visual, along with an estimated time frame as to how long a task should take. When the piece of mail was passed to another person or department, this was also filmed. Most of the time, this occurred in a batch process where as work was completed it was put into a basket. The completed work in the basket was routinely picked up at certain times during the day and delivered to the next department so another task could be done to it. At each one of these waiting points, a sign was made to show the best and worst situations. The best situation was that a piece of mail was completed and put in the basket for the next department, just as the mail was being picked up. The worst was that the piece of mail was completed and put into the basket right after mail was picked up, so that piece of work would have to wait until the next time mail got picked up before the processing could continue on it.

VSM is an essential part of the Lean process. It helps make visible the entire process one step at a time throughout the different tasks and departments. It's a true representation of what is occurring in the product process. When the mapping of the entire current environment is completed, then work can start on goal-state improvements. It's important to understand that it would be a wrong assumption that "all" changes created by the Lean process are always going to bring about beneficial results. The process is a trial and error process in that sometimes the changes that are going to be made might adversely affect the final product outcome. Even though an idea might seem to be able to improve performance greatly, it's only theory until it's actually put into production and then measurements are taken to validate it.

Many times instead of looking at the actual process that drives improvement, the quantitative numbers drive the improvement, for example, when there are lots of defects, the improvement effort is concentrated only on improving defects. The solution might reduce waste of not having as many defects, but the solution increases waste in several other *muda* catagories. Therefore, the big picture doesn't change. For example, to reduce defects, a new process is built where all logic will be double-checked. In the *muda* category of defects, the number of defects decreases, so waste has been reduced for that category. But in the category of motion, waste increased because of the double-checking. So the entire process needs to looked at and a goal state decided upon.

For creating the goal state of peak efficiency and performance, one can leverage the knowledge acquired in Chapters 12 through 14 that covered process engineering, quality, and continuous improvement. This includes the log chain concept and specialist versus generalist. The easiest improvements for identifying and removing and changing are the waste (*muda*) that occurs in the processes and procedures. Most of the time, look to change the processes so that there is a continuous flow. Do this by removing many of the steps that have a stop and start, along with removing as many hand-offs as possible.

In order to create the best process, there might be a need to change how work is passed from step to step. Almost always the product is pushed through the process in an assembly line. But once in a while a better process is a pull at certain spots. Think of it like a grocery store. The dependency on the amount of material coming through the process is based near the end of the process with how much the customer purchases. What is sold in the store triggers what is pulled into the store. This concept can be applied at certain spots in the process to increase efficiency. There might be a resource restriction in a certain area. Instead of forecasting when people are done and giving them deadlines that most of the time are not met, do a pull process. Instead of deadlines and timelines, just queue up work for the person so that when they are done the next piece of work is ready. Timelines and deadlines are based on estimates that usually end up being inaccurate.

Many tasks can take longer because there is more to the change than originally expected, or they could take less time because it ends up to be a simple change. If it's easier, the person will work slower to meet the deadline. If the work is harder than expected, the person will work extra hours to meet the deadline, which adds stress and reduces quality. When the work is pushed, the performance is based around meeting the deadline generated from the estimate and not what the true capacity of the person is. With a pull process there is no waste when a task ends up being simpler than expected. As soon as the worker is done she can start the next task. When it takes longer, there is less stress because work is not based around a specific deadline. Allowing adequate time to complete the task increases quality. The pull process can easily be used in IT for development. A list of tasks can be created indicating the order in which they should be done. As a developer finishes the current task, the next one on the list is assigned.

An example of the pull concept is a claim system in insurance. Work is assigned to a claims examiner based on the location of the claim and not the volume. If a severe storm goes through a claims examiner's territory, they could end up being bombarded with pending claims that need to be worked and closed. They have two options: (1) work at their normal pace, which ensures quality but will make them look bad on their review because of the number of pending claims; or (2) ignore quality and take shortcuts to close claims as fast as they can to get their pending claim number down. Neither option is a win–win situation.

Instead of the storm driving the number of pending claims an examiner gets, a system should be in place to limit the number they can have. If the claims examiner is at their maximum limit that they are supposed to have, only when they close a claim will a new one be pulled into their workload. If the claims examiner is at the maximum number of pending claims and a new one comes in for him or her, the system will automatically route the claim to another claims examiner who is not as busy but is qualified to handle claims in that territory.

No matter what processes are used, once the goal-state VSM is done, the most important part comes next: implementing the necessary changes. Unless there is a measurable change, people including upper management will feel as if it's just another futile attempt at improvement. Then like all the other improvement initiatives that show little or no return, Lean will be looked as something that does not work.

The Lean lead needs to build a simple implementation plan. The plan needs to include what is planned on being done and when. It must be in a step-by-step process with a timeline. Before the implementation there must be documentation created on how the tentative improvement change will be measured. If it's allowed to wait until after implementation to define the measurement, people who are creating the performance results will pick out only the positive results that occurred to communicate the status of the change. The negative results will fall by the wayside. The last step before implementation is the communication of the change. This should include what and why things are being changed, along with the expected results.

The implementation is nothing special. How changes get implemented in a company is unique to each company. After the implementation, follow-ups should be conducted with the affected areas and the effects measured. Even though it's not part of Lean, these follow-ups and measurements must occur several times over a specific time span. When changes occur, rarely will the full results show themselves immediately. It takes time for people to get up to speed on the changes. Most people are hesitant of new processes so they naturally work slower in the beginning, but once they see that there are benefits, plus the fact it becomes part of their everyday work process, then speed and quality increase. Only by talking to the users and taking measurements several times can the true effect of the change be reported.

Along with word Lean, the word *Kaizen* is normally mentioned. It's a Japanese word for continuous improvement; it usually indicates a gradual, orderly continuous improvement, without a large capital investment. This is accomplished by finding and eliminating the wastes that exist in an organization's systems and processes. This is totally different from the traditional management style. The traditional system is referred to as *management by exception,* which translates into the "If it isn't broken, don't fix it or improve it" approach. *Kaizen* and Lean take the opposite approach: It's best to always challenge the existing systems and processes no matter how well they are performing. The purpose is to always be looking to find ways to add improvement and value, which were the same goals and concepts related to Deming's wheel and continuous improvement.

16

Six Sigma

Lean adds improvement by increasing the process flow via eliminating wastes in the process. Another improvement tool is called Six Sigma, which involves improvements occurring through reducing process variations.

If you deal with improvement or are in upper management and trying to find ways to improve quality, you have probably encountered the terminology Six Sigma. Six Sigma originated in 1986 from Motorola. It seeks to improve quality by looking at the outputs of processes. This can lead to identifying and removing the causes of defects. At a high level Six Sigma is a disciplined methodology that uses data and statistical analysis to measure and improve a company's operational performance by identifying and eliminating defects. By looking at statistical data and loading it into varies formula's, Six Sigma can indentify processes that need improvement.

Within Six Sigma, there are certificate levels, or belts, the most common of which is green. People who have achieved a green belt have been taught enough about Six Sigma to apply the principles to their current work. People with a black belt oversee the green belts. Black belts work 100% of their time doing only Six Sigma. Consider them as consultants to the project to make sure Six Sigma is followed. There are other levels, but these are the most important two for the present discussion.

Six Sigma projects follow one of two project methodologies. Both follow the same concept of the Deming wheel of Plan-Do-Check-Act (PDCA). The first project methodology is geared toward improving the existing business process and is called Define-Measure-Analyze-Improve-Control (DMAIC):

- Define: Normally the project starts with the idea that an existing process can be improved upon. To do this, the problem that is stopping improvement from happening, along with all the measurable data available, must be clearly captured. A good problem statement is,

"Defects in the wheel assembly area have increased by 25% over the last two quarters." It's clear, concise, and measurable.

- Measure: Six Sigma is about statistical data. In this phase all the relevant data is captured around the problem. It includes data from all the inputs into the problem process, along with data around the outputs. The data selected to be measured needs to be defined and justification given as to why it is being captured. This is to ensure that the data being captured has value to the process. Monetary value needs to be assigned if the problem is removed. This can be based on increased profitability or cost savings.

- Analyze: Using proven statistical tools, the data is analyzed to see whether the problem is real and can be solved. Sometimes a defect is caused by a random occurrence that is happening at which Six Sigma is not capable to solve. The volume and overall effect of these random defects are so small that it is not cost justified to address them, even if they could.

- Improve: If in the analyzing phase the data shows that the problem can be solved, then the project moves into this phase. By looking at the data and using many different data analysis techniques, the Six Sigma team can try to come up with solutions to improve the process. The goal is to find the root cause of the problem and fix it.

- Control: After the improvement has been implemented, measurements and controls must be put in place to make sure the improvements stay in place. Any deviations from the goals can easily materialize into process defects that will take away from the gains acquired.

The second project methodology is geared toward projects that are creating a new product or process design and is called Define-Measure-Analyze-Design-Verify (DMADV):

- Define: This time what is being looked at are enhancements and new functionality. Instead of stating what needs to be improved, it needs to be stated what new business functionality is needed along with the measurable increase that will occur. It needs to be documented how this will be measured. A good statement is, "By adding imaging capabilities in the processing department, the overall expenses will be reduced by 25% in that department." It's clear, concise, and measurable.

- Measure: This is the same as the DMAIC process. Gather all the relevant statistical data around the enhancement that will be made. Include data from all the inputs, along with data around the outputs. For the data that are selected to be measured, define the justification in terms of quality to ensure the data being captured have value to both the current and future process. Awareness of product capabilities and risks is necessary.
- Analyze: From the collected data and goals, the Six Sigma team comes up with a high-level design to meet the project requirements and goal. Sometimes it's realized at this point that the goal of the project cannot be obtained. The proposed change does not match the proposed improvements stated in the define phase. If this does happen, it needs to be documented that the best solution found will not meet the business goals. Maybe the goals of the business partners needs to be reviewed to make sure they are accurate, or maybe a lesser solution will be used that will obtain almost as much efficiency as the best solution. Negotiation needs to occur to arrive at the correct decision on what to do.
- Design: The high-level design is turned into fine details with tangible tasks and measurements. The best possible solution is found, along with justification on why it is. To justify this, walkthrough simulations may be needed. This all needs to be approved by the customer before moving onto the next phase.
- Verify: Before full implementation verification needs to be obtained that the design works as planned. Prototyping and small pilots introducing the new functionality into production can be used to accomplish this. The purpose is to get the changes into the hands of the owners as smoothly as possible without interfering with their existing workload. Most of the time by moving slowing through the implementation process there are no work disruptions and enhancements very quickly get verified that they work as planned.

What Six Sigma does is to group together a wide range of quality tools that can be used in each of the individual phases no matter whether DMAIC or DMADV is used. Such tools used are analysis of variance, axiomatic design, business process mapping, chi-square test, control chart, correlation, cost-benefit analysis, design of experiments, failure mode and effects analysis, general linear model, histograms, quality function deployment, Pareto chart, pick chart, process capability, regression analysis, root cause analysis, run charts, taquchi methods, and taquch loss function. It allows the statistical effects of a problem or issue to be examined to solve it. Because it's based on statistical data, forecasting and trending can occur. Sometimes low performance and poor quality can be identified before anyone notices it.

Six Sigma can be relatively sophisticated, along with which comes high-price resources that are solely responsible for implementing and supporting Six Sigma. When initially started in an organization, the Six Sigma skill and knowledge do not exist in the organization so there is a cost in training, along with probably bringing in outside Six Sigma consultants to implement it correctly. Since Six Sigma is primarily based around statistical information, the techniques for defining and capturing the data can be relatively complicated sometimes. In a manufacturing environment where there can be true measurements for a unit of work, the statistical information gathered can be concise, accurate, and easy to gather. But for other industries that deal with service and information, gathering true statistical measurements is not easy to come by.

Much like all the latest and greatest technology and concepts, companies need to take a serious look at the startup cost, learning curve, and expenses to keep Six Sigma up and running. The benefits from Six Sigma can be great if executed correctly. But so is the risk of failure if it's not executed correctly.

17

Workplace Efficiencies and Distraction

In today's business world as new technology was brought in to improve performance, the new technology also caused distractions that rob most users of their performance. The correct controls and training were never done when the technology was implemented. Now these distractions have become part of the workplace and can be difficult to eliminate. The only thing that can be done is to be aware of them and try to reduce the effects. Whether in management or a team member on a project, people need to understand these distractions and control them for performance reasons.

E-MAIL

The very first type of e-mail tool I ever saw was a mainframe tool called SYSM. There was nothing really fancy about it. I don't believe you could even store any of the messages sent. It did though open my eyes up on how dangerous it could be. The system could use a wild card character so that you could send the SYSM message to more than one person. By accident, on a very personal note the wild card character got put in the address of the "Sent To." Within seconds, 10% percent of the company received this very personal note.

A couple of things must be considered when working with e-mail. When talking either on the phone or in person, we can hear the other person's tone of voice during the conversation. By that single factor we can tell if what we are saying is being understood by the other person or if it's angering them. E-mails don't allow for this. They are a one-sided communication by the person typing the email. Even though e-mails can be sent back and forth, without hearing the other person's voice there is no idea if the conversation is offending the other person or if they understand and agree with what is being written.

An e-mail is hard copy. It's the same as if a person has handwritten a note and mailed it to someone using the post office. Logs tell when the e-mail was sent, who it went to, and when the other person actually opened it to read. It's a well-documented trail that allows a hard copy to be produced at any time. E-mails are stored on a server personal computer (PC) for the receiver to pick up when they are ready. These servers are backed up on a daily basis and stored for years. Most people assume that if they delete the e-mail it's gone forever. That is a wrong assumption because of the backup process. With the possibility of needing an important e-mail in the future, all companies have a common process in place to retrieve a deleted e-mail. So any e-mail, even ones deleted years ago, can easily be retrieved.

A handwritten letter takes a lot of effort and can be sent to only one person. But with e-mail it's really simple to forward one to another person or a group of people. The person who originally sent the e-mail has no control over to whom it might get forwarded. A common mistake is that the person who started the e-mail vents on something or someone. They send it to a coworker as confidential. But the coworker still forwards it to someone else. Now the e-mail that was supposed to be between two people is out into the open, and the venting remarks can be seen by everyone.

Let's discuss how e-mails rob performance. Normally on a daily basis many daily communications come from the company. Most do not pertain to a person's job, but employees still need to read them just in case it might. Then there are the personal e-mails from friends inside and outside of the company, plus family members. And who can resist a good joke that is sent to you, which you end up passing on to your friends? Things such as compnay e-mails are a good way to communicate, but all these take away from the normal workday.

When I first started in the information technology (IT) profession before e-mail, the rule was that if an IT worker was scheduled to work 8 hours day, the employee normally worked only 6.5 hours. A total of 1.5 hours each day were lost because of lunch breaks that take longer than normally scheduled, bathroom breaks, trips to the vending machines, conversations around the water cooler, and going to and from meetings. E-mail is not the sole cause, but in today's workplace on the average a worker is probably working 1 hour less. So now today on average probably only about 5.5 hours of work is being done during the entire 8-hour work day.

For several months during certain phases of running a large project, I can receive over 120 e-mails daily. Let's play with some time statistics with the consequences of receiving 120 e-mails daily. From those 120 e-mails, half do not require a response back but still need to be opened and read. Let's say each of these e-mails takes 20 seconds to open and read, which totals 20 minutes out of your day. Looking at the other 60 e-mails that need a response requires 20 seconds to read each one and then the time it takes to type the response. If a person can type really fast and knows exactly what they want to say without much thinking, let's estimate that these take 1 minute to type the response per e-mail—that is, if the response can be kept short. With 20 seconds to read and 1 minute to type the response, that's 1 hour and 20 minutes to handle the 60 e-mails that need responses. All total, to handle 120 e-mails a day it will take 1 hour and 40 minutes out of every day. If a person gets only 30 e-mails a day, which is very common, and they all need to be responded to, only half of them with short responses, this totals 25 minutes each day to handle just e-mails.

When a person misses a day of work, it becomes worse. In the example of receiving 120 emails per day, now there are 240 to address, which translates to 3 hours and 20 minutes of work. And if a person takes a week's vacation and does not answer e-mails during that time, when they come back they have over 8 hours to spend just on e-mails to get caught up. The e-mailing by itself has become a necessary skill that each employee needs to develop. Without training and knowledge in how to use it effectively, employees and the company will be robbed of time.

Using the same time statistics only with a different situation, let's say an e-mail was originally sent to 12 people and four times the e-mail comes back to the original sender asking for more information. Each time all 12 people have been copied. For each time it gets sent, the e-mail consumes 20 seconds of time of each of the 12 people, or a total of 4 minutes. Even though the originator has sent it five times, someone has sent back a reply four times. So almost everyone has received nine e-mails. Take into account the fact that one person each of the nine times has typed a reply (1 minute), which is a total of 9 minutes. Adding up the time for everyone to read (4 minutes each, times 9 times received, equals 36 minutes) and the time to type the responses (9 minutes). This one e-mail has consumed about 45 minutes of the company's time. For a large corporation there could daily be 100 of these types of e-mails that go back and forth with everyone copied in. If there was 100, this translates into 4,500 minutes per day, or 75 hours a day.

In today's business environment there is no way to get around e-mail, but individuals can help control it. First, make sure an e-mail is the correct communication tool. Is the content going to generate a lot of questions? If it is, then call people to get the answers before sending out the e-mail or set up a short meeting. Sometimes the meeting might have to be only with the one person asking the questions. Even through an individual might not have started the initial e-mail, at any time anyone on the mailing list can recommend that a meeting is held if it seems like there will be an endless chain of e-mails.

Another bad habit that is costly is on a resend or forward of an e-mail. Is it necessary to copy everyone on the reply? It's really simple to do and everyone does it, but it is seldom needed. Review the address list, and delete the people that do not need to be included. When a person is working toward a solution, they need only the core people affected or people who can make the decisions to be involved. Later, after the decisions are made and all the information has been gathered, then inform all the other people about the outcome by copying them in. Even the conversation from prior e-mails can be included.

Something I call shot gunning also occurs with e-mailing. I call it this because with one simple reply it can create mass confusion and uncertainty. Working on many enterprise-wide projects that are bringing change about on a large scale it's impossible to keep everyone informed all the time. So after all the research is done and the stakeholders and upper management have approved the changes, then normally an informational e-mail is sent out to everyone to validate the actions that are going to occur. Most of these e-mails go to over 100 people. Even though at the end of the e-mail it's always stated in bold letters: "If you have any issues, concerns, or feedback on the above, please contact only me directly," most of the time this is not what happens. Instead, someone uses the reply to all option on e-mail when sending back their questions, concerns, or many times just to vent. It's okay to question something, but by sending back the reply to everyone the person has undermined all the work that has been done before.

The normal effect of shot gunning a reply is that once one person starts to question the decision then doubt comes into play. This in turns adds to more e-mails being sent by and to everyone. It spreads like wildfire, and pretty soon 10 different e-mail conversations are occurring and on each one everyone is being copied. To stop the spread of confusion, large meetings and personal phone calls are necessary to control the confusion. It can take weeks of work in damage control to get back to the point of when the original e-mail was sent. When the person that started the shot-gunning it is talked to, most times they had not spent the time to read the original e-mail fully, nor spent time to think it over. They initially did not understand what the changes were and why, so they responded quickly and without much thought.

To reduce the waste that can occur with e-mail usage companies need to take ownership of monitoring it. As much as I hate control, there is no other way around it. They need to do spot checking to make sure correct e-mailing protocol is being followed. They also need to have regular training for all employees who use e-mail. E-mail will never go away because it's part of the business process. But the value it brings to the company can be increased if there are controls around its usage.

INTERNET

In the mid-1990s I gave a presentation to the president of a company I was working for. In the presentation I mentioned how the Internet was going to change how business was going to be done. Instead of our customers having to physically go someplace to purchase our product, they could now do it over the Internet. We could bring the function of purchasing into the customer's home. We could also advertise all the products that we sold over the Internet, which would change how marketing would be done. Plus another benefit was if a customer selected a specific item over the Internet we could gather information from the customer so that other similar items we carried could be attempted to be cross-sold to the same customer.

The president was not impressed with the presentation until the search capability over the Internet was explained to him. All of sudden there was a large interest from him. He wanted us to search for expensive Bentley cars on the Internet. The last hour of the presentation we ended up looking up cars. Something that could have made the company millions, the president showed little interest in. But when it got to nonbusiness he was very excited. And since that day I have always wondered why does a company allow full access to the external web? A company demands that their people work harder and longer to get more results, but then the same company gives full access to the Internet. For most users the external Internet is not a requirement for them to do their job. It could actually be classified as a distraction to the employee.

With the capabilities of windows to quickly switch from screen to screen, users believe it's easy to hide that they are searching the web. Years back another person and I decided to make a game out how many times we could catch a person surfing the Internet. We caught the person 22 different times in just one day researching stock market picks on the Internet. They thought they were fooling everyone by quickly changing over to an Excel spreadsheet, but it was easy to see no work was being done on the spreadsheet.

The common trend is that a company's performers rarely use the Internet for nonrelated work. They might once or twice a day check the weather or some other common sites but spend only a couple of minutes doing it. Otherwise the rest of the day they are busy working. For many of the below average works, though, it's is a different story. They are constantly on the Internet checking sports scores, doing fantasy leagues, looking at the latest funny videos. Even to me, instead of doing boring company work, it sounds like a much more exciting day looking at videos, checking the stock market, sending and receiving jokes, and strategizing for a football fantasy league.

Before the Internet it was very easy to identify and manage the subpar worker. Since there were no distractions at their desk to consume their day, they would have to go to other places away from their desks to help fill in their day. You could find them at other people's desks, in the breakroom, or standing at the water fountain, or sometimes they just might disappear for an hour and nobody knew where they went. Most of the time they were disrupting other people's work. As a manager it was easy to visually see this happening. Now with all the distractions of the Internet, e-mail, instant messaging, and cell phones, these same people no longer have to leave their desks when they become bored. They have all the tools and technology at their desks to keep them entertained through the workday.

INSTANT MESSAGING

My daughters used to pick on me for the longest time because I never carried a cell phone or it was turned off when I did. Also at supper the rule was supposed to be no cell phone texting. With today's cell phone technology anyone at any time can interrupt what you are doing with a simple text message. My personal time and our family supper time were not something that I wanted someone else to easily interrupt.

In the workplace the same thing is happening with instant messaging. For the few people who might not know what it is, it's the ability to send very easily and quickly a personal note, just like texting on a cell phone. Without having to accept it, the receiver gets a little box with the message in it. If used correctly it could be a valuable tool, but most of the time it is not.

Imagine leading a large change and a large number of people are involved. Very easily the lead can have five to six different instant messaging conversations with different people going on at the same time, none of which they started. Because it's so easy and quick to use, people without hesitation will start an instant message session on some of the simplest things. The person who pays the price is the lead, who through the entire day gets bombarded constantly with instant messaging. Each message, besides taking time away, makes the person start and stop what they were doing before—all waste. Many times people leading major changes will turn this feature off to get work done. As for the cave dwellers and fence sitters, instant messaging is just another tool that can be used to interrupt others and pass time without even having to leave their desk.

CONTROLLING WORKPLACE INEFFICIENCIES

I have listened to several people in upper management who have visited the off-shore sites before making a decision to outsource overseas. When they got back they all were very impressed with how the company's overseas employees worked. The common process is that when a developer started to work they had to log in that they started. Each time they took a break or there was a long distraction, they would log off. Naturally the outsourcing company knew representatives were coming in to see their operations, so it's unknown if this occurred every day, but if it is, this the work ethic of the global competition.

Many people are probably upset with the idea of controlling or even removing some of these distractions, such as access to the Internet. But then again, most of the performers in a company who work hard most every minute during the workday are also upset. These performers are trying to make the company great, yet they sit beside other workers who spend most of their day abusing the Internet and e-mail. It's never that the low performer sees what the performers are accomplishing and stop the abuse. It's just the opposite. The performers at some point ask themselves why I'm I working so hard compared with others around me. So the performer's work ethics change to include more distractions such as surfing the Internet, which reduces their productivity.

The consequences of all of this is a work force that works toward being mediocre instead of toward becoming high performers. Many companies realize this and already have restrictions around the Internet, e-mails, and cell phones while at work. Companies that still allow these distractions have lowered their full performance potential. The sad part of this is that upper management does not choose the hard path and remove or control many of the distractions to help increase performance for their internal employees, which would increase return on investment (ROI); instead they take the easy path and outsource jobs to cheaper labor to increase ROI. The responsibility of reducing these distractions is not solely upon upper management. It's the responsibility of all management from the top down to the front-line management to work on controlling it.

One last thing that is probably not too surprising. When the Internet first came out and was not available in companies, people used to go home and surf the Internet many hours each day. Now when I find someone who is continuously abusing the Internet I like to ask indirectly how much they use the Internet at home. Surprisingly, most do not. They do enough surfing the Internet at work that there is not a need to do it at home.

It's only theory, but at some point companies will have to address these internal distractions. Currently, to keep showing good ROI the common tool used is outsourcing with cheaper labor. But what is occurring each year with the world economy, the salary gap between the regular labor and the cheap labor keeps shrinking. At some point companies will have to look elsewhere to improve ROI. One place would be to take a long hard look internally at the waste that is occurring.

GETTING STARTED FOR THE WORKDAY

If we are covering waste that affects performance, then we need to cover what happens in the beginning of the workday. In the old days a person turned on a green-screen monitor on their desk and was working in under a minute. In today's world with all the technology and software that is used to do our work, startup does not happen that fast. In today's world it requires the time-consuming task, for example, of starting up the Windows software, which includes going through a security process that requires entry of a user ID and password partway through the process. After Windows is up and running, then the e-mail system needs to be started up. If the company does not have an automatic process to use the user ID and password from the Windows sign-on, then those have to be entered again partway through the e-mail system startup. In the end almost 15 minutes once a day is spent just getting ready to work. Sometimes a software system will stop working and the only way to get it running again is to shut down and restart the computer, which requires another 15 minutes. Even at the end of the day to shut down all the programs and then the computer itself can take up to 5 minutes.

Let's say in a company there are 1,000 employees who each need to start their PCs up each morning. With 15 minutes for each person, that equates to 250 hours each day being spent just to get the tools ready for a person to work. If a person works 8 hours a day, which nobody does, this equates into the cost of 31 people just to get the PCs ready for people to work. Earlier it was mentioned that out of an 8 hour scheduled day, there are only about 5.5 hours of work being done. You might have been skeptical when it was first mentioned, but as things are pieced together on what happens during a typical day, it becomes easy to see the 5.5 hours might be very close to the daily average production rate.

The problem is not getting any better. As newer items are being created, such as widgets and RSS feeds, the startup time is only increasing. This leads to more waste.

It was once stated to me that most people, when creating a word processing document, use only 2% of the capability of the software. So the other 98% of the functionality is not required. In the business world much is the same with software and features of the tools that everyone has. If a survey was done to identify all the things that would be required for a worker to do their job, the list would probably be a simple spreadsheet, word processing, simple e-mail system, and access to the company system that they receive and do their work from. Don't get me wrong; I think some of the new technology that is loaded on everyone's PC is pretty cool such as RSS feeds. But I struggle with how it adds value to the company by the workers using it.

Upper management needs to look at the tools and features that are being loaded each day on all the PCs. There needs to be a business reason and cost justification for each tool and each feature within the tool that gets implemented. Since PCs started to be used in the business environment, this has been an issue. The process has been that, when new technology comes out, everyone is given it with the hope that workers will find a use for it. This ends up causing waste and confusion by having another feature or tool that does little or nothing to help with doing a person's job.

18

Technology

Everything seems to evolve around technology. With technology come the processes and procedures created to make the technology get the best results. To better understand how to improve processes, there needs to be some knowledge on the technology. Either the technology can control you, or you can control the technology.

A good example of what technology could do was the process at Radio Shack for reordering and restocking of merchandise. I'm familiar with it because for about two years I was a sales associate with them in early '80s when it was first being automated. Radio Shack, with all its small circuitry parts, carried about 2,000 individual products.

Before the information technology era, the process was all manual. Items sold were hand written on a sales ticket, along with the price. There were no cash registers so the sales ticket had to be manually totaled and sales tax applied. At the end of the day these sales tickets were used to help mark on an inventory list that was paper what was sold.

Every two weeks an order was put together from this inventory list. The order was mailed overnight to the distribution center. Once the distribution center received the order then they would start to put together the order, which took about 2 weeks to do. Finally about 3 weeks after placing the order, the merchandise would arrive in the store. But there are many gaps with that process.

If right after an order had been placed to the distribution center, a customer came in and wanted three of the same items but only two were in the store, the store would have to wait 2 weeks before another order could be placed. At best the customer might have to wait almost 5 weeks before receiving its merchandise. I say at the best 5 weeks because it was unknown if the item was in stock at the distribution center. If the item was out of stock in the distribution center, the store never found out until the placed order arrived in the store. The shipping list would show that the item had not been filled. So the item would have to be ordered again in the next order. Now we are talking another 4–5 weeks. The customers sometimes had to wait 2–3 months before getting their item. This was not very customer oriented.

Technology changed this. The first big step was the transmittal each night of what was purchased during that day. The technology that led to this was the invention of the personal computer and a communication device called a modem. Instead of having to wait every 2 weeks to place the order, the store order was being built as soon as the item was sold. With using this new technology 2 weeks had been removed from the process because information was being sent to the distribution center every night. With the new technology, stores also had the ability of knowing immediately when an item was out of stock at the distribution center. Instead of stringing along the customers every 4–5 weeks that their items might come up in the next order, a report was sent back to the store showing what was going to be sent and what was not in the order. Delivery dates becamse more realistic because of the technology.

The Information Technology Age really started when the computer mainframe processing became common in the early 1970s in most companies. Even though it was costly, in the millions, it still became a necessity to compete with competitors. What the computer mainframe brought were the functions of entering data, editing data, storing data, manipulating data, retrieving data, and printing the data into a format. The early entry process was labor intensive with paper cards needing to be punched and then run through a card reader for the mainframe computer to translate. Because it was labor intensive and there was a large possibility of error, only the minimal amount of information needed to complete the transaction was captured. Several other types of improvements were made to get data into the mainframe, but the next big step of evolution was when terminals were invented to enter data into screens. This technology is still used today. The original terminals had one color and 80 characters per row with 24 rows per screen. Development cost was low because skills and knowledge to code these screens were fairly simple to learn. Cost stayed low because everyone in the world that was doing development was using the same tools. There was no business reason to pay someone high wages when there were hundreds of thousands of other people with the same knowledge and skills. With the small terminal screen size there was a limitation to the functionality and complexity that could be done, but all the competitors had the same technology and the same limitations.

But technology keeps changing for the better. Mainframe processing got faster. Print changed from impact printers that printed only in black to laser printers that could print in multiple colors at speeds exceeding 120 pages a minute with print on both sides of the paper. There were many more options and technology paths that a company could take. This is where, in terms of technology, companies started to separate themselves. A company could try to stay with the latest and greatest technology on the market, but that meant that it was in constant technology change. Plus, leading-edge technology is always very expensive. A large part of the information technology (IT) annual budgets was just based around purchasing of new technology.

The other approach companies took was that they would not let technology drive their business. Instead they had the business needs drive the technology. The approach was that unless there was a true business need the company stayed with the existing technology. Companies that took this approach normally had a much lower IT budget than those that were always installing the latest technology. If the IT budget did increase it was because of growth or because manual processing was changed to automation.

Even if a company was not on the path of always purchasing the leading-edge technology, it still got caught up in the upgrade process. Each year data could be processed faster than the year before, and the capability to store it increased drastically. Companies became power hungry for data of all types. Hence, everyone had to keep upgrading because of the increase in data. Nobody would say no to the data requests. In the early 1980s, the company I worked for needed only 250 fields of data to issue and support a homeowner insurance policy, and 25 years later, an insurance company carries over 2,500 fields of data for a homeowner insurance policy. Each year businesses keep asking for data.

Businesses cannot be solely blamed for always asking to enter and store more data. IT management is also part of the problem. IT rarely would say no to the business requests because it justified asking for more funding for the next coming years. Computer technology was all new so there were really no guidelines or examples to follow. Once companies started down the path of capturing any and all data, it became an addiction to keep gathering more and more. When business partners were asked what specific purpose and what value the data would bring, often the response was, "It would be nice to have." It would also be nice to have an unlimited amount of resources and funding too, which IT does not have.

The next technology that changed everything was the invention of the personal computer (PC). Even though PCs started to be able to do simple functional tasks in the late 1970s, it was not until the late 1980s that PCs become powerful enough, reliable enough, and cheap enough that they started to become common in the business environment. It was also the same time that networks started to become common in business for the same reasons. Just like the mainframe terminals, data could be entered, edited, manipulated, stored, retrieved, and printed with PCs.

And this is where companies started to get into big trouble. Most of the time companies jumped to the PC infrastructure too early and without any cost justification. Business processes and procedures were not utilizing the technology to its fullest. Instead of reducing cost and resources the new technology added to both. Besides the initial high cost to purchase the equipment, new employees had to be hired to support the new technology. A business department might be reduced by two staff members because of the new technology, but three to four IT people would have to be hired to support the new technology. It was not until the early 1990s that PC technology started to be cost justified on a large scale in an organization.

The next step in technology was the Internet. In the early 1990s the web started to take off. It grew at the speed of light because in the beginning it was easy to program, and programmers could see their results immediately on their PCs. Want to see the source code of a web page? Open up any web page. At the top of the screen is probably the option of VIEW on the web viewer. Click on SOURCE, and a person will see the code that generated that web page. Today the code is very complex but in the beginning it was fairly simple. Techies and geeks jumped on this technology. Code could be copied from someone else's web page, modified to a person's liking, and then put back on the web for everyone to see immediately. I remember the first time someone figured out how to do automation on the web. Within 48 hours it had spread to other web pages throughout the world. This was really impressive—not because of the automation but because for the first time in history within a couple of days a new idea or functionality had been communicated throughout the world without using radio, television, or newspaper. Instead it was a new communication tool called the Internet.

When personal PCs became cheap in the mid- to late 1980s, people could afford them for home use. In their spare time they started to design and prototype different web programming languages. Many of them even went as far as to market their version. Never had this happened before.

In the past there were only mainframe programming languages. Because of the cost to purchase a mainframe there were few people just playing with languages in their spare time. Today there are over 600 different languages available for development. A list of these can be found at *http://en.wikipedia.org/wiki/Alphabetical_list_of_programming_languages.*

Time has been spent on the history of technology to understand what is happening today in terms of technology. What is today's leading-edge technology might not even be in the top 10 tomorrow because of new functionality introduced and rapidly deployed. The technology tools purchased and how these tools are used within a company can be the cause a large amount of wastes.

Many times the primary goal of a project is to find the latest and greatest technology on the market and then try to use it for the next development project. In large companies for web page development this happens all the time, and it's obvious. Each internal web system will consist of at least four to five different programming languages so that the combination is unique to that system.

There are two large issues with always using the latest and greatest. One deals with the learning curve for new technology. When a new web language is brought in odds are nobody within the company has expertise knowledge in using it. So either an outside person (very expensive) who knows the language must be brought in, or time must be spent to get the internal staff trained. Most companies tried the option of training their own staff because they believed the costs would be lower. When this option is used the first systems that are built on the new technology are normally pretty bad. Nobody fully understands how to use all the features and functions that it was originally purchased for. It's easy to read about all the fancy things something can do, but it takes knowledge and experience to make the fancy things work. Initially the cost was low, but massive savings were never realized because of bad design and processes for the new systems. Once a system is built, it almost never goes away, and rarely does it get totally rewritten to work properly, because there is always something else more important to do.

In the past there have been many examples of the cost and issues with bringing in new languages. Companies seem to never learn. When the COBOL programming language was created it became very popular because it was fairly easy to learn, and it was the same language no matter what company you worked in. Cost to do development was kept low just because of those two key factors. In the mid-1980s companies started to go back to a language called Assembler. It was a more efficient way of executing code, which would allow more data to be processed by the processor. The issue was that Assembler was harder to learn and even harder to code it correctly to get the high performance out of it. Very few people had the skills and knowledge to use Assembler code correctly. Since it was a specialized skill, people with these skills were in demand. A person with Assembler skills could almost set their own salary. Many times it was not a single person, but groups of Assembler programmers leaving a company because another was offering a lot more money. The original company after losing most of their Assembler programmers realized that they needed to increase their salary scale for this specific skill set just to retain Assembler programmers to support their existing programs. So they increased their pay scale more than the competition. Programmers who left a year ago would then come back to the original company. So the competition would have to raise their pay scale to get the programmers back. It got to a point that an Assembler developer was making more than most IT front-line managers. And were they getting the high-performance results by coding in Assembler? Nobody really knew because benchmarking comparisons were never really done to see if the function coded in Assembler had better performance results than the same function coded in the common development language of COBOL.

In the mid-1990s this trend started again, only this time it happened with the web development languages. As new languages such as Java came about, companies had to have them because on paper they looked great. With it being new and something only a few were good at, the web developers again could set their own salary. Many web developers have been making six figures since the mid-1990s, which is much more than what many front-line managers are making today.

The question that is never asked is what does the new technology bring a company? In insurance for the last 40 years the core functions are of data entry, editing, manipulating, storing, retrieving, and printing of data have changed only slightly. About the only change that has occurred is that it's necessary to do business on the Internet. So now web development is a requirement for entering and showing data.

As for the common users of the Internet system, they really don't care and don't need to know what web language is used when they use a web system. Much like common users of a word processing software that uses only 2% of the capability, all the fancy stuff is of no use to them. So it's unknown why a company would want to keep bringing in new technology with the learning curve and expense that adds little value or no value to the company.

Another factor is that with each new technology another layer of complexity has been added. Again, using web languages as an example, a couple of languages might be used to display the web page, a couple of others might be used to format and store the data, and then a couple of other languages might be used when processing the data. It becomes so complicated that a person hired off the street with expert web development skills still needs to be trained to understand how things work in the organization. The programming style used in a company becomes proprietary to that company. This normally equates into higher cost to support and maintain, along with lower quality because of the uniqueness. Another issue with bringing in many different languages over a period of time is that each system within the company becomes unique. If experienced internal web developers wanted to transfer and work on another system in the same enterprise, they have to go through a training and learning process to understand the languages used in that specific system. It becomes a barrier for when people want to transfer from one application system to another within the organization.

A couple of times I have heard it called system waste or technology debt. It occurs in both the PC and mainframe environment. In the mainframe world when a new system is developed very few people are initially needed to support it. The primary reason is because the core infrastructure is designed around ease of updating, and the design is consistency throughout the entire system. The waste occurs because in the mainframe the old logic is almost never taken out or upgraded. When new concepts or technology comes along, only the places that need it gets changed. An example is currently the latest technology that deals with being able to connect from the mainframe to web-based systems across multiple platforms, both internal and external to the company. Only in the spots that the new functionality is needed are changes made with the the new technology. Other spots that would greatly benefit by the new technology are not changed because the change only specifies to add the new functionality. These are the most painful and costly in the future. The next time someone needs to make changes in these spots they need to come up with different designs, development, and testing for the two different solutions in production. Another factor of technology debt is the individual programmer who might not understand the base infrastructure of the system and codes unique logic that does not match what others have done. All of this leads to a system that becomes inconsistent in both infrastructure and logic.

Slowly, or in a few cases I have seen very rapidly, the system becomes very complex to maintain. This leads to more defects and longer delivery time to do things, which translates to more staff required to support the system. At some point the company will need to make a decision to rewrite the system because the growing IT expenses are decreasing the profitability of the company. The rewrite usually removes the bad design and the inconsistent infrastructure so that the system is once again simple and consistent. This leads to ease to maintain, fewer defects, and few resources needed to support it. It's very costly to rewrite a system, but it's only a one-time cost that will reduce future expenses.

System waste can also occur on purchased software. At the college where I worked there was a purchased software package that handled the grades, registration, class scheduling, and many other administration tasks of the college. Every several months new software versions were sent out from the company for upgrades and fixes to problems. The base system without any modifications was called the baseline. Since many colleges do things slightly different, the system was flexible so that each college could make modifications to suit its needs. But as a college made these changes, it kept getting further away from the vendor's baseline version. The software company in its maintenance agreement supported only the baseline. When it made software upgrades it was concerned only with making sure the baseline worked. Many times custom modifications would stop working after the software upgrades. Since it was outside of the baseline version, the code either got fixed by paying additional money to the software company to resolve them, or the users of the system needed to hire and train additional staff to support the system. With routine upgrades to the baseline from the company, it was a never-ending additional cost.

Many projects start out with what is called a mission statement explaining the reason for the project. Incorporated into this mission statement are phrases like *leading edge, state-of-the-art,* and *market leader.* People believe that this includes the technology also. So there are discussions around what technology to use first. As soon as they get close to finalizing a decision, then new technology comes on the market. Instead of proceeding and continuing with the technology already decided upon, the project team stops and analyzes the new technology. It becomes a never-ending process with no final decision being made on the technology direction. I have even seen several projects well into development stop and change direction on the technology because something new came on the market. This constant changing of direction adds time to the project and also adds thousands of dollars to the project, plus it wastes the effort that was already done.

Small companies, which can bring change about quickly and cost-effectively, don't have this issue. They don't have the spare resources to look at what is the latest on the market. Instead they take the approach of finding tools such as only one or two web languages that are robust and that fit their needs both in the short- and long-term and make sure that the company supplying the tool is stable and plans on continuing to enhance its product. Small companies then build their systems and, most importantly, a knowledge base around the development tools selected. Very rarely will they stray from their technology plan.

Whether technology or business processes, large companies need to not stray from their plans. If improvement needs to be done most times it should be done in small steps and working on the existing environment to remove the wastes from it. If a proposed change is going to change the infrastructure, a study of short-term and long-term effects needs to be done. IT and their business partners must negotiate a business solution that fits into the existing system infrastructure. A solution that appears to meet short-term needs of functionality, cost, and delivery can easily add complexity and inconsistency. Long-term this equates into increased defects and more staff to support the system, which translates into additional costs of hundreds of thousands of dollars over a decade.

You might be thinking you don't need to know this stuff because this is knowledge that only upper management needs to make a decision on whether to allow the new technology. This would be a wrong assumption, especially in large organizations. Upper management only gives the approval to bring in new technology. Lower management and front-line workers actually are the ones that will suggest, research, and then create the proposals for new technology. Whenever a person sees a proposal to bring in new technology they need to question the value it will bring. Even after it's been approved by upper management and a developer is assigned to work with new technology, there should be a challenge to see the documentation on the purpose of the technology in the company and expected value it will bring.

19

Contractors

CONTRACTOR BEHAVIOR

It is normal for today's companies to have contractors on staff. Every company I have worked for has used contractors in some shape or form. But most companies have also just jumped into the process of using contractors without much planning and thought in the beginning. Many times instead of helping the situation the contractors will only add to the confusion, backlog of work, and low productivity. It's not that contractors' knowledge and skills are bad but that they are put into a position to fail. To understand the duties and responsibilities of a contractor, we need to take a look at who they are, when to use them, and how to use them in the most efficient manner so that they add the most value.

Contractors have a slightly different set of work values and priorities. Although contractors take great pride in their work, their primary loyalty is to their company they represent and not the company they are doing contracting work for. This makes a noticeable difference.

When polled, contractors agree that their purpose is not necessarily to do things right but instead to get things done on time. They are contracted to do a specific task in a specific amount of time. If they notice that there is a better way to do something, they almost never speak up because they are thinking more in the short-term versus long-term. There is little understanding of the organization's history so they don't understand the full cause and effect of what they are changing. Because of this, they can make changes that contradict a pattern or logic that has been followed for decades. In addition, when the task is completed and their contract is up, they are gone. There is no incentive to think long-term about how the change will be supported and modified in the future.

Regular employees tends to think more long-term about what is changed and to take a more active role throughout the project because they will be around to support the changes after it's been implemented. They pay attention to the details of the change and ask questions about why things are being changed. In years to come when there are questions or when enhancements must be made to their changes, people will come back to them for the history and knowledge of the original change.

There are two primary reasons for contractors: (1) They bring knowledge that does not exist in organization; and (2) they fill in a resource void that is needed to complete a task in a given time frame.

CONTRACTORS FOR KNOWLEDGE

The biggest project I have ever worked on had outside consulting contractors assigned for a multiyear project. The project was to reengineer the business structure of the personal lines of two companies—St. Paul Insurance and Kemper's Economy Fire and Casualty—into a one-company structure. The contractors were brought in not to run or direct the project but instead only as a support and consulting resource. The contractors taught the project team on such things as project methodology, team building, and project engineering. As the project team came across things that we thought might be beneficial to the project, the contractors were asked to go out and find material or subject matter experts (SMEs) for us. At the start of the project the constructors spent the entire day with the project team. As the project progressed the team needed the contractors less and less. By the time the project was half over the project team no longer needed the contractors to sit full time with the project team. Enough of the contractors' knowledge had been transferred into the project team that the project could be accomplished on time and within budget without much of their help.

The key is to make sure contractors hand off their knowledge to the team. Many times contractors on a project team play too big of a role on a project. The worst situation is that a contractor is brought in because they know of a new web language that needs to be used, and they do all the development. This happens far too often because there is a need to get the project done as soon as possible with the new web language. Here are the problems with doing this. Even though an experienced contractor can probably do the development very quickly and with high quality, it does very little for the company. The company gets the code developed quickly, but from there it starts to go downhill. None of the regular employees will understand the logic completely. If asked to make changes after the contractor is gone, the staff will have very little knowledge of how to do it. Even support for the changes becomes an issue because the regular employees don't understand why things are coded the way they are. There is no knowledge transfer when the contractor does most of the work. All that is left is the code and not the knowledge on how it works.

If the purpose is to use a contractor because of a specific knowledge or skill they have, then their primary duty should be training and being a mentor to the regular employees. At first it might be slow with inexperienced developers. But in a short time, as their knowledge increases the inexperienced developers' combined output would be much more than a single experienced contractor doing all the work. It's tempting to have the contactor maybe only do the most complex task on a project, but it still should not be allowed. For speed it would be best to take the best one or two employees who have picked up the knowledge and have them code the complex task under the direction of the contractor. Even if the contractor is telling the developers line by line what to do, at least the developers have a chance to ask questions as to why things are being done. After the contractor is gone, the knowledge is not, and thus a good understanding of how to support the changes is retained.

Bringing in a contractor to share knowledge can be used in many different situations, such as to teach employees how to write accurate business requirements and to help implement project methodology, process engineering, quality, IT, and business process improvement.

CONTRACTORS FOR FILLING A RESOURCE VOID

The other reason to use contractors is because there are not enough resources in the company to do the work. The knowledge is in the organization to do the tasks, but there is backlog of work or issues that the regular workers cannot get to. We wish work was at a constant rate, but it seldom is. For 6 months there might not be enough work to keep the regular employees working. Then the next 6 months there might be work to keep every employee working double shifts. Companies need the ability to gear up for when there is more work then capacity, and the ability to gear down during bad times such as when business drops. During bad times the worst thing a company can do is to add negativity by laying off employees because of being overstaffed. So companies' full-time employee staffing numbers tend to be conservative. To handle the additional work, contractors are used. Contactors offer the ability to add resources without having to add long-term cost and commitment.

A contractor normally doesn't get company benefits such as health insurance, retirement funds, and long-term disability. Earlier in my career when I wrote project proposals, I had to factor in not only each employee's salary but also another 20–25% in benefits. So for a project if one internal resource was used with a base salary of $100K, the true cost to the company ended up being $120K–$125K. This is a large difference in calculating the cost of a project if only the base salary is used versus the actual cost the company has to pay when benefits are calculated in.

The easy fixes are not an issue with using contractors. Such things as simple maintenance or small projects are easy for them to complete successfully. Given simple instructions, contractors can complete changes with little system or company knowledge. When the changes start to become complex, then using a contractor starts to cause trouble. Without spending months on training it's impossible for a contractor to understand what they are changing, along with all the effects of the change.

This brings up a quality issue. A contractor has no idea what and how to do a complete unit test to validate their changes because they don't have the full system knowledge. They cannot understand all the possible effects that would happen because of the change, so common things that need to be unit tested end up being missed. If it is missed in unit testing, hopefully it will be found in the system testing phase. But defects found in the system testing and later phases cost a lot more in time and resources then if they were found in unit testing phase. The testing cost difference will be covered in detail later in the book, but for now just know that for system testing it's more formal with documentation and traceability, which slows up the process and costs more.

Contractors somehow need to be given instructions on what to change. The common tool is to write up detailed technical specifications. These get handed off to the contractor so that they can do development from them. The big mistake with this process that occurs over and over again is assuming that with little support contractors can work from these written technical specifications to make complex changes. Every time this process is used it causes problems and defects.

The worst project that I have ever seen had 716 system testing defects. It used the process of handing contractors technical specifications and then giving them little system support. On that project the few overseas contractors I talked to were knowledgeable with coding. But each one admitted that without knowing the systems and business knowledge the technical specifications were just directions with no meaning. The felt like they were developing blindly. This greatly increased the possibility of creating defects, which it did.

USING CONTRACTORS SUCCESSFULLY

We talked about what does not work. Now let's address what seems to work consistently. If adding contractors for additional resources, then assign a mentor to work with them. The person should be a subject matter expert (SME) of the systems that are being changed. The SME needs to be almost in contact daily with the contractors. They also need to routinely check the work that is being done. Not all the work needs to be checked but just enough to verify that the contractors are staying on track. The contractors themselves like this approach because they feel they are not blindly making guesses as to what really is wanted and what the development instructions say.

To ensure that the SME is communicating with the contractors, besides the mentoring the SME should also do the more complex development work and testing. One reason to do this is that it creates a team effort on the work. Sometimes when a mentor is assigned they have a tendency to not spend as much time and dedication on the daily communication. They meet, but it's just a quick status check. The other reason can be connected to the Lean concept and wastes. Why spend time training a contractor on understanding the complex parts of the system when at some point they will leave with this knowledge? This can be classified as waste. Another reason is that the SME will not only be faster but will also be able to make sure the original design requirements, which are probably complex, will work within the system.

Another approach to using contractors is to pull people from an existing team to do the project, and then use a technique called backfill to fill their emptied position with contractors. With the project team consisting of full-time employees, everyone has system knowledge and experience. Besides being completed faster because there is almost no training needed, the quality through the project phases is of high standards because of the company and system knowledge on the team. As for the contractors backfilling in the regular employee's job, with a small amount of training and mentoring they can do simple and routine changes without causing too much disruption or quality decrease.

The backfill process also allows employees to instill pride in their systems, which increases engagement. When the project is over and they go back to their normal position and tasks they get to maintain code and functions they helped develop. When a contractor does the new development, the employee ends up having to support the work the contractor did. An employee is never going to take personal pride in work others have done. A person can never underestimate the power of pride in ownership of something, which can be called the thumbprint philosophy. It's the ability of an employee to see within the company beneficial changes that they did in the past. It could be a new field on the screen, a new report being used by a department, or a new process that is being used in a department. Most employees never get a chance to be able to bring about change. So when a chance does come up, take a serious look to see if you can get internal employees and not temporary contractors to do the development.

The reason this option is not popular is that it requires more hands-on management. Management first has to come up with what resources can be replaced with a contractor. Most managers like to keep their smartest and best people closest to them. The belief is that project enhancements are needed for growth, but the routine maintenance keeps the systems going and is the bread and butter of the organization. They make resource decisions, such as to how to use contractors, based on playing it safe and keeping their best people in maintenance.

OVERSEAS CONTRACTORS

This is a hot topic in companies. In terms of tasks that require little company knowledge and skills to do the job, the trend is to move the work overseas. Even with the cost of more defects and less product being produced, the lower labor cost is attractive. But when it comes to tasks that require technical knowledge and needing to understand the past to know how to bring change about for the future, the true benefits with moving work overseas become blurred. To be consistently successful both in the short- and long-term in IT, there needs to be knowledge in the company, the systems, and the business product.

Many variables are involved with overseas contractors. The following discussion assumes overseas contractors who work on the other side of the world (12 hour difference) and have little company or system knowledge for which they will be doing development. It's also based around the viewpoint of a conventionalist that requires data to validate that the decision is adding value to the company.

Chief information officers (CIOs) are under pressure to do more with less money. So when there is a promise of the possibility to reduce labor costs drastically by using cheaper overseas labor, it gets their attention. On the surface it seems to make sense. But like Lean management, many times when one area changes a process to reduce cost, then another area's cost automatically goes up. Overall, the cost has only been shifted. The total effect is little or no cost savings overall.

A person will rarely hear or read that the benefit for outsourcing overseas is to increase productivity or quality. Instead, the primary reason is to reduce labor costs. This is accomplished by replacing one internal worker with an overseas contractor who gets paid a fraction of the normal salary. But many new variables affect the flow and performance when this happens.

One variable is the different time zones. Work is hard enough even with everyone working in the same location in the same time zone. I have run a couple of large projects with team members in the four different United States time zones. It causes delays because the entire team is together for fewer hours. Many times, to get an answer or to finish something there is a dependency on someone in a different time zone. Instead of quickly getting an answer, there is a time delay until the person comes into work. If the person is working in the afternoon on the West Coast and the answer needs to come from someone on the East Coast, it's going to be the next day before an answer can be received. With workers on the other side of the world, different shifts are involved. When it's noon in the Rocky Mountain time zone in the United States, in India on the other side of the world, it's midnight. Process engineering and Lean management emphasize looking for delays built into the process. Split shifts are an obvious waste.

Testing is another variable. Without system knowledge and history, any unit testing that the developer is responsible for will be poor quality. Changes to logic in one spot many times will affect outcomes in another spot. Without understanding this, things will be missed in testing. Internal developers have access to other developers to ask questions at any time in person, whereas overseas contractors need to work through the SME assigned from the company to get their questions addressed. But because of the different time zones direct verbal communication is difficult. Most questions are first tried to be addressed through emails. If that does not work then a meeting is set up with one party having to call in late at night, in order to catch the other party at work. All this extra effort in communication can be classified as waste.

System testing checks that the visual functionality is working as requested and that none of the existing logic got broken. To accomplish this, a person is required to have knowledge in the system's overall functionality and business user processes. The best qualified specialist is someone who works closely with the business partner on a routine basis to visually see how work is done. This requires someone from inside the company to fill the system testing role. Many times the area with this knowledge is called the Test Office. This means overseas contractors are on one side of the world, and Test Office testers are on the other. When the Test Office finds a defect, it will need to be documented and then routed back to the overseas contractor. With the split shifts, one day has been lost just to notify the contractor that a defect has occurred. Then there is the fact that Test Office staff are normally not technically people, so their documentation on the defect is not technical either. Many times additional information is needed from the Test Office to understand the entire problem. Each time additional information is asked for, one more day is added to the time it takes to resolving the defect. Instead of being able to resolve a defect quickly and keep the workflow going, there is stoppage for both the Test Office and the overseas contractor, which equates to waste.

Most of the overseas contractors with whom I have worked are very knowledgeable and good with their development skill levels. However, some have shared that they don't like the time differences and the work process. The process makes them feel as if they have blinders on and are being held back. When a contractor needs a quick answer, it cannot be done most of the time because their SME contact and Test Office staff members have gone home for the day. They are also given very narrow instructions as to what to do. Overseas contractors have to trust that the coding instructions are 100% accurate, because without system knowledge they will not know. Internal developers do not have these issues. To validate or to get clarification or even additional training to make the change, they can just walk over to someone in IT and within minutes obtain the knowledge they need to correctly do development.

Companies currently choose between two options to try to leverage the cheaper labor overseas. The first one is to create developer centers overseas and have most development done there. To get the company and system knowledge into these centers, representatives from overseas come and work in the company for a limited amount of time to get this knowledge. Also, regular employees are sent overseas routinely to help train and mentor the overseas contractors. Between these two processes the goal is to raise the knowledge in the overseas development center to a level that they can take on much of the development in the company. It's based around the concept that everything can be documented and that the company and system knowledge can quickly be transported.

The other trend to leverage overseas contractors is to select specific tasks that overseas contractors can easily do. On a per-system basis a percentage of workers are overseas. For example, if 10 employees are assigned to a system, 20% need to be overseas contractors. Besides lowering the cost of labor, the belief is that 20% of the work being done in that system is simple enough to do that most anyone can do it with not much guidance. This concept is already being used in all companies: A certain percentage of developers have different titles of senior developer, IT specialist, and developer. Each has a different pay range and type of work. The option of using overseas contractors has introduced a cheaper labor source that does the same things a beginning developer would get assigned to do.

It's a common process that the work assignments do not go directly overseas to the contractor. Instead, a middle person from the overseas company first reviews the work assignments. Most of the time this person is located within the company, but they could also be located overseas. The work and technical specifications are explained to this overseas coordinator, who is then responsible for assigning the work to the company's contractors overseas. The single point of contact to the overseas contractors is used to help with communication and scheduling of work. However, another handoff has been added to the process.

No matter what the process is to get the work to the overseas developer, most incorporate more people into the total work process. Breaking down the processes with just using all internal developers the originator of the change gives it to the developer. The developer writes up the technical specifications and then completes the change. Here just two people are involved. A common process when using overseas contractors is that the originator gives the work to an internal developer. The developer creates the technical specifications on what needs to be changed. This documentation is then handed to the overseas coordinator, who then takes the work and assigns it to the overseas contractor. A process that used to have only two people to complete now has four.

One criterion to obtaining speed to market and quality is to use processes with few handoffs as was discussed with Lean management. The more handoffs there are, the more risk for miscommunication and understandings. More handoffs lead to a longer process, since each handoff requires a repeat of the communication on such things as what is changing, why it's being done, how to test, and how to implement. And what happens when the written documentation from the developer is not complete or something is documented wrong? If you start with bad instructions, then it's 100% guaranteed the final results will be bad.

Even with all these factors and barriers that can cause waste and failure, the biggest issue is that most companies do not have in place the correct performance and quality benchmarks to tell if outsourcing is beneficial. IT development is unique in that there are hundreds of ways to do the same thing so it becomes hard to measure performance and quality accurately. A company needs to make sure it has the right benchmarks to measure the overall benefits.

Cost is certainly reduced when an internal developer is replaced with a cheaper labor overseas contractor. But there are also expenses with more people involved: defect increases, more rework, delays, more handoffs, and lower performance. The purpose of the discussion on outsourcing is to make sure that companies truly are adding value to the company, both short and long term.

In my circle of friends, many times we have discussions around what ifs. Like what if the Internet suddenly goes down throughout the world for several days? Could a company still do business and survive? Outsourcing has been one of those what if conversations. Whether true or not, the conversation leads to the possibility that outsourcing is only a temporary thing to increase return on investment (ROI). Poor countries that suddenly start to get an influx of money are going to have their economy grow rather fast. One financial input of making this happen is outsourcing that is done to these countries. Another financial source is the large number of foreign workers who are employees working in the company. Many of these workers send money they have saved back home to help out their families. Even the trips back home to see their families help

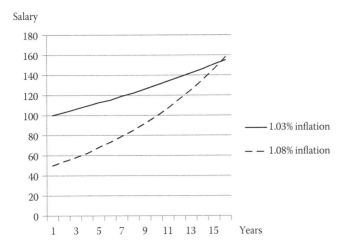

FIGURE 19.1
Forecast of salary based on 3% and 8% inflation rates.

improve the country's economic growth. Five years ago a company could save labor cost by 50% by outsourcing. But with salaries rising much faster in poor countries, today that same company might be saving only 33% by outsourcing. It becomes predictable that the salary gap will narrow fairly quickly over time. If and when that happens, the interesting question becomes how much of an advantage does a company have if it retains its developers and grows its knowledge versus using a large percentage of overseas contractors?

To help explain the trend, one country has an average salary of $100 an hour, and its average yearly inflation factor is 1.03%. Another has an average salary of $50 an hour and an average yearly inflation factor of 1.08%. In about 16 years, salaries will match between the two countries as long as salary increases match the inflation factor increases each year. Figure 19.1 shows the merging of salaries. In manufacturing when the salaries get close, they do what is called "moving to a new frontier," which means moving the plants to a cheaper source, such as China. In IT, though, system, company, and development knowledge are primary assets. It will be interesting to see what will occur when salary bases get closer. One view is the company that retains most of its IT knowledge will have a competitive edge. Another view is that, just like manufacturing, IT will find another new frontier with cheap labor.

20

Defects

So far the material covered in this book has encompassed most activities that occur daily in a company. One key area left to cover in the daily work environment is defects. Lean management has its own classification under *muda* just for defects, because there is so much waste that goes with it. In a perfect world there would never be any defects. But we don't live in a perfect world. Defects are part of the normal work environment. The more unstable the environment is, such as making major changes and enhancements to stay competitive, the more defects there will be.

EFFECTS OF DEFECTS

Most people really don't take the time to understand the negative effects a defect has on a company. Here is one way to think about defects. First, you pay the person to make the changes. Then you have to pay another person to fix what was not done correctly the first time. If defects get out to the general consumer, then there are additional costs to replace the defective work. Defect items do not just magically get switched out with good ones. There is additional cost in transportation of the replacement. And last, as more defects get into the public hands, more customer service and support staff are needed to address each defect. A large number of defects can become costly to a company and hurt the profit margin.

On the intangible side, defects lower the customer's confidence level. Customers want to go through the process of purchasing a product only once. The expectation is that it will last almost forever. When it doesn't meet their expectations because of a defect, then their confidence level drops in the product. Customers don't keep their feelings to themselves; they broadcast them to everyone they know. You can think of the negativity that a defect creates much like dropping a stone in the water. The initial point of impact (customer) will cause a large water displacement. As ripples go outward from the point of impact, they slowly reduce in size. The closest people around the customer will hear about the defect, who in turn will tell other people. As the story of the defect is handed down and gets further away from the impacted customer, the severity of it decreases. But the story still leaves an impression or warning to those people that hear it to maybe stay away from that specific product. The product could be anything such as toaster, lawn mower, insurance policy, or service or food at a restaurant. For example, when you ask a friend about a new restaurant you want to go to and they said they had bad service and undercooked food, there is a very good chance either of those responses (defects) will cause you not to go to the restaurant. Even though you personally never had the experience, you are going to take your friend's word for it and probably never go there.

It's rarely talked about, but defects also affect internal employees. If there is a serious issue with defects in the company, then usually there is a large backlog of defects to fix. The backlog often is addressed by having employees working overtime to reduce the number of them. With more and more new defects coming in each day and the amount of overtime it takes just to stay current, employee morale lowers and stress increases. If the product is bad, it's really tough for an employee to take pride in the company.

If a large part of your resources are used fixing and resolving issues, then they are being taken away from doing enhancements. This reassignment of resources to work defects means there will not be enough resources to do new enhancements. Completing these enhancements could be critical to the company staying competitive.

Earlier the book addressed the cost of defects once they got out to the general public, but what about when a defect is found in the project process before it gets implemented? When a defect is found in unit testing, there is low cost to get it resolved. Since the developer is the only one testing in this phase, he or she can quickly make changes and retest. When a defect is found in later testing phases (system, integration, and release phases), there is a noticeable cost in time and labor. In these later testing phases, the test office staff is involved. I'm going to go into detail just to show all the additional steps and time that go into fixing one single defect. While going through the process, just think of this: If there never was a defect none of it would have to be done.

When a defect is found by the test office, it's normally entered into some type of reporting system that keeps tracks of them. The developer accesses this reporting system to get the general information on the defect. When the developer has information about the defect and how to resolve it, more documentation is added into the reporting system for the defect. All defects do not necessarily get fixed the first time. Sometimes it might take three to four times before it's actually fixed correctly. Each time a defect reoccurs, the process of development and testing must occur over again, which adds cost.

Most of the time there is only one process to report and document all types of defects, so the process is designed around being able to handle the needs of the most complex defects. Thus, a small defect that takes only 5 minutes to fix and unit test gets incorporated into the process of large defects. The defect process to handle large defects many times can take 30 minutes to properly document and another 60 minutes of sitting in a meeting that covers the cause, effects, and when the fix will be implemented. So the small defect that takes only 5 minutes to fix takes over 1.5 hours. There is always a much larger percentage of smaller defects than large defects, so major waste occurs because a complex lengthy process is used for something that could get the same results if a simpler, shorter process was used.

This is a common theme throughout this book: The work needs to match the process, and not the other way around. Defects are no different. At least two processes need to be created for defects. One process is for the most complex defects that might occur. The other process is to handle smaller defects. Both processes should have guidelines around when one is used versus the other.

CAUSES OF DEFECTS

In my career with all the major and small projects worked on, I have never seen anyone deliberately cause a defect. If people are not deliberately causing defects how does one happen? Miscommunication is a common factor, which can be defined as inaccurate statements or information missing that is required for the action to be done successfully. This miscommunication ends up in the documentation or verbal communication that occurs.

Instead of spending time to make sure everything is accurate, statements are made that are untrue or unclear. When this occurs at the beginning of the change process the bad information continues down through the process. Decisions and design are made based on it. At some point it gets realized that the information is bad and a defect is created. In the common project process that could be classified as linear, most defects are not found until in the later phase of development and unit testing has started.

The other type of defect is a system-generated result. This would be similar to a defect a machine makes in manufacturing. Even though the input is accurate, the process itself causes a defect to occur. Chapter 14 discussed building a widget that was folded a couple of times with a five-sided star on both sides. The original process was prone to defects no matter how careful the work was done. Randomly at some point in time a widget would not be created correctly. When the process was changed to reduce the number of handoffs and some steps were moved around, the possibility of creating a defect was reduced.

This same concept occurs with processes. As processes add more handoffs and complexity, the process itself is introducing more spots in which a defect can occur, which increases the possibility of defects occurring. It becomes a catch 22 in that when companies have issues with the number of defects, they create more complex processes to try to stop them from happening. By doing this they only add to the problem. The defects initially do go down, but it's only because of the amount of additional resources and the priority given to the defects. Once both resources and priority are moved to other things, then the defect counts go back up and might even increase because with the more complex process there are more spots in which a defect might occur.

It would be wonderful if processes could be made to eliminate all defects, but they don't. There is always some unique situation—whether machine or human—that will always create a defect. Attaining zero defects in most situations is impossible. The best that can be done is to greatly reduce the risk of having a defect. This is not to say that each defect does not need to be analyzed, but every defect does not need to be resolved. For system-generated ones it might not be monetarily feasible to make changes to eliminate them from happening. Even Six Sigma addresses this by originally stating that the quality goal is to obtain 3.4 defect parts per million (PPM) opportunities. It would be impossible and also very costly to attempt to obtain a defect ratio of 0.00.

W. Edwards Deming's point #3 states that processes need to be created so that instead of opening up the possibility of defects occurring they will eliminate defects. If the possibility of defects is eliminated, then no rework and mass inspections are needed. Companies need to look at their processes and make changes to reduce the possibility of defects. Fewer handoffs in a process is a good start. Proper staffing of work is another process.

Most companies don't understand this. They continue to use the same process over and over again that is creating in-system defects, which are out of the control of the users. Even companies that are trying to improve quality rarely look at first changing processes to eliminate defects. Instead, their first priority is to create more processes that deal with reporting and controlling. If average people are put into a bad process, the outcome most often will be failure. But if those same average people are placed into a good process, the outcome most often will be success. This translates into greatly reducing defects by just improving the process.

21

Knowledge Base for Project Work

Up to this point, the book has discussed the many knowledge areas that exist in everyday work. Many are the basic building blocks required to be successful for the next level of complexity, which is project work.

It started in Chapter 2 with acquiring knowledge around management. Without good management a project has little chance of success. But what is good management? In order to understand that, the 6 disciplines of Management Best Practice—leadership, negotiating, problem solving, ability to influence, decision making and communication—were explained. For better definition the pyramid process of goal state, outcomes, and tools & inputs was covered to help further explain each discipline, along with being able to identify tasks that can be done for improvement. Another aspect of management is how it's applied. Depending on a person's style and the type of work managed, each manager is unique. But each must work toward a common set of goals, which led to the discussion on the 25 points of leadership from Jack Welch, along with Servant Leadership from Robert Greenleaf. These are concepts to help accomplish that.

Projects, especially medium to large in size, are unique in that the project management team that is leading the change will often be different people than the managers that are the system owners that the changes will be put in. Both need to work together for resources needed for the project, along with agreement on system design changes from the project. In a perfect world everyone would work together toward the same goals. But in the real world that does not happen. There are IT managers, as well as business partner managers, that are the performer type, who will do everything to help the project, and then there is the cave dweller type who will do very little to help. It's critical to understand this because a cave dweller most times is a project constraint that will increase the chance of failure.

Even though every project can follow the same process, each is unique in what it is trying to accomplish and the size of the project. By making changes to the process in certain types of projects, performance and quality can be increased greatly. To understand how to do this, we have discussed the knowledge on topics such as process engineering, Lean management, continuous improvement and quality. Part of the discussion was also on the base concepts of generalist versus specialist, and waste that can occur in such steps as transportation, inventory, motion, waiting, overproduction, overprocessing, defects and Deming's wheel of Plan-Do-Check-Act. When working on a project most of these items come into play.

A project is a team concept. Just putting together a group of people without much thought will greatly increase the chance of failure. Selecting people for the team based on balanced behavior patterns of influencer, driver, steadiest and conventionalist instead will increase the chances of success. But the team performance can be improved even more quickly and can attain a very high level if the process of Forming-Norming-Storming-Performing is applied as part of the team building process.

The importance of understanding this knowledge is that these things have a direct effect on the outcome of the project. Starting in the next chapter the topic turns specifically to project work and structure. It covers what makes up a project, the different project types, different processes to do a project, and qualifications to lead a project through its different phases. It's the combination of both the knowledge already acquired and the knowledge about to be learned that are factors involved with success, or failure, of a project. When this knowledge is used correctly, all types of projects can be consistently completed with excellent quality, under budget, and early delivery.

22

Project Selection Criteria

For a company to maintain its market share and even to grow, it must always be finding ways to make its product better. This involves bringing change about, which translates into project work. Project requests can come from anywhere. Some projects can be simple to execute, and others can be very complex and take years to do. All changes cost money, and all changes should bring beneficial change about. The issue that companies have is controlling what projects should be done.

Small companies have an advantage over large companies in project work. In small companies when a project request is being done almost all management in the company knows the cost and benefits of the project. With limited resources, only the projects that bring the most benefit with the minimal cost are selected to be done partly because of the overall management awareness. It's an automatic prioritization process. And when a major project is almost complete, a small company will check the project priority list against the current needs to make sure the next project is the most important one to do. It also helps that only a few projects happen at a time because of the limited resources of smaller companies.

In large companies, at any given time there could be 100 different projects being worked on. Coordinating resource and scheduling to get all this work done on time is a major effort, especially for large projects that involve multiple systems across the enterprise. Everyone should know what is suppose to be important to complete because of the benefits it will bring, upper management will make a few of the projects a top priority because of the benefits they will bring, but many of the lower areas involved with making the project becoming a reality could have different views and opinions as to what are their priorities. Having managed many large enterprise-wide projects across multiple systems, I know that this is a big issue. Even though upper management might say it's a top priority, once the request gets down to the lower departments the priority gets lost. In the lower levels the top priority is maintenance and fixing defects as soon as possible. With some resources already tied up on other projects, a new request for resources to work a top-priority project causes a resource availability issue. There are just not enough people in the group to do it all. In the end something suffers. It can be maintenance, fixing defects, or other projects that have already been started but are having some of their resources moved to the new top-priority project.

For a project that is labeled as a priority, resources will always be found and assigned because upper management wants it done. For the other projects that are not classified a priority there are issues with resourcing. Departments affected and that need to do development for the project will not supply any resources in the timeframe needed. The only option is to delay the project until the department can supply resources. But often by the time the date arrives that the resources are supposed to be available, a high priority project comes along and the resources get assigned to work that instead. Completing on time a high priority project is much easier than a project that has a lower priority.

Can large companies control this? I say yes, and it starts with the number of projects approved to be done. The first company I worked for was Kemper's Economy Fire and Casualty. There was a rule that any project (whether technology or process changes) got approved only for one of two reasons: (1) to remove a potential that would hinder us from processing policies (like mainframe upgrades and printer upgrades) or (2) because the project could be cost justified in 18 months after implementation. If the payback took 24 months the project rarely happened. Many of the project proposals (white papers) showed detailed cost and projected cost savings. There are several benefits of this process:

- Cost on technology always goes down over time. What is expensive today might be half the price a year later. Even though nothing else has changed, just the reduced cost of the technology will change the return on investment (ROI) a project will have for the company.
- Not many projects each year met the 18-month rule. Because of the smaller number of projects, the number of people who supported and did development work was kept small.
- With the reduced staff and control over the projects worked on, the organization could turn on a dime if a project suddenly came up that would reap major benefits.

- To reach justification, all benchmarks around the change needed to be identified and a cost dealing with a unit of work needed to be defined, even down to a keystroke. If new fields needed to be added to gather more data, the time to add that data was in the proposal.
- Most projects are a business's guess on what the customer wants and what the company needs in the future. So with a longer payback period, there is an increase of the risk never reaching the payback point because of customer, market, and competition changes; 18 months was as far as we wanted to see into the future. Anything beyond that time it becomes more of an educated guess as to the results that would be obtained.
- In continuous improvement the process is about taking many small steps to reach peak performance. So it is with the 18-month payback rule. Most often it deals with concentrating on the smaller improvements that will cost justify themselves very quickly. But most companies are always concentrating on making major changes, trying to bring about large amounts of improvement. They tend to spend little time and effort on the smaller changes. I like to say that they try to hit a home run in quality and performance by doing large projects. In contrast, the 18-month payback rule is like hitting a bunch of singles over and over again.

Kemper's Economy Fire and Casualty Insurance was purchased by St. Paul Insurance in the 1980s. St. Paul Insurance had no 18-month rules, so it had many more projects going on simultaneously. Many of the projects had payback points of years, if not decades, into the future. It seemed that if the business request was logical and within reason, then a project was done to do it. The emphasis was around giving business whatever it wanted if it seemed responsible. Both companies sold personal lines insurance in about the same number of states and sold basically the same product. The St. Paul systems were complex, with many features and functions that added little benefit. Once these new features and functions were in the system, they needed to be maintained and supported. Because of these differences the Kemper's Economy Fire and Casualty information technology (IT) department consisted of around 100 employees, whereas St. Paul Insurance had over 500 people supporting its systems—over five times more people.

You might think Kemper's Economy Fire and Casualty systems must have been simple and built around old technology. Wrong! Most of the systems and processes were wrapped around the leading-edge technology of the time, so much so that vendors such as IBM and Xerox routinely came to the company to work and learn with us as we developed and implemented it into projects.

When a detailed comparison was done between the systems of the two insurance companies it was revealed that Economy's systems were more efficient and effective in terms of not only technology but also the business process. Economy's systems were designed around the business workflow. The systems presented seamless data important for business users to do their job. Users flowed through data from the Claims, Correspondence, Billing, Comments, and Policy Master systems without even knowing it. Even before Lean management was a mainstream concept, Kemper's Economy Fire and Casualty was already removing as much waste as possible from the business flow. The St. Paul systems at the time worked differently. A user first had to visually identify that the policy was a home, dwelling fire, auto, or commercial policy. Then the user keyed in a transaction code to start the system that the policy should be in. Only then could the policy number be entered. Once the policy number was entered, then the data in that system would come up, but it was only data in that one system. If there was information on other systems such as claims, billing, or remarks system, the same process of keying a transaction code to start the system and then entering the policy number was repeated. This was not very friendly and was costly in terms of usage because of manually having to jump from system to system. Once in the system the user then might have to page through several different screens to find the needed data. For example, at renewal time for a policy, underwriters who needed to review a new claim that occurred needed to see only a couple of pieces of data in the claim system to do that. The process was to start the claim entry system with the code, enter the policy number, then page through a couple of pages of screens to find the necessary data. On the screen are probably 60 other nonrelevant fields that they had to sift through it to find their data. This led to a great deal of wasted time just to navigate through the data. In addition, there was a big learning curve, which is another cost. Not only did underwriters need to do this for Claims, but it was the same for such systems as Billing and Comments that routinely were needed to look at.

Besides limiting the number of projects approved, the 18-month justification rule also had another benefit. It made people in the organization start to think of changes in terms of adding the most company value. It was part of the company culture. In light of W. Edwards Deming's 14th point (see Chapter 13), the 18-month rule was part of the process to get everyone involved with the transformation of the company into a cost-effective efficient market leader.

Companies get into trouble today because they are trying to do too much that does too little to their immediate bottom line. Small enhancements can always be done to improve performance and quality, but there is never enough time or money to do that because the top-priority larger projects are consuming all the funding and resources. These large projects many times have payback periods far into the future. It's a guess as to when payback will occur. It's wonderful to guess at what might happen in the far future and the possible returns that it could bring. But the farther out in the future the cost justification point is, the higher the risk that the return will not be realized because of such things as company direction changes, competition, and the economy.

23

Project Characteristics

PROJECT SUCCESS VERSUS FAILURE

What are the criteria for a project to be classified as a success versus a failure? In the past it was easy for a company to see if a project was successful based on final cost and the delivery date, but now these points are blurred. *Descoping* and *additional phases* help blur the final outcome of the project. The first time I heard these terms was in a large company. I could not believe that because bad research, estimates, and wrong assumptions were made in the beginning of the project, parts of the project deliverables could be descoped out of the project, or additional phases added, and the project could still be successful. I'm not saying that everything can always be identified early, but many times descoping and additional phases are used to hide bad research and wrong assumptions.

With all the different criteria there could be over a dozen different classifications for the final outcome of the project. We will work with only three here: *successful, challenged,* and *failed.* There are four benchmarks (cornerstones): delivery on time, on budget, good quality, and has all features and functions requested.

Successful

The project, when completed, has met all four benchmarks. Does this mean it has to be to the penny and to the hour that it was originally specified? No—most companies have a plus–minus factor of 3–10% on tangible items such as final cost, number of defects, and delivery date. So a float factor gets applied to the final results.

Also, on large projects there will almost always be changes to the original cost and specifications. There are so many unknowns in most large projects that the project goal can be classified only as a dream or vision when first estimates are required. As the project progresses, a better way of doing it could be identified, or maybe as the vision or dream starts to materialize, the original request is not exactly what the business needs. These are valid reasons to change the original request. A formal process such as a request for change (RFC) allows for documentation of the changes, the cost involved, and whether the delivery date is being changed. These RFCs get incorporated into the original estimates and requirements. As long as the adjusted costs, delivery date, and functionality from the RFCs are met and the quality measurement is met, the project can be classified as a success.

Challenged

The project is completed and operational, but one criterion used to measure success is outside of float ranges. Maybe the delivery date was missed by several months or there was a cost overrun of several thousand dollars, but all the other factors that measure success were still met. This would classify the program as challenged.

The majority of projects fall into this category. For example, when a project gets behind, one common option to get it back on track is to add more staff. This will make cost go over the expected range, but quality, delivery, and functionality criteria will all be met. Instead of adding staff, another option is to shorten testing. When that happens most times the project criterion of quality will not be met, but all the other criteria will be.

Failed

The project missed two or more of the success criteria. It was delivered late and there was a cost overrun, or maybe the final product was delivered without full functionality. Many times projects try to hide their failure by using descoping and additional phases. By reducing the amount of work and the functionality that was originally promised, it appears the original project success criteria are being met. But the truth is, usually when either of these two words are being used it means the project is failing to meet two or more of the criteria of cost, functionality, delivery date, and quality.

The worst type of failure is when the project gets canceled before it's completed. If you work in a small company you probably have never seen this. The first time I came across this I was shocked. Millions of dollars and numerous man-years of labor had been spent to try to develop a new front-end system for users. As cost overruns occurred and a delivery date kept getting extended far out into the future, upper management decided to cancel the project. It got down to whether to keep spending money and resources in a bad situation. Even though attempts were made to change project team members, project leadership, and even the name of the project to get away from the stigma with it, in the end they were no closer to the delivery of project. The flaws that existed in the project were never found or fixed. Putting good people into a bad process did not fix it.

LAW OF CAUSE AND EFFECT

> For every effect in your life there is a specific cause. Everything that happens has a cause. Failure doesn't happen by accident. Success doesn't happen by accident.

Analyzing why a project fails makes sense, but it also needs to done when there is success. Put "Failure" at one end of a line and "Success" on the other end (Figure 23.1). If we know and understand what works for a project, then there should be little guessing as to how to sustain most projects near the end of the line with the title of "Success." Instead, companies spend all their time analyzing only projects that end up being near the other end of the line, "Failure." Without having data on what actually works in your environment, it's only a guess or an assumption as to why a project failed, so it makes sense to start with what we know works.

FIGURE 23.1
Linear scale of possible outcomes.

So why do some projects fail and others succeed? There are always many reasons for a project's success or failure. It can be bad instructions, the project team makeup, the project methodology process used, lack of the management best practices disciplines (leadership, problem solving, ability to influence, negotiation, problem solving, communication), and even

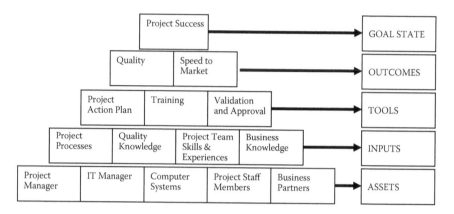

FIGURE 23.2
Pyramid to project success.

lack of commitment from upper management. To understand this better, the next few chapters will cover project management, project control, consultants, project staffing, and just plain stupid processes.

To help with this, a pyramid concept is going to be used (Figure 23.2). Each level has a purpose. By no means is this complete, and you can argue that some might not seem to be at the right level. But the purpose of this is to give a general understanding of the pyramid concept for projects.

In this structure one of the foundation blocks could be weak, but the project still could obtain success. Take, for instance, a weak IT manager. If the rest of the foundation blocks are strong, then all the inputs listed at the second level will be good. And if all those are good, then the rest of the upper levels will be good. But take more than one out at each level and it's a good possibility failure will occur.

IDENTIFYING THE CAUSE

The most common process companies use to identify reasons of success or failure is a process called lessons learned. It's normally a meeting after the project has been completed. Team members get together to discuss what went wrong and what went right. One flaw to this approach is that it's normally done at the end of the project. The process is designed to help the next project instead of the current one. Another flaw is that because the project is over and everyone wants to move on there is no attempt to do a root cause analysis (RCA) to find the detailed reasons things happened. A high explanation is given and accepted as to the cause of the problem. Not much time is spent trying to identify all the causes of the problems and the possible things that could have been done differently. In addition, the documentation almost always falls into the black hole along with all the other documentation and is never seen again. Hence, several months later when a similar project is done with a different project team, the same mistakes reoccur.

Another common process that companies have in place and don't use correctly is RCA. Companies normally use this process when there is a common defect but never apply it when a project is having problems. Many times the root cause is that parts of the project methodology are not being followed correctly. A common problem is that the project methodology's check and balances processes are not done correctly, or even not at all. Thus, bad research, wrong requirements, bad estimates, and incorrect staffing are approved and passed down to later phases. A process outside of the project such as RCA would help to identify what is happening. A trigger that maybe a RCA needs to done for a project would be if the words descoping or additional phases are ever mentioned. Another warning sign would be if there is a large number of RFCs occurring to change the original requirements.

One project team had stayed mostly together for several projects. They averaged around 70–80 RFCs on each project. Most other teams that worked on similar projects averaged under half of that. If the project team had done an RCA, they would have discovered that the process they used to write their business requirements and get approval was the cause of all the RFCs later in the project. Besides missing many business requirements that IT needed in order to do their development, many of the requirements were wrong assumptions on how things worked. The only way to fix the project plan was to create the many RFCs. Research would have also revealed that checkpoints in the project process were having the wrong people invited to approve the documentation. Only management from the third level up were being invited to the approval process. People at that level do not have the detailed system knowledge to know whether things are missing or misstated.

For those who do not work on projects and don't know how serious this is, let's say you purchased a piece of equipment that has a hundred different parts in need of assembly. Not only are the assembly instructions missing steps, but also many of the steps are misleading and wrong. Imagine the frustration you would have trying to put it together. Now imagine you are starting to develop a $2 million project in which the instructions are wrong and incomplete. It can be very frustrating and stressful.

24

Effects of Project Failure

When a project starts to miss its project phase milestones (i.e., dates and deliverables), something must be done to fix it. One option is to assign more resources; the problem here is that this adds additional costs, plus there are never spare resources just sitting around. So the only other options available are descoping and additional phases.

When descoping occurs, the business partners are naturally upset. Originally they had agreed on a delivery date, the functionality they would get, and the cost. Putting it in a different perspective, a customer who walks into a brand-name fast food place and orders and pays right away for a combo meal, which they expect to get a drink, fries, and a hamburger. Instead, let's say they get only the drink and fries. It's taking longer than expected to cook the hamburger. The person behind the counter asks the customer to sit down and they will bring it to them. After a while, they come to tell the customer it's going to cost another $2 for the hamburger because it had to be descoped from the first order. To get the sandwich an additional phase of a second order will need to be created. The customer doesn't get any money back from the first order even though it was not their fault. Instead they have to pay for the second order, plus they have to wait another 15 minutes before they get the hamburger. This is the same concept business partners have to live with when descoping and additional phases occur on projects.

If this happened just once at a fast food place, the customer would never come back. Business partners are captive, so when projects have problems they have no other place to go. They often keep their frustration to themselves. If your company is having problems with delivery of projects, I challenge you to go to your business partner and have an honest talk. In one company, descoping was done so often that in the business customer survey there was almost zero confidence that information technology (IT) could deliver a large project on time and on budget. The business partners never complained because the issue had been going on for such a long time and nothing ever changed even when concerns were voiced in the past.

This, though, changed almost overnight because of a single occurrence. The company had a true chargeback system in place. The internal IT department had almost no money because it was all given to the business side of the company. Business would then contract with internal IT for both maintenance and development work. This seems like a good checks and balance process to keep IT from overspending and to produce results. A business department had requested the internal IT department to develop a web-based front end for one of its business entry systems. The IT department went off and developed a state-of-the-art system with many fancy features in it. The problem was that IT never really checked back with their business stakeholders to make sure it was what it needed. Naturally, the project went way over budget and was very late in delivery. When it was finally completed, the business stakeholders hated it and did not want to pay for it. In this true chargeback environment, the chief executive officer (CEO) made the decision that the business did not have to pay IT for the new system. Plus, the CEO said that if internal IT could not deliver on time and within budget, maybe an external company could do it better. So the business department contracted with an outside software company to have its system built. It was delivered on time and with only the functions the business originally requested.

IT management naturally got excited about this outsourcing. If it could be done once, it could be done again. Hence, for the first time IT had to take a serious look at how it did things and make some major changes. This department finally realized that missing deadlines and going over budget were very unhappy experiences for their businesses partners. For the first time, IT saw itself as being arrogant sometimes regarding the needs of the business. IT staff members designed and created things based solely on the technology and then guessed as to how it could be applied to the needs of the business. Things changed almost overnight in how IT worked and treated its business partners. Business and IT communicated better as to what was needed and how to go about doing things. One change was that the different management levels no longer relied solely on status reports to understand what was occurring. Instead, both business and IT management began to get more involved with the day-to-day activities of project work to understand the true status of the work being done. The end result was that a larger percentage of all projects started to be delivered successfully.

A project that starts to go bad is like a small ripple. It's very easy to correct things when it's just a small ripple. However, when nothing is done to correct a project early, it can become a major tidal wave very quickly, which then makes it very hard to make corrections that will still allow the project to meet all the benchmarks for success. With the previously mentioned company, opening communication and getting management more involved throughout the project allowed small problems to be identified and fixed early so that they did not become large problems. It was a simple process and concept that cost no money to implement. This illustrates W. Edwards Deming's point 14 (see Chapter 13): "Put everyone in the company to work to accomplish the transformation. The transformation is everybody's work." Because of the threat of outsourcing and losing jobs, all IT management were forced to transform how they interacted with their business partners.

25

Controlling Failure

In planning change, all the planning is around success, which we like to call the happy path. But there also needs to be some planning and knowledge around failure, which can be called the sad path. Let's face it: Many parts in a large change can and will fail. Most great business leaders understand this and have processes and procedures to control failure and get things back on track.

As a person gains experience and knowledge in what and how a process works, a by-product is that they can see barriers, problems, and bottlenecks well into the future before they become large; this is called being proactive. It would be easy to step in and immediately demand changes on a project to make it right, which goes against one of Jack Welch's leadership points of managing less. Jumping in and taking over immediately on a failure can be damaging to a project and its members. Just like the philosophy that new management needs to spend time to understand the company and systems before making any changes, the same thing is true of projects. What makes projects so much fun is that each one is very unique because of requirements, design, cost, and resources. Until time is spent understanding what is not working and why it's not, it's only a guess that the changes being made are going to make the situation better.

Remember the log chain concept and replacing weak links? Finding the weakest parts in the project process and fixing them will get the best performance increases. And how do we go about finding and fixing things that are wrong? We go back to the same continuous improvement process of Deming's wheel. Plan-Do-Check-Act (PDCA) from Chapter 13. This simple process can be used to improve a lot of things.

A small failure is actually good for a project and the team. If success happens all the time, then people tend to get sloppy. They take things for granted and don't pay attention to the finer details. If someone steps in and corrects them before they fail, then team members start to expect that all the time. At some point someone will not be looking over their shoulders, and a mistake will not be caught. The reality is that a single point of checking is better than having multiple points of checking. It also ties into W. Edwards Deming's point 3 (see Chapter 13): "Cease dependence on mass inspection. Eliminate the need for inspection on a mass basis by building quality into the product in the first place." With multiple points of checking, an assumption is made that the other people checked their points thoroughly, which is what Deming covers on page 30 of his book, *Out of the Crisis*. A real life example are the party crashers of President Barack Obama's first State Dinner in November 2009. Even though their name was not on the list, since they showed what appeared to be a valid invitation they got through the first checkpoint. Many other levels of screening occurred, but the assumption at each checkpoint was that the other checkpoints would have turned the couple away if they were not supposed to be there. This brings up a golden rule: Never assume, always validate. The most common way to control small failures is through communication before or at the time the work is being done. Ask questions such as: Does the developer understand the instructions and goals? Is the worker planning on validating their test plan and results with someone else? Are the developer's decisions based on assumptions or facts? The purpose is to make the sure the developer understands what needs to be done, how to do it, and that he or she has the knowledge and skills to accomplish it. Open communication is the best way to address small issues and problems before they become large ones.

Large failures, as you would expect, are the most dangerous. This type of failure should never happen with the correct processes and procedures being in place and being followed. In a project methodology there are always several checks and balances throughout the project life span to make sure things are accurate. It takes neglect on a number of the control processes for a large failure to happen, but it does. The most common cause of project failure can be traced back to the earlier project phases. The output from these early phases is very poor in terms of defining the *what*. There was more emphasis on meeting the deadline for the task than on creating quality material people can work from. This happens because a couple of controls are neglected. One is that the right people are not involved with the process of creating the documentation. Another is that the approval process for the material is not done or the wrong people are asked to approve it.

For small and medium-sized projects, the consequences are normally small when processes are not being followed correctly. But when under stress with a large project, a bad process can have severe effects. For the project team that ended up having 716 defects in testing, tracing the cause of defects revealed that the requirements document was missing half of the instructions, or the *what* for the project. And many of the requirements in the document were unclear and wrong assumptions. Even though the issue was identified by the development team 6 months before implementation, the core project team did not want to concern upper management that there were issues. Status reports to upper management showed the project was on track. The truth of the project status came out about 1 month before implementation. After several heated discussions with upper business and IT management, it was decided that only one-third of the project could be delivered on time; two-thirds were descoped from the original release, and two additional phases were added to complete the original proposed project. Even though 716 defects were found in testing, once in production the finding of defects continued for over a year. The cost of defects, descoping, and adding two additional phases moved the final delivery date just under 1 year past the original delivery date.

If there appears to be a failure occurring, action needs to be taken immediately. Most of the time the mistake is made by waiting, hoping the problem will correct itself. When it seems like there might be a small failure, an informal process such as direct communication can be used to get things back on track. But when there seems to be a large failure, then a more formal process needs to be followed immediately, such as the root cause analysis (RCA) process. Someone suggesting that that there might be major issues is enough to trigger an RCA. In the worst case, if an RCA is done and finds that everything is correct, the only thing wasted was some time to get everyone on the same page. But is that so bad to make sure everyone understands what is occurring? In the best case a major issue is found and corrected before it had time to affect the project objectives, goals, and timelines.

26

Project Methodology

Projects require a roadmap, directions, or a template to bring everything together. A project can be thought of as having two parts: (1) the intangible items, or the art of the project, and (2) the tangible items, or the form of the project. Quality, improvement, performance, process engineering, and management are the intangible items that compose the *art* of the project. This chapter discusses the project methodology, which tangible, is the *form* of the project known as the form.

Failure rate is very high when it comes to information technology (IT)-related projects—higher than what most people even suspect. A web search with the keywords "IT project failure" will return numerous web sites that contain different studies that have been done. Each study is different in how and what is being measured and who participated, So there is no way to compare them. However, we can look at a category such as "success" and check across all studies to see the trends.

One group that routinely gathers information on project work and then creates reports is The Standish Group that started in 1985. I subscribe to their email newsletter . The first survey they published on IT project failure was in 1995 and it was called The Chaos Report. Since then they have continued to do company surveys to gather information around IT project work. They have many charts, including one that shows probability of failure based on number of people involved, estimated cost, and length of project. As it would be expected, as projects get larger with number of people, cost, and length of time to complete, the success rate goes down—so much that once a project cost climbs into the millions, there is only a single digit chance of the project meeting the success criteria. Since The Standish Group has been capturing IT project information for over 25 year, they are a good source to check regarding trending. And the trend is not good. As they reported in their newsletter and at their website (http://

www1.standishgroup.com/newsroom/chaos_2009.php), their "CHAOS Summary 2009" report showed a decrease in success rates. Based on being delivered on time, on budget, and with required features and functions, 32% of all projects succeeded, 44% were challenged, and 24% failed. This was a downtick in success rates from the previous study. The 2009 results represented the highest failure rate in over a decade. One would think that, with all the project knowledge and project methodologies, things would be better than they were in 1999. With an average of only 32% success rate, there is a lot of room for improvement when it comes to projects.

Being a conventionalist that needs data, it's important to understand the percentages above. These percentages represent thousands of projects of different types and sizes from hundreds of companies. In your environment the percentages could be higher or they could be lower. Surprisingly, most companies do not take the time to track project success rates defined around size and type of project. Instead they group all projects together and at the end of the year there is report showing a certain percentage was completed on time and a certain percentage was not. Without detailed benchmarks, there is no way to validate changes in processes, such as using a new project methodology.

A project methodology is nothing more than a high-level plan on what is going to occur in a project. Let's say there is a need to get groceries. We first need to get dressed. Then we need to go to the grocery store. Next, we walk up and down the aisle getting the groceries. Then we need to pay by going though the checkout line. Then we drive home with the groceries, and, last, we need to put the groceries away. Using this example we could create a grocery methodology for each time we needed to get groceries. The general steps would be as follows:

- Get dressed
- Go to store
- Select groceries
- Pay for groceries
- Drive home
- Put away groceries

Does this mean that each time we go to the grocery store it will be exactly the same? No. Different clothes will be worn, different stores could be shopped at, cash instead of credit could be used. So each time we go grocery shopping it's different.

Despite the differences, similar steps happen each time. Each one of these general steps is called a phase. These phases must always occur in the same chronological order. Imagine what the outcome would be if you did the "Select groceries" phase without doing the "Get dressed" phase first. We would be naked in the grocery store.

When we talk of a project methodology, we are talking about nothing more than a series of general phases (steps) that will occur and the order in which they need to occur. All project methodologies generally have the same phases, but each methodology follows a different order and execution. Search the Internet, and you can find over 100 different project methodologies.

I cannot speak of every project methodology that is on the market, but the various ones on which I have worked can be categorized into two general types: (1) linear; and (2) spiral. Depending on the type of project, one will get better results than the other. For small, simple projects, there is no need for project management. Most companies have a threshold so that if the project appears to be below a certain number of hours and affects only one system, formal project management does not need to be applied. As the project gets larger or affects more than one system, it becomes necessary to have some type of project control, which is what project methodology is mostly about.

Most project methodologies have been on the market only for the last couple of decades, so they are fairly new. Examples are Prince2, Method123 Project Management Methodology (MPMM), and Project Management Body of Knowledge Guide (PMBOK). PMBOK is from the Project Management Institute (PMI) and probably is the most recognized and used on the market. PMI was first founded in 1969 by a small group of people who wanted to share process information and discuss common problems that occurred during a project. In 1987 PMI published a white paper called "Project Management Body of Knowledge Guide." In 1994 PMI took its knowledge to the next level and published a book of concepts. Since then it has released several other editions of that book.

PMBOK is good, but you have to take it for what it is. It's designed to handle a wide range of projects such as construction, software development, and automotive business. To handle this diverse set of users, the material has to be general enough to fit all situations in which it might be used. By following it to the letter, the same concepts and techniques for software development are being used to build a jail. Think of any project process taken directly from the book as a generalist approach. Thus, companies must modify PMBOK to their project structure to fit specific usage, or in other words hone it into a specialist process. This increases the chances of success and improves performance.

To show how simple modifications can be done to fit a company's needs better, the PMBOK project structure will be covered at a high level. PMBOK breaks down the project process into different knowledge areas: project integration management, project scope management, project time management, project cost management, project quality management, project human resource management, project communication management, project risk management, and project procurement management. All these things deal with the tangible tasks that go with a project. Table 26.1 provides definitions for each area.

A formal project methodology is really detailed, and Table 26.1 shows just a small part of it. Not shown in the table are the countless activities and tasks for each action step in the Characteristics column. So hundreds of processes might be improved depending on the situation. If we apply the pyramid template with Goal State, Outcome and Tools & Input as the different columns the PMBOK structure would look like Figure 26.1.

Remember when we applied the pyramid template to improve the management best practices disciplines (see Chapter 7)? The same process can be used to modify the project methodology to best fit the company's environment. The goal state and outcomes are pretty well set in stone based on the project methodology being used. These are also intangible items that cannot be measured directly. But the Tools & Inputs section is where modifications can be made so that the methodology best fits the type of development the company does. The columns to the right are the tangible actions that people can execute. They also can be measured to see if improvement is occurring. Once again, it's not about making major one-time changes but instead making small changes numerous times. A company that builds bridges would require the same goals and outcomes as an insurance company. But the Tools & Inputs would differ somewhat so that the project process fits the different type of projects better.

A company can track whether the changes it is making to the project methodology are beneficial by using the log chain concept and the continuous improvement process of Plan-Do-Check-Act (PDCA). Once again, continuous improvement is about making small adjustments and measuring the results. Find the weakest part in the project methodology. It might be something that causes a bottleneck or conflict or even failure in the environment. Replace it with something so that the enhancement becomes one of the strongest points in the project process. Repeat the process again and again, trying to find the next weakest link each time and then improve upon it. In a short time the project success rate will start to go up because the project methodology is being molded to fit the company usage instead of the company having to be changed to fit the project methodology.

We talked about modifying the project methodology to meet the company's needs. A company can have several different types of projects. At one end of the spectrum are simple projects based around updates and small enhancements. At the other end are large complex projects that involve building a dream or vision that starts with many unknowns into reality. To be consistently good at project delivery, companies need to have more than one project methodology to handle the different types. One methodology might be designed around projects that have few unknowns but is labor intensive. Another project methodology could be for medium-sized projects only. Yet another project methodology could be for large, complex projects that mostly start out as a dream and unknowns. Before

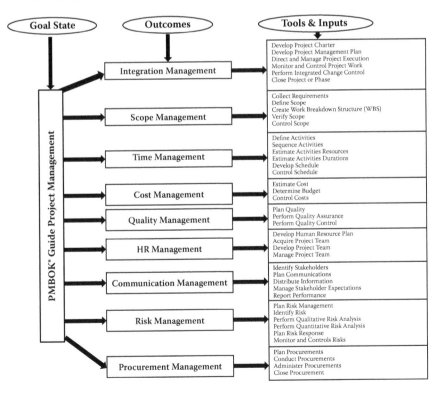

FIGURE 26.1
PMBOK guide.

TABLE 26.1

PMBOK Knowledge Areas

Knowledge Area	Description	Characteristics
Project integration management	The processes and activities needed to identify, define, combine, unify, and coordinate the various activity processes and project management activities within the project management process group.	Develop project charter: The process of developing a document that formally authorizes a project or a phase and documentation of initial requirements that satisfy the stakeholder needs and expectations. Develop project management plan: The process of documenting the actions necessary to define, prepare, integrate, and coordinate all subsidiary plans. Direct and manage project execution: The process of performing the work defined in the project management plan to achieve the project's objective. Monitor and control project work: The process of tracking, reviewing, and regulating the progress to meet the performance objectives defined in the project management plan. Perform integrated change control: The process of reviewing all change requests, approving changes, and managing changes to the deliverables, organizational process assets, project documents, and the project management plan. Close project or phase: The process of finalizing all activities across all of the project management process groups to formally complete the project or phase.
Project scope management	The processes required to ensure that the project includes all the work required, and only the work required, to complete the project successfully.	Collecting requirements: The process of defining and documenting stakeholder needs to meet the project objectives. Define scope: The process of developing a detail description of the project and product. Create work breakdown structure (WBS): The process of subdividing project deliverables and project work into smaller, more manageable components. Verify scope: The process of formalizing acceptance of the completed project deliverables. Control scope: The process of monitoring the status of the project and product scope and managing changes to the scope baseline.

Project time management	The processes required to ensure timely completion of the project.	Define activities: The process of identifying the specific actions to be performed to produce the project deliverables.
		Sequence activities: The process of identifying and documenting relationships among project activities.
		Estimate activity resources: The process of estimating the type of quantities of material, people, equipment, or supplies required to perform each activity.
		Estimated activity duration: The process of approximating the number of work periods needed to complete individual activities with estimated resources.
		Development schedule: The process of analyzing activity sequences, durations, resource requirements, and schedule constraints to create the project schedule.
		Control schedule: The process of monitoring the status of the project to update project progress and managing changes to the schedule baseline.
		Activity definition: Identifying the specific activities that must be performed to produce the various project deliverables.
Project cost management	The processes involved in estimating, budgeting, and controlling cost so that the project can be completed within the approved budget.	Estimate costs: The process of developing an approximation of the monetary resources needed to complete project activities.
		Determine budget: The process of aggregating the estimated costs of individual activities or work packages to establish an authorized cost baseline.
		Control costs: The process of monitoring the status of the project to update the project budget and managing changes to the cost baseline.
Project quality management	The processes and activities of the performing organization that determined quality processes, objectives, and responsibilities so that the project will satisfy the needs for which it was undertaken.	Plan quality planning: The process of identifying quality requirements and/or standards for the project and product, and documenting how the project will demonstrate compliance.
		Perform quality assurance: The process of auditing the quality requirements and the results from quality control measurements to ensure appropriate quality standards and operational definitions are used.
		Perform quality control: The process of monitoring and recording results of executing the quality activities to assess performance and recommend necessary changes.

TABLE 26.1 (*Continued*)

PMBOK Knowledge Areas

Knowledge Area	Description	Characteristics
Project human resource management	The processes that organize, manage, and lead the project team.	Develop human resource plan: The process of identifying and documenting project roles, responsibilities, and required skills, reporting relationships, and creating a staffing management plan.
		Acquire project team: The process of confirming human resource availability and obtaining the team necessary to complete project assignments.
		Develop project team: The process of improving the competencies, team interaction, and the overall team environment to enhance project performance.
		Manage project team: The process of tracking team member performance, providing feedback, resolving issues, and managing changes to optimize project performance.
Project communication management	The processes required to ensure timely and appropriate generation, collection, distribution, storage, retrieval, and ultimate disposition of project information.	Identify stakeholders: The process of identifying all people or organizations impacted by the project, and documenting relevant information regarding their interests, involvement, and impact on project success.
		Plan communications: The process of determining the project stakeholder information needs and defining a communication approach.
		Distribution information: The process of making relevant information available to project stakeholders as planned.
		Manage stakeholder expectations: The process of communicating and working with stakeholders to meet their needs and addressing issues as they occur.
		Report performance: The process of collecting and distribution performance information, including status reports, progress measurements, and forecasts.

| Project risk management | The systematic process of conducting risk management planning, identification, analysis, response planning, and monitoring and control on a project. | Plan risk management: The process of defining how to conduct risk management activities for a project.
Identify risks: The process of determining which risks may affect the project and documenting their characteristics.
Perform qualitative risk analysis: The process of prioritizing risks for further analysis or action by assessing and combining their probability of occurrence and impact.
Perform quantitative risk analysis: The process of numerically analyzing the effect of identified risks on overall project objectives.
Plan risk responses: The process of developing options and actions to enhance opportunities and to reduce threats to project objectives.
Monitor and control risks: The process of implementing risk response plans, tracking identified risks, monitoring residual risks, identifying new risks, and evaluating risk process effectiveness throughout the project. |
| Project procurement management | The processes necessary to purchase or acquire products, services, or results needed from outside of the project team. | Plan procurements: The process of documenting project purchasing decisions, specifying the approach, and identifying potential sellers.
Conduct procurements: The process of obtaining seller responses, selecting a seller, and awarding a contract.
Administer procurements: The process of managing procurement relationships, monitoring contract performance, and making changes and corrections as needed.
Close procurements: The process of completing each project procurement. |

Source: PMI, *A Guide to the Project Management Body of Knowledge*, 4th edition, Appendix F, Author, 2008 (with permission).

each project is started there needs to be a decision on what methodology to use. If you put average people into a bad process, the outcome often will be failure, but if you take those same average people and put them into a good process, the outcome most often will be success. Starting out with the right process for the type of work being done will help reduce the risk of failure.

27

Project Phases

DOCUMENTATION

Before we cover the different project phases, we need to discuss documentation. Documentation is the primary tool that ties all the phases together. For each project phase, several different types of documentation are suggested to be created. In the first phases the project needs to have the structure defined, so the documentation contains such things as a communication plan, project structure that will be used, roles and responsibilities of the different project titles, and business alignment of who is sponsoring and driving the work. Some project processes have over 20 different templates for just the first project phase. Once the project gets started then there are different documents for such things as reporting defects, test strategy, release plan, business requirements, architecture changes, design, return on investment, and risk report. And near the end of the project documentation such as implementation check list, technical specifics, test data, and postimplementation validation report is needed. The tendency is that as the project gets into the later phases fewer documents need to be created. Instead of 20 in the first couple of project phases, fewer than 10 documents might be created in the last phases. All total, a project management process could have around 60 different documents that are suggested to be created. A project team could spend the time to fill out every document on a project, but depending on the type of project being done many of the documents will add no value to the success of the project.

As stated before, a company that is marketing a project management process creates it so that many different types of businesses can use it. The same is true of the documentation. The documentation templates are designed for general usage for a wide range of projects and lines of business. Many of the sections in these documents may have no bearing on the project for which they will used. When a company selects a project management process it needs to realize that modifications should be made to it along with the required documentation to fit its specific needs.

The project team at the beginning of each phase needs to decide what documents it needs to create for the specific type of project just for that phase. After that it needs to look at each template and modify them to be specific for the project. Do this by removing, modifying, or deleting sections out of the template. A key to a successful project has nothing to do with the amount of documentation that is created. Instead, a key to success is that the documentation created must be simple, clear, concise, and accurate so that everyone can understand it and work from it.

In a perfect world everything would be 100% accurate and complete the first time. But in the real world, which is where we work, things are missed, inaccurate statements are made, or the needs of the business partners change midproject. A project is consistently changing, and documentation updates need to be made to reflect this throughout the project time frame. When creating the format of documentation, a key consideration is that it must be easily updated. If late in a project it's realized that a business process needs to be redesigned because there is a better way to do it, then it must be easy to update all the documentation that already exists such as the business requirements, solution scoping, design, architect, technical specs, implementation, and testing documents.

Once those documents are updated, then comes the communication factor. It must be easy to communicate the changes to everyone using the different documents for their work. Even though most project methodologies have a formal change request in place to document the changes that come up, if the original documents are many and stored all over the place, it's an issue in keeping all documentation in synch and people informed of what is current.

So how is good documentation created? It's just common sense that fragmentation of similar data over several documents increases the risk of miscommunication and misinterpretation and adds confusion. The fewer documents there are, the lower the risk. A successful process is to select the different documents that are known to be needed. In each document remove the items that do not pertain to the project that is being done. If there becomes a need later in the project, it can be added back in. The goal is to start out as simple as possible and build on that.

Once the different documentation has started to be created, merge documents that are trying to accomplish the same thing.

There are many benefits of merging documents together. One is that with fewer documents there is less chance of redundancy of data in different documents, since many documents require similar information. Information can be found easier and faster. If data is scattered in many different documents, it takes time to scan the various documents to find what is needed. When changes do occur, fewer documents need to be changed. With more information in a document and fewer documents, people have a better chance of understanding versus jumping from document to document trying to understand what is occurring. When creating the documents and the format, consider what best will work for the people that need to use them. Sometimes people forget that documentation they create is not for themselves but for others to work from.

The format and control of the documentation is one task of a project that, if done correctly, can greatly increase performance and decrease the number of defects that occur. Think back to the project with 716 defects found in system testing. Project team members followed the project methodology as closely as possible and created numerous documents that had little value to the project but only added confusion. They did not merge or modify any of the document templates, so when there was a need to make numerous changes because of missed information and wrong assumptions, it became mass confusion. There were documents from system analysts, business analysts, architects, technical leads, and test office. Many of these people had more than one document that needed to be updated when changes were made. Even though a formal update process was in place nobody really knew what was current and accurate because there were so many people involved and because the number of documents kept changing. Many times documents containing similar information had different directives. What was in the scope document was different from what was in the business requirements document or the technical specification document. This lack of control over the documentation and the inconsistency among documents was another key factor that led to low productivity and a large number of defects.

In summary, the concept is to not be afraid to modify the documentation format to better fit the project needs. By no means am I saying to create one large document with all the information. Instead, look at the content of what is needed to make the project successful, and then format your documentation around that. Last, when you do make a new document template by merging others together, validate the final format with the project team. Many times they can give input as to how to improve the template even more. They themselves might even change the format of their documentation to better fit the project. The purpose is to have all documentation consistent for that project.

PHASES

When I first started working on projects in the 1980s, the company I worked for never had such things as a project methodology or phases. One or two IT people would take the lead and gather all the information and then turn it into changes. There was little validation that the analyzing was complete or accurate. Development started once the one or two IT people felt they knew what the business partners wanted. Many times the final proposed design was not what business wanted. A project would be partway through development, and people would realize that a major requested item was missed. Until things got straightened out with more analyzing, development would slow to a crawl or even stop. Most of the time design changes had to occur. The outcome was that the project would be delivered late and over budget because of the rework that needed to be done.

Another common occurrence was that once the change was tested and ready to implement the technical people forgot to send out user communication or training before the changes were implemented. A few projects I know of even got delayed because they had to wait until proper training was done. Only the people with a lot of experiences with project, system knowledge, and working with their business partners directly could deliver successful projects consistently before project methodology. In the first company I worked for there were less than five people with the skills and experience to successfully lead medium and large projects.

A project methodology breaks down the project into smaller phases. Each phase has a certain purpose and a specific chronological order that it follows so that each phase can be managed. There are start dates, stop dates, and deliverables for each phase. A good example of the benefits that project methodology bring is that normally in one of the early project phases there is always a task dealing with defining how the implementation will occur. Because this task is early in the project process, there can be proper planning, training, and communication on how the change will be implemented.

There can be classified two general project methodology types. One is called a linear process, and the other is a spiral process. For now we are talking of the linear process. Some project methodologies consist of nine different phases, and others have five or less. Each project methodology has slightly different names for its different phases. For our discussion a seven-phase approach will be used: (1) initiation; (2) analysis; (3) design; (4) development; (5) testing; (6) implementation; and (7) postimplementation.

Again, the number of phases used is a suggestion. Each project in a company is unique. Whether you want to use four or nine phases should depend on the type of the project. To many times, companies implement formal project management without being able to modify the phases and what is delivered in each phase. Because of this lack of flexibility projects don't obtain peak outcomes because the process does not match the work that needs to be done.

In a project management methodology the earlier project phases are designed around organizing the project by doing such things as setting up budgets, defining what the project is supposed to be, the best people to be involved, and defining what business is truly asking for. The later phases of a project deal with executing a project plan in terms of development. So keep in mind that the best person to lead the first phases is someone who knows how to organize and handle financials, while the best person to handle the later phases is someone with the technical skills to lead the development and implementation of the change.

INITIATION

This phase is the start of a project. The top priority in this phase is to put together a core project team. The team's responsibility in this phase is to gather the initial high-level requirements around what needs to be accomplished—not how to do it but *what* and *why* to do it. The *how* behind a project will be defined in later phases.

The information gathered defines what probably will change and what probably will not be changed. Project terminology used in this early stage will mention things as being in scope or out of scope for the project. It's very high-level information and probably fits into the 80–20 rule: 80% of the information defined now will probably be true throughout the project; the other 20% of the information is based assumptions, which until later phases will not be known whether it's true or not true. So some information from this early phase is expected to be changed as the project progresses.

After all the high-level information is gathered, then a very high-level estimate of the entire project cost is made. Since the information is at a high level and without any details around how to accomplish the change, it's acceptable for the estimate to be as much as +/–100% in this phase. There will be several other chances to revise this estimate in later phases. This first estimate is only to inform the business partners that will be financing the project whether the project is a $100K project or a $10 million project. Besides the high-level estimate on the entire project, another estimate is normally included. This second estimate covers the cost and time frame to complete only the next project phase. With only high-level information finer details need to be gathered to make a correct decision on whether to proceed.

The outcome of this phase might be as simple as a document with just a couple of written objectives or as complex as a thick manual defining all the expected outcomes and objectives that are trying to be accomplished. The purpose is for the business stakeholders to define the rationality behind doing the project. A term for the final product is the *scope document.* Its purpose is to lock down early what is being requested. In the old days before formal project management and scope documents, it was a moving target as to what the final product would be. What the business stakeholder would request today could be different in a couple of weeks in their minds. Many times there would be discussions later in the project as to what was originally agreed upon. Everyone hates doing documentation, but creating scope documentation is a far better option than arguing with your business stakeholders over what had been originally agreed upon without having anything in writing.

The last task in this phase is to review all the information and make a decision as to whether to proceed to the next phase. The approval process is fairly simple. The business partners that asked for the request and the core project team reviews the scope documentation that was created. There might be additions, deletions, or changes to the documentation. By no means does approval to proceed mean the project is 100% approved. It only means there is justification to gather more information to see if it's still feasible.

So who is the best person to lead this first phase? The phase's primary deliverables are to organize the project in terms of getting it started, initial resource allocation, budgets, and project expectations. Project managers are trained in these tasks, so they would be the best individuals responsible to get them done.

ANALYSIS (SOLUTION SCOPING)

This phase, sometimes called the solution scoping phase, takes the project into deeper detail. The scope document created in the initiation phase is used to define finer details called *business requirements* or just *requirements* in this phase. A requirement is a statement specifically on what the business wants. It can deal with a certain look or functionality that is needed. The requirement statements should *not* be written around *how* to do it but around *what* and *why*.

Most of the time projects start out wrong because the business requirements are stated using *how* verbiage. The *how* is supposed to be done in the later stages of design and development. Confused? Think of a couple that wants to build a house. They can document all the "what": how they want the house to look and why. But for the house to become a reality it will take design and construction knowledge from architects, electricians, plumbers, heating, and construction experts to define how it will be done. This is similar to the business world. The technical people need to be responsible for the *how,* or else it will lead to bad design and development. In the project roles and responsibilities, normally the people who create the requirements are called *solution analysts*.

Once all the requirements are gathered it's time to get another estimate, only this time the estimate needs to be around the +/–50% range. Through the analysis phase the technical side should have been part of the process. There are two reasons for their early involvement. One is to bring a different mind-set to gathering requirements. Technical people will think differently about the change than their business partners will, so the final requirements will be more complete and accurate. The other reason to have them involved is for this estimate. With technical people being involved in the phase they will be able to give a quick and accurate estimate of what it's going to take to accomplish the project. This estimate in the analysis phase needs to have the cost broken down on each functionality so that individual items can be questioned as to the benefit and cost that they will bring. This almost never happens and should be done if a company is serious about costs, quality, and performance.

At this point return on investment (ROI) needs to be applied to the requirement. This is where small companies excel and large companies fail miserably. In a small company because of limited resources and money, only the required changes for a project get approved. Functionality or enhancements that could be classified as *nice to have* are normally not done. It's self-monitoring because in a small company most everyone in different management levels and departments are aware of the changes that are pending. Large companies on the other hand do not have this self-controlling process.

What occurs in large companies is that in medium-sized to large projects, many requirements get built into the project based on personal wants and needs and not because of the value they bring. When business stakeholders are questioned about the ROI on a nonessential requirement the response normally will be that it would be nice to have. Think of it as how government works. When voted upon, a government bill, because of the benefits it will bring to everyone, will have enough votes to make it law. Because it's known it will pass, government representatives attach personal pork belly projects to the original bill. If the pork belly project had to stand on its own it never would be passed because it only brings benefit to maybe a few congressmen's districts. This is the same concept for project requirements. What gets attached to an approved project are enhancements and functionality that add very little value to the company but cost resources and time.

In large companies the financial times dictate how closely projects are examined and what is being requested. In good times they are interested in building by trying to become a market leader. Cost does not seem to be a factor involved with many of the projects that are done. Companies take risks because they have large amounts of money and resources to gamble with. In tough times they start to look at the ROI on projects, but only at the project level. On projects that get approved, nonessential requirements are still included. There is no process in place to get rid of them. So even in tough times when a large company thinks it's watching its cost, it is still spending money on changes that will add little or no value to the company.

On large projects, there is probably an average of 10% of the requirements that are personal wants (nice to have) that cannot be cost justified. If a company is doing $100 million in large-scale development, this translates into $10 million being spent on work that is adding little value to the company. If companies wanted to control this and reduce development cost, at the end of the analysis phase there should be a process to justify each requirement with an ROI. By no means is adding a process to validate each project requirement the only cure to reduce project cost, but it is a large step to make sure the work that is being done is the most important to the company needs and not someone's personal wants.

A simple process that works successfully to identify the low value requirements is to rank each one. A scale is built with a value at one end that represents "absolutely needed." At the other end of the scale there is a value representing "nice to have." Business stakeholders that asked for the project then assigns one of the values from the scale to each requirement. When a rough estimate is given at the end of the analysis phase two different ones are created. One estimate is based on all the requirements being done, even the "nice to have" ones. The other estimate given is if only the "absolutely needed" requirements are done. With these two estimates a cost range can be created based on if only the required changes are made or all changes are made.

At this point another approval process is gone through. Since there is more detail of what is expected with the business requirements, the estimate range needs to go from +/–100% to +/–50%. As mentioned earlier, if a knowledgeable IT person has been on the project during this entire phase, he or she should be able to very quickly give the estimate.

DESIGN

Up to this point only the project's *what* and *why* have been gathered and documented. This has been accomplished by the scope document and business requirements created in the earlier phases. Now it's time to create the *how*. In this phase the technical people start to become the key drivers behind the project. Business stakeholders and the analysts have done their part in defining what they want, and it's now up to the technical professionals to build it. The first step is to create documentation around the *how*. These normally are called *architecture specifications* and *technical specifications*. This documentation details the architecture changes and building tasks that are needed to fill all the requirements that business has asked for.

There are countless numbers of formats for the technical specifications. There can be documents on the architecture, design, and functionality and then a different document for each individual item that needs to be changed. I'm not going to go into detail. Just think of different construction documents that are required to build a new house. Besides the material list and core set of blueprints for the house, there are blueprint sets for the plumbing, electrical, heating, and landscaping. This is similar to dealing with projects. Everything that defines how things will be done gets documented in this phase. When the design is complete, the core project team of business stakeholders and designers can go back through all the business requirements and validate that the design documentation design will cover everything, which is called traceability.

Near the end of this phase all the unknowns, questions, and gaps on how to accomplish the project should have been identified and resolved. With the information gathered, a detailed estimate can be given. The estimate will contain the hours needed to complete it along with the type of resources that are required to complete the project. The type of resources is needed because a special skill or knowledge might be needed for a specific task. The cost and the availability of this specialist affect the project outcome. Defining all these things items helps with the accuracy of the final estimate at the end of this phase.

In this last phase before development, one of the tasks is to approve the functionality that will be done and the cost of developing that functionality. If the ranking process of "absolutely needed" to "nice to have" was done on each requirement, there will be a detailed information on the cost of doing the "nice to have" requirements. At this time if the cost of doing the project is too high, very quickly the core project team can work on removing some (or all) of the "nice to have" items to reduce the cost. What occurs if the items are not ranked and there is a need to reduce costs? Then the project has to go back to the analysis phase and rework the solution to reduce cost, which is very time-consuming. It should be noted that later, when the spiral methodology is discussed (see Chapter 29), some of the processes involve ranking requirements. The process is based around doing the most important work first and then working down to less important things.

Another task in this phase is to come up with a timeline of the tasks that need to be done along with the delivery date. This will drive how many resources are needed. If a project is 2,000 hours and does not need to be implemented for 1 year, one person could possibly do that. But if the same project needs to be done in 1 month, then 12 people need to be assigned. This is all documented before the final review in this phase because there might not be enough internal resources to complete the project. External contractors might have to be brought in to complete the project on time, or maybe the timeline needs to be changed to match the resources available.

Once all the resources have been assigned, then the final estimates can be given. There is the final estimate on the delivery date and the final estimate for total cost. Once again, these are reviewed to see if the project should proceed. A project might be put on hold at this point. Even though it's a good project, there could be other projects that will bring better benefits. With limited money and resources it's better to do the higher-priority projects first.

Some people might think putting a project hold at this point would waste a lot of time and money. It does not. At this point the vast majority of the work left is all development and deals with execution. These are things for which the technical staff are primary responsible. If development is not started for several months after design is completed, the only additional work or waste would be to pull the original project team together for a quick review of the existing documentation to identify if anything has changed.

Often, two important designs get missed in this phase. Even though it's in the middle of the project process, how to test the changes need to be decided, along with how to implement the changes. These are just as important as the primary design work. Remember that before there was formal project management, implementation and testing were rarely thought of until the project was mostly completed. Even with formal project management many times these things are not completed when they should be. People put a low priority on them because they want to get started on the next phase, which is development. But not having a plan in place early for testing and implementation adds a risk that these tasks will not be ready when they are needed.

DEVELOPMENT

From this point on it's about execution of the approved project plan. To do their work correctly developers can leverage documents created earlier such as scope, business requirements, solution scoping, architect, and the finely detailed documentation of technical specifications. Monitoring must be done to ensure that the plan is being followed. Status reports are routinely sent out to all stakeholders on the status of development. No matter how much research or analysis was done earlier, once in development technical staff will find things that have been missed or misunderstood as to how things actually work. In addition, the business market is changing every day, which includes during the development phase. Business stakeholders might request some enhancements to fit the current market needs better.

Depending on the project methodology, testing can be part of the development phase or a separate phase by itself. Again, use your own discretion on what best fits for the project. If the change requires major testing throughout the enterprise, then there are benefits to having testing as a separate project phase. If testing is minimal, then include it as a task under development. Either way, testing is only about executing the plan that has been created and agreed upon in the design phase.

TESTING

In the small organizations for which I worked, there was no formal testing process. The developers did all the testing with very little input. Once they thought everything was tested then the changes were put into production. Many defects got into production that could have been prevented if testing would have been expanded just a little to include more people. In large enterprises it becomes a necessity to have a formal testing process. There could be 10 people making changes within one system. One system normally is but a part of long stream of systems in which data are passed from system to system. To keep control of what is happening and to make sure what is being changed does work throughout the enterprise and meets the business request, a formal testing process is required.

To know what to test and check, the test plan is created from the business requirements and the technical specifications. For all changes that have been documented, it needs to be defined how it will be tested, or what is called the test case. This ensures traceability from the business requirements to the technical specifications to what was actually developed. Each test case needs to take into account the full effects that occur when the change happens. These test cases are then used to create the test plan. Test plans will be covered in more detail shortly.

In a formal testing process the developer first codes and then does unit testing. The primary goal of unit testing is to look at the actual code as it's executed to make sure the changes work. This step in testing puts the emphasis on the testing of the data and logic that changes the data. Other testing steps will put the emphasis on the inputs and outputs of the systems. Unit testing is the only testing step that technical people control. Normally at this step there is no official process to report defects. What was done to resolve a defect is seldom documented because the developer will quickly make changes and then test the logic again. When unit testing is completed then the changes are handled over to a Test Office team that does the next step of testing called system testing.

The primary goal of system testing is to check the input and outputs of the system to make sure it's working according to the project requirements. The Test Office verifies that things that have been changed, such as reports, print, input and output functionality, and editing, work as planned. They also make sure things that were not changed also work as they have in the past. Many times a change in one spot will affect something that was not supposed to change in another spot. A way to think of it is that the tangible items that can be seen are tested. That is about all the Test Office can check because they are not normally staffed with technical people.

The testing a developer and Test Office do might sound like a duplication of the testing, but it's not. A system might consist of 2,000 different data fields, but when data is entered, printed, or retrieved for viewing, only about 500 fields are used. The developer must validate through testing that these internal fields that nobody can see are working correctly. The Test Office, on the other hand, checks only on the visual things such as print and screen functionality. An example is a data field called roof type. Internal in the system a roof type of copper might be stored in a data field as CO, but every place it displays or prints it will appear as "copper roof." Primarily, the developer would check to make sure a CO was being stored in the field. The Test Office would check screens and print to make sure that copper roof is being displayed.

Earlier it was mentioned that a test plan consists of test cases that define what needs to be tested for each change. The test plan in the system testing step can consist of several different test runs, commonly known as cycles. In the insurance industry we first have to check new business, so that is done in the first cycle. Then in the next cycle the new business policies created from the first cycle are used to test cancels and amendments (changes to policies). Only after a policy is canceled in the second cycle can a reinstatement be done to the policy. So only in the third cycle is it possible to test reinstatements. Last is testing of the automatic renewal of a policy to another term. This requires yet another cycle to be run. On large projects there can be 20 or more cycles with hundreds of test cases (policies) in each cycle. All this is needed to check out all the possible situations affected by the change. Testing sometimes can take several months to complete because of the number of cycles and the number of test cases to check in each cycle.

When system testing is completed, then the next step of testing is called integration testing, which is very similar to system testing. The only difference is that many systems are put together in a cycle run so that data can be passed from the start to the end of the enterprise process. The purpose of integration testing is to make sure all the changes in each system work together. The Test Office team controls this step again. They build a test plan and enter the data but on a smaller scale than in system testing. The reasoning for the smaller number of test cases is that because of the number of systems being tested at once there is not enough time to run several multiple cycles with hundreds of test cases in each cycle.

The last testing step is called release testing. In release testing a large amount of current production data is copied and used to run through all the changed systems. Using production data allows a large amount of data to be used through the systems with minimal effort. It tries to address the situation of missing unique situations that never got thought of and tested. Up to this point the test data was controlled by what the developer or Test Office could think of. In release testing what is being tested is controlled by what is current in the system. Using production data is just another process to help reduce the possibility of a defect getting into production.

Summary of Testing Steps

1. Coding and unit testing:
   a. Developer responsible for.
   b. Developer keys data for testing.
   c. Testing focus is on detail data changes.
   d. No formal test plan required, but recommended.
2. System testing:
   a. Test Office responsible for. This team normally does not understand the technical changes.
   b. Test Office keys data for testing.
   c. Testing focus is on visual inputs/outputs. It could be how something is printing or how something is functioning.

    d. All changes, even simple maintenance changes, must go through this step.

    e. Testing is around only one or two systems.

    f. Formal test plan required before testing begins in this step.

    g. Test plans can consist of many cycles with hundreds of test cases in each cycle.

3. Integration:

    a. Test Office team completes.

    b. Test Office keys data for testing.

    c. Testing focus is on data flowing between systems to make sure changes made in one system does not have a negative effect on another system that receives data.

    d. Many times simple changes that have low risk of changing other systems don't go through this step.

    e. The test plan consists of fewer cycles then the system testing step, but still can have several cycles to make sure all transactions are tested.

4. Release:

    a. Test Office team completes.

    b. Data is replicated from production. No keying of data by anyone.

    c. Very similar to the above integration testing step, only in this step large amounts of production data are processed instead of test data created.

    d. Testing focus is on serious conditions that will cause major production defects.

    e. The test plan consists of a few cycles. The purpose of this step is to thoroughly test the systems that are changing by using a large amount of data.

IMPLEMENTATION

Implementation is similar to development and testing. There should have been a plan created in the design phase on how this was going to happen. In the design phase it might have been a high-level plan without much specifics. Detailed specifics would be added to the plan during the development. Normally the first thing for implementation is communication that gets sent out to all users and stakeholders explaining what is about to happen. Many times this communication might be sent out a couple of times, with the first notice being sent months before the change is actually being implemented. Training might also be needed so that users— not only business users but also other technical staff such as developers or operations—are operating at peak performance at the start of the change. Communication and training needs to be done for all users affected.

The implementation plan itself needs to be documented and reviewed several times even after approval is given. If it's a large project the week before the implementation there might be a meeting to walk through the entire implementation plan with everyone affected. This is done so that everyone has a chance to address any questions and to make sure everyone is ready for the change.

POSTIMPLEMENTATION

Just because a project goes to production it does not necessarily mean the project is over. Most companies have what is called a warranty period on the changes after implementation. If problems occur because of the new changes, the problems and cost to fix them come back to the project team to resolve during this warranty period. The project team has the best knowledge of what was changed so they are the best qualified to fix defects correctly and quickly. They are the specialists of the change. Another task after implementation is the off-loading of knowledge to the people that will need to support the changes. Most of the time the people who do the building and development don't have to support the change in the future.

The last steps deal with closing down the project. When the warranty period is almost over it's a good time to ask everyone that worked on the project for input as to what went right and what could have been improved. It's called the lesson learned process. Bad things that happened, along with how they could be improved next time, are included with the good things that happened during the project. The methods to gather this information can be a meeting or a questionnaire or an e-mail. As mentioned earlier, it's a good process that creates valuable information that could be leveraged for future projects. But what negates the effort is that nothing becomes of this information. Besides no actions to change any of the processes, the documentation disappears into the black hole into which most documentation falls.

For a company's best practice, the lesson learned documentation from all projects should be centralized in one spot that is readily accessible for everyone. Even though it pertains to what occurred on the project, its true purpose is for improvement on future projects by learning from past experiences. In this way, people can go to one location for key information on possible pitfalls to watch for and things that worked in other projects that added improvement.

The very last task is to close down the project. The project manager creates the final financial and status reports. In the final reports are the final cost, defects, and a grade as to how well the performance benchmarks were met. The performance benchmarks are around how close the final cost, delivery date, functionality, and quality met the originally estimates. At this time the project can get classified as a success, challenge, or a failure.

28

Factors That Affect Projects

PROJECT ESTIMATES AND STAFFING

An estimate is the key factor used to decide whether to proceed with a project. As discussed earlier, there are several chances to give estimates during a project. The first estimate is vague because of all the unknowns. Business has only an idea of what they want. Later estimates given in the project process will have a narrower variance.

The issue with any estimate is that once it's given it can never be taken back. Decisions are based on these estimates, and people are held accountable for them. When an estimate ends up not being in the acceptable range, then there is a demand to know why. On estimates that appear to be high, business stakeholders will almost always ask why. After some discussion and negotiation of what makes up the estimate normally it gets changed to a smaller number. Most of these high estimates are discovered early because of business stakeholders questioning the high estimate.

The estimate that is too low for the work that needs to be done is the most dangerous. Business stakeholders normally do not question these because they believe they are getting a bargain. Usually these low estimates are not found until after development has started. At that point it's too late to stop. The only option normally is to find more money and resources to continue the project. One project was supposed to be delivered in 1 year and ended up taking 3 years to complete. It ended up being classified as a failure because it missed the benchmarks of delivery date and cost. If the original estimates had been correct the project probably never would have been approved. In rare occasions projects get canceled even after millions of dollars had already been spent on development. Upper management gets tired of the estimates on cost and delivery dates that are always wrong. Without the confidence of even getting closer to the completion of the project, upper management can either keep putting money and resources into the project, not knowing when or even if there will ever be an outcome, or can just cancel the project. It's a tough decision to make.

Most of the time the estimates are inflated because of the process and lack of knowledge as to what is happening. Here is a firsthand experience. On a large project I was playing the role of project manager. Underneath me was a technical lead who was assigned to get estimates from several different systems. At the system level the technical lead worked with the managers of the many different systems. The managers in turn asked their developers for the actual estimate. Because of my technical background, when the estimates came back I knew they were inflated. After doing some research, I discovered that each level was inflating the numbers by 25%. If the developer had originally estimated 100 hours of actual work, they would inflate it by 25% to 125 hours because of the unknowns of the work needing to be done and not knowing who would be doing it. This estimate was then given to their manager. The manager in turn also inflated it by 25%. Now the estimate was 156 hours. Then when the technical lead got the estimate from the manager they did what they had always done on all prior projects. They inflated that estimate by 25%. The original estimate of 100 hours now had become just under 200 hours because of the different levels inflating the estimate they received by 25%. A project with an estimate of 9,000 hours at a cost of around $1 million is far easier to get approval than a project estimated at 18,000 hours with a cost of $2 million.

Estimates also need to include the resource skill level that will be used to complete the project tasks. An expert in a system can easily do a task in half the time and with fewer defects as a person new to the company. So the skill level has a direct effect on the final cost. Most of the time estimates based on three skills levels should be requested. The first skill level is that the best qualified person in that group does the change. The second skill level is that an average person does the change. The last estimate is based on someone doing the work with a low skill level, such as a new employee or contractor. All three estimates based on skill levels end up in the estimate. Remember that when an estimate is asked for, normally an actual person has not yet been assigned to the task. A specific qualified person might be in mind to do the change when an estimate is asked for, but because of something with a higher priority that person might not be available for your work. A new person could be assigned instead whose performance is lower, so the estimates need to reflect the unknown staffing factor.

Most people don't understand the seriousness of having inaccurate estimates. Let's say an estimate is inflated for a project. Does anyone think that once the actual work is completed the project will be delivered early and well under the estimated budget? Those inflated hours become part of the project because of our human nature and the project linear timeline process. Most people given a 2-week time frame to complete an 8-hour task would wait until near the end of the second week to complete it. Very few people will complete the task the first day it was assigned. It's human nature to procrastinate on what needs to be done until the last second. So when these inflated estimates in labor and time get incorporated into the project plan, do not expect that they will be found. People will work slower to meet the estimates given. Just think back to how many times we have heard something such as, "I'm not going to start it yet, because I have until Friday to get it done." This is one of few flaws in what is called linear project methodology, which is based on start and stop dates for a task. With bad estimates a great deal of waste goes unnoticed.

There are a couple of ways to control bad estimates. The first is to validate the estimate a couple of times to make sure they are accurate. Go directly to the front-line person who initiated the estimate to understand how it was obtained. Was the estimate based on an expert making the changes, an average person making the changes, or someone with no experience? Ask whether inflation factors are in the estimate, and, if so, how much. All these questions need to be asked to ensure that the estimates given are accurate. Then build the project plan based on these estimates with acceptable inflation factors.

Another way to control inflated estimates and to reduce wasted time is to break apart the actual estimated hours to complete the task from the inflated hours. It is still necessary to go directly to the front-line person to get the initial estimate and inflated estimate. For each phase all the inflated hours go into a separate category by themselves. It can be broken down further, but never down to the task level. The concept is to have a place that can be used to get extra hours for when a task overruns their true estimated amount that was not inflated. This concept of breaking out inflated hours by themselves is called float.

Using the float concept a primary timeline is created based on whether everything worked perfectly and the estimates are 100% correct with no inflated factors. A secondary timeline is built with float hours. Resources work from the first timeline, which is a shorter one since inflated factors are taken out. It was previously mentioned that it is human nature to procrastinate and work backward from the due date. If a person cannot change human nature, change the process. Instead of giving someone 10 days to complete a task, give them 8 days.

The benefit of using the float concept is that the delivery time is shortened. Let's say that for a project 100 tasks each took an equal amount of time. The estimates given show that the project will take 120 days to do but each estimate was inflated by 20%. Taking the inflated hours out, the timeline would be shortened to 100 days. When the plan is executed, if half of the tasks got completed on time without using their inflated hours and the other half had to use their 20% inflated hours, then the project would end up being delivered at 110 days, 10 days earlier.

Another benefit to the process is that if a task is not completed by the initial completion date, it's a trigger to check with the developer regarding the status. Most of the time it is just taking longer than expected, but sometimes issues need to be addressed. Identifying and addressing them as soon as possible helps complete the task, which in turn keeps the project on track. Another benefit is that this concept challenges the developer more. It pushes the resources to increase their performance. Most of the resources like this process. If by chance the first date was missed, they do not feel the stress and sense of failure that comes when a task misses its deadline. With the float process developers know the first date was based on if everything was perfect and that they have a second chance to meet another date.

Another option to control bad estimates deals with the project methodology that is used. Most common project methodology deals with linear phases. In a linear project process estimates are required to set up a timeline from phase to phase and task to task. It's based around approvals for phases and start–stop dates for each task. Remember when Lean management was discussed (see Chapter 15)? For quality and performance there needs to be fewer wastes such as stop–start tasks and the many handoffs. A process that follows that concept is spiral project methodology. In spiral development there are very few start and stop dates, and it does not depend on estimates as much. Spiral development puts the majority of emphasis on the development. This will be covered in Chapter 29 when linear and spiral project methodology concepts are discussed.

Here is another example of estimating gone wrong. There was a project request to change how rating was done in California. Over a time span of 9 months, two different times our business partners had come to information technology (IT) and asked for an estimate. With a different person calculating the estimate each time, the number that came back each time was 660 hours. At that cost, they did not have enough money in its budget to do it. As a last chance it asked for it to be reviewed again. This time we broke down the actual work estimate versus the inflated estimated hours. To do that the best qualified person to do the development was identified. That person then gave an estimate based on doing the changes himself. By changing who gave the estimate and specifying specifically who would do the majority of the work, the estimate changed from 660 hours to 120 hours. This fit the budget, so the project was approved.

To validate the 120-hour estimate and to ensure nothing was missed, research was done as to why the two prior times the estimate was 660 hours. The first thing we found was that the two original developers were not the experts in the part of the system that needed to be changed. Since they were unfamiliar with that part of the system they increased the estimate slightly to adjust for that. Their initial work hours were 150 hours. Then they applied the standard inflation factor of 25% because of all the unknowns they had since they did not understand that part of the system. Since they did not know who would do the project they then doubled the estimate to 400 hours on the basis that in the worst case scenario someone new or a contractor might end up doing the work. For testing, the Test Office had a standard formula that test hours are based on 50% of development time. It did not matter what the requirements or scope document said. So another 200 hours got added for testing because development was 400 hours. This made the estimate 600 hours. Last, there are miscellaneous items such as meetings, status reporting, and e-mails related to the project. This again was a standard ratio of 10% of the total hours for development and testing, so another 60 hours were added for a total estimate of 660 hours.

By finding the experts in the systems and asking for them to define what needed to be changed and then getting a commitment from management that the experts would do the change, the estimate for actual work was 80. For testing hours, instead of using a standard formula of 50% of development. The Test Office was talked to about what the changes were and what needed to be tested. The estimate they came back with was 30 hours. Last were the miscellaneous hours for meetings and so forth. As a team we talked about what was really needed versus using a formula. As a team we agreed there was only a need for 10 hours. When the project was actually completed, it took 125 hours, which included creating the proper documentation, testing, and meeting times.

By understanding the process of estimating and staffing the project correctly, the performance increased over five times. If the project had been approved at 660 hours, in light of human nature and procrastination, most of those hours probably would have been used. Process and procedures such as doing estimates are a requirement for a business to exist, but understanding them and being able to identify and remove the wastes that exist in them is what makes a company a market leader versus staying in the middle of the pack.

29

Spiral and Linear Project Methodology

Even though I had read articles on different project methodologies early in my career, it was not until working on a project with a consulting firm that my eyes were opened to how other project methodologies worked. Up to that point I had used only the most common methodology, called waterfall or sometimes linear methodology.

The consultants presented several different project methodologies. They went through each and then did a comparison of the strengths and weaknesses of each one. Some strengths of a methodology might be structure and documentation, but their weaknesses were speed of delivery and quality of the final product. All of the different types of project methodologies could be categorized as being either a spiral or linear project methodology.

SPIRAL PROJECT METHODOLOGY

Some of the earlier names for this methodology are rapid application development (RAD), joint development, and prototyping. They all follow the same simple concept, which is basically going through a series of steps over and over again during some phases of the project. These repetitive steps are often called iterations. As each iteration is gone through, small changes are made to improve the final product.

The spiral project methodology concept of iterations can be traced back to the inventor of quality, W. Edwards Deming, and his wheel Plan-Do-Check-Act (PDCA; Figure 13.1) and continuous improvement. In 1988, Barry Boehm took the concept of spiral and modified it into Boehm's spiral software development plan for projects (Figure 29.1). It's a little more complicated but still does the same core process of iterations. Instead of PDCA, Boehm's cornerstones are as follows:

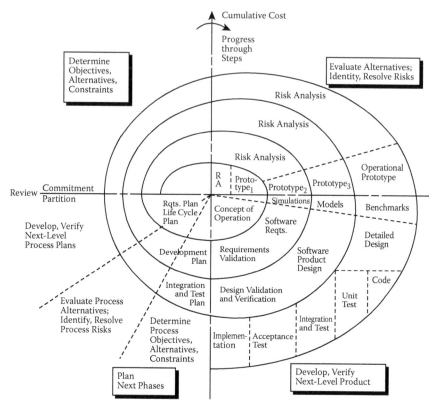

FIGURE 29.1
Boehm's spiral software development process.

- Determine objectives, alternatives, constraints
- Evaluate alternatives; identify, resolve risks
- Development, verify next-level product
- Plan next phases

In the example it spirals through each section several times. If you look in the lower right quadrant (the develop phase) of Figure 29.1, it starts out on the first iteration (near the center) with just the Concept of Operation. On the next iteration through the phase it builds on the Concept of Operation by adding the Requirement Validation and Software Requirements. On the next iteration through this phase there is Software Product Design and Design Validation and Verification. On the last iteration through that phase it covers the final coding, testing, and implementation. In the center it started out as a dream or a vision. By the time of the last iteration it had become a reality.

For projects that use a spiral methodology, the first iteration should deal with setting the objectives, or what are called cornerstones. Only three to five are necessary. For the project I was part of that merged the business side of two companies into one, the only cornerstones that upper management gave to reengineer $1B in premium were as follows:

- Take the business side of two companies and merge their processes and culture into one company structure with one culture.
- Make the new company better in terms of service than either of the old two companies.
- The business model had to be virtual. In other words, the infrastructure to do business could be placed anywhere in the world.
- The solution had to be cost-efficient.

The objectives or cornerstones should almost never change. Throughout the project life cycle the design and approval process will be based around these cornerstones. It's very easy over time for business stakeholders and the project team to wander off course of what the project is trying to accomplish. When the cornerstones are in place from the beginning, there is always a static point of reference to go back to when decisions and approval are needed. The best solutions are the ones that meet the requirements of all the cornerstones (Figure 2.2).

In a spiral methodology, since one of the phases is to build it (the "do" in PDCA), almost every time you will hear the term *prototyping* in this methodology. On the first couple of iterations prototyping will not occur. After some high-level details are defined, prototyping can begin. It allows team members, along with stakeholders, to see some visual results. It starts out as maybe some drawings that show at a high level what the final product is supposed to look like. At some point it starts to turn into a tangible reality. At first there might be no functionality, but as each iteration is completed more functionality gets added until the final product is arrived at.

If the origin of spiral development started with the Deming wheel and Boehm created the first spiral process for software development, then the next evolution of spiral development happened in 1991, when James Martin introduced a project process called rapid application development (RAD). It follows the same concept as Boehm's spiral methodology in that several iterations and prototyping are involved in the process. The primary difference between the two is that Boehm's spiral methodology is based on an iteration having a time frame of 6 months to 2 years to complete. This concept was geared for extremely large projects that deal, e.g., with development of a new airplane or creating a new drug. Martin's RAD methodology has a much shorter time frame—about 2 weeks—to go through an iteration and is geared more for the business world by using speed to market to stay competitive. RAD also introduced a new process called timeboxing. It's important to understand because it explains the outcome differences between spiral and linear when a project has things go wrong.

Timeboxing breaks down the project into small separate time periods. Each timebox has its own deadline, budget, and deliverables. The deadline will almost never change for a timebox. A timebox could consist of one or a couple of iterations. What can only change in a timebox period is the deliverables. If the timebox deadline appears it will be missed because something is taking longer to do than expected, then the least important deliverable in that timebox is removed and moved to the next timebox. Since RAD is an iteration process, in the next loop that deliverable will be accomplished.

The difference between timeboxing and descoping is descoping takes the deliverable and totally removes it from the current project plan. If the deliverable is still needed then another project plan must be created for the descoped deliverable to be developed. In RAD the deliverable is just being moved to a later timebox within the same project. In a linear project process when a deliverable is behind a couple of things almost always happen: (1) more resources are brought into the project, which translates into a cost increase; and (2) shortcuts, the most common of which is testing which affects the quality, are taken to try to meet the deadline, which affects the quality. Even with increasing resources and taking shortcuts, many times the deadline is still missed. There are four main benchmarks when managing projects: cost, deliverables, quality, and time. So out of the four benchmarks in a linear process, when the project gets behind the only one that might meet the original estimate is the deliverables that were promised. The other three—cost, quality, and time—will be missed.

It's just the opposite when using RAD and timeboxing. When a timebox period appears to be behind schedule, the least important deliverables are removed. Because the amount of work is being adjusted to meet the deadline for the timebox, there is never a need to add more resources. If the deadline and the resources are both fixed, then for that timebox period the final cost will also be fixed. Since it's possible to remove work from a timebox, there is no need to take shortcuts such as reducing the testing time to still meet the deadline. So in general it works just the opposite of linear methodology. The deliverables are reduced so that the three benchmarks of cost, quality, and time are always met.

Overall, it might be necessary to add another iteration to a later timebox or to add a new timebox. Both will increase the final cost and time. But generally the least important deliverables keep getting moved down to further timeboxes. Near the end of the project, often the business partners see no benefits of doing these less important deliverables in the last iteration. Most can be classified as "nice to have" and are not required for the project to still meet the business needs. Businesses stakeholders usually request implementing the project without them.

The next evolution step of spiral project methodology was in February 2001 with the introduction of Agile. The story goes that for 3 days at a ski resort in Utah, 17 representatives from fairly new methodologies of extreme programming, scrum, dynamic systems development management (DSDM), adaptive software development, crystal, feature-driven development (FDD) method, and pragmatic programming met to discuss software development processes. Their discussion was around processes that were the opposite of the commonly used linear methodology, which is document driven and classified as a heavyweight in terms of delivery and resources needed. From this meeting a document was created called the Agile Manifesto, later shortened to Agile.

Agile is the latest buzzword. The core principles behind this methodology are for the following to occur:

- Deliver valuable software early and continuously
- Frequently deliver working software
- Welcome and adapt to changing requirements
- Demand daily communication between business stakeholders and development
- Demand direct communication between business stakeholders and development
- Build projects around teams of motivated people
- Trust and support the teams
- Allow teams to work at a pace that can be sustained forever
- Allow teams to organize themselves
- Allow teams to reflect on their successes and failures
- Strive for simplicity in design and execution
- Strive for technical excellence in design and execution

Comparing what was happening with the traditional linear process, Agile methodology attempts to improve the project process in the following ways:

- Results of development are directly and promptly visible.
- Since the users are actively involved in the development of the system, they are more likely to embrace it and take it on.
- Basic functionality is delivered quickly, with more functionality being delivered at regular intervals.
- Eliminates bureaucracy and breaks down the communication barrier between interested parties.
- Because of constant feedback from the users, the system being developed is more likely to meet the need it was commissioned for.
- Early indicators are given of whether the project will work or not rather than a nasty surprise halfway through the development.
- System is delivered on time and on budget.
- The users have the ability to affect the project's direction.

To make these improvements, Agile uses one key principle, which is the 80–20 rule. Agile believes that 80% of the solution can be developed in 20% of the time it would take to produce the total solution. Thus, the methodologies concentrate on the 80% that is known and leave the other 20% to be addressed in later iterations. This also follows the concept that the most important items are discovered first. The other remaining 20% of the unknowns should be of medium or low importance. This is the justification Agile uses for not having all the requirements for the final solution before development begins.

Most of Agile's methodology uses the iteration concept at some part in its process. To be distinct, each uses it in different ways. Iterations, prototyping, and processes that require almost daily communication with business stakeholders throughout the project are the factors that add quality and performance. Let's take a look at a few Agile methodologies.

SCRUM

I have worked with scrum a couple of times, once on a project in a crisis mode and once on a project that, because of business necessity, needed to be done yesterday. It's a simple process but has proven to greatly increase productivity.

With understanding the 80–20 rule and that the most important things are always identified first, a backlog of unknowns and tasks can quickly be created. The team, including the business partners, sets priorities on what needs to be done first. This is done by having a daily 15-minute meeting. Yes, daily! These meetings first cover what happened since the last scrum meeting the day before. Then discussed are any barriers, questions, or unknowns that need be addressed, along with how and when these will be removed and who is the owner of getting these results. The last part of the meeting deals with what the group thinks can be accomplished before the next day's scrum meeting. The discussions go rather quickly since there are only 15 minutes and no more. If other topics need to be addressed after the 15 minutes, they need to wait until the next day's meeting. The short time frame guarantees that only the most important topics are discussed.

Scrum actually has two iterations. There is the daily iteration of the meetings, and then there is longer iteration around a unit of work. Work and tasks are grouped together to create a unit of work that will last around 30 days. These 30 day units of work are referred to as sprints. It's not a requirement, but usually at the end of that time the business stakeholder should be able to see some type of a prototype.

Near the end of the project, many small things are still left to address, and there are still a few unknowns. Instead of a meeting daily, meetings can be reduced to two to three times a week. By the late stages of the project, the core team has seen and is very familiar with the prototype (at this stage it's not really a prototype since it's almost ready for production). Instead of grouping things together for a 30-day sprint, just address them. Figure 29.2 illustrates the scrum process.

EXTREME PROGRAMMING (XP)

XP has five primary philosophies: (1) need to improve communication; (2) need to seek simplicity; (3) need to get feedback on how well you are doing; (4) need to respect everyone's point of view; and (5) need to always proceed with courage. The process itself consists of about a dozen different points or practices:

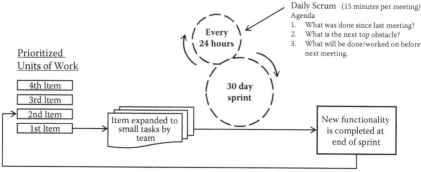

FIGURE 29.2
SCRUM project methodology process.

- **User story planning:** Development proceeds in very short iterations of 1–2 weeks typically. In the initial planning features are broken down into very small deliverables, called stories. These are captured requirements that are in the user's words. They are small, concise, and testable. Included in each story are different scenarios of what is supposed to happen, along with any business interactions that might occur outside of the system. These stories are estimated by development and then given back to the customer for approval. Either high-cost or low-business value may require changes in what is supposed to be delivered in the next iteration.
- **Small releases (building blocks):** XP emphasizes small, simple, but frequent version updates of the application. Newly developed code will instantly be incorporated into the prototype or release. Even though development iterations is around 1–2 weeks, releases do not have to follow that. Most times in a 1–2-week time period very little can be implemented. Instead, the release interval can be anytime, with a maximum of around 2–3 months between each release.
- **Metaphor (standardized naming schemes):** Developers and programmers must adhere to standards on names, class names, and methods. With the speed of development and the merging of code continuously, guidelines needs to be in place and communicated beforehand for consistency to occur.
- **Collective ownership:** In XP methodology all code is considered to be owned by the whole team and not an individual property. Hence, all code is reviewed and updated by everyone.

- **Coding standard:** Styles and formats of coding must be the same to enable compatibility among team members. This approach results in more rapid collaboration.
- **Simple design:** The simplest design that suffices for the task at hand is the right design. More complex and general design may become needed later, but not now. Do not get burdened with complexity when it is not needed.
- **Refactoring:** The application should be continually adjusted and improved by all team members. It needs to stay clean and to conform to the standards. This requires extremely good communication among members to avoid work duplication.
- **Testing:** Every small release (called building block) must pass tests before being released. XP's uniqueness in this aspect is that tests are created first and then application code is developed to meet and pass the challenges of those prewritten tests.
- **Pair programming:** XP programmers work in pairs. All code is developed by two programmers who work together at a single machine. Every couple of hours the programmers switch. The expectation is that pair programming produces higher-quality code at the same or less cost.
- **Continuous integration:** Software builds are completed several times a day. In this way all developers can avoid work fragmentations because they are continuously releasing and integrating code together.
- **Sustainable pace:** Development is based around a marathon and not a sprint. Working 60 hours a week for a month straight is not acceptable. This wears down team members both mentally and physically. Instead work is laid out to fit within the normal 40-hour work week.
- **On-site customer:** The customer must be viewed as an integral part of the project. The customer must arrange to be available at all times to ensure that the project is on the right track.

Figure 29.3 shows what XP looks like at a high level. As with all process there are strengths and weaknesses. Some of XP's weaknesses are as follows:

- When the team is large there is a difficulty in coordinating the work and making it production ready all the time.
- With little documentation and the flexibility to change the design and features at any time, if not managed right the project could become never-ending.

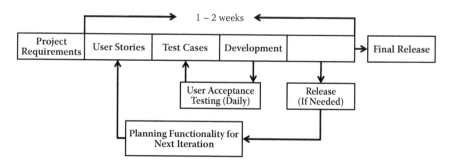

FIGURE 29.3
Extreme Programming (XP) project methodology process.

- Predicting the precise delivery of features is tough to do. There was a quick estimate done at the start of the project, but there were not too much tangible data to base that estimate on.
- Pairing programmers is controversial. A single programmer that is skilled and knowledgeable can work more efficiently than assigning someone else to work with him. Having another person look over his shoulder only slows the pace. If two programmers have low to medium skills, pairing becomes even more questionable. In the perfect world, both are supposed to work together. But in the real world that does not happen. The programmer who is not doing the coding at the time has a tendency to spend time socializing with the other half of the programmers who are also not working. This in turn leads to the paired programmer who was supposed to be working to also start to socialize. With the right people, the right work, and the right controls this could work. But in the real world, everything is not perfect, so waste ends up occurring.
- During the developing it's been mentioned that it's easy to stray from core standards. With the many releases it's very easy to start down an architecture path that is not compliant with the rest of the organization. Once these changes are in production, it's almost impossible to get them out. Hence, it leads to system instability.

I have been involved with this process only once, so I don't know if it was executed correctly or if it was used for the correct project needs. The dual programming lasted 1 month, and then the team switched back to single programming. The experienced programmers on the project had a tough time sitting behind someone while the other person coded. Also when they were coding they did not like others looking over their shoulders questioning them. It was not that they did not mind the input, but that it was continuous. They would be working through ideas in their minds about how everything was supposed to fit together as they were developing, only to have that train of thought interrupted constantly. Continuous integration was another area that caused problems. At first it was done around breaks, lunch, and before we went home each day. The problem was it took time to do each one of these. Even though there was not much conflict with the many updates, when someone coded a defect it affected everyone on the team. Since the entire team owns the code, at first we had the entire team work on the defect. Without understanding all the criteria of the change that caused the defect, normally only the pair of developers who worked on the logic originally worked on the fix. The rest would give some input, but there was a lot of waste in sitting around until it got fixed. The process was changed several weeks into the project to revert the code to the last known working version for everyone and then have the group that caused the defect to fix their logic. It stopped the waste of people sitting around while the fix was done and also allowed everyone to continue with development. But again there was waste in the time it took to revert to older versions.

DYNAMIC SYSTEMS DEVELOPMENT METHOD (DSDM)

As with all the other Agile methodologies, DSDM has very similar core concepts, including the following:

- Active user involvement
- Team empowered to make decisions
- Focus on frequent release
- Iterative development, driven by user feedback
- Changes reversible in case a certain change does not work out
- Requirements initially defined at a high level because possibility of rework is built into the process
- Goal is fitness for business purposes, which translates into business need being more important than technical perfection
- Integrated testing done all the time
- Collaboration and cooperation among all interested parties

DSDM uses the short fixed length concept of timeboxing, along with iterations. Even though all the requirements are not known in the beginning, DSDM uses a priority process for the ones that are known. This helps to identify what truly are the most important things to be worked on first. The process is simple as giving each requirement a ranking. The levels are as follows:

- M: Must have requirement
- S: Should have if at all possible
- C: Could have but not critical
- W: Won't have this time, but potentially later

These rankings come into play with timeboxing. As has been discussed before, for timeboxing the importance is around delivery time, quality, and controlling cost. The least important is the deliverable that was stated to be completed by the end of the iteration. If functionality needs to be removed from an iteration because work is behind, the ranking allows a way to identify the ones that have a lower importance.

Depending on the research and who you talked to about DSDM, there could be a different number of phases and stages. Most of them are simple, such as the pre-project phase. It deals with obtaining funding for the initial project. Another phase is called postproject phase and deals with benchmarking to make sure the changes in the system are working effectively and efficiently. This phase covers items such as support and maintenance. The following is a description of DSDM phases.

Study

In this stage there are two deliverables: a feasibility study and a business study. For the feasibility study the change or problem is defined along with the feasibility of creating a technical solution for it. It's also verified that DSDM is the best development tool to be used. The business study is also done here. The business requirements are specified at a high level. There is little research done so what is not known stays unknown at this time.

Functional Modeling

This is an iterative process that occurs many times. The main focus in this phase is on building the model through the iteration process. Before moving into development there will be several passes of building a model to match the business requirements. During each iteration, both will be tried to be improved. The model and requirements are improved through demonstration and communication with the user.

Design and Build

This phase stresses ensuring that the models are satisfactorily and properly engineered to work in the company's environment. The model is then actually built and tested. Testing is done by both technical and business partners to ensure that everyone understands and has a chance to approve the work done so far.

Many times once a component gets into the design and build stage it will be pushed back into the functional modeling for more work because of unknowns, questions, and issues, along with clarification. Because of all the unknowns in the beginning of the project, do not be concerned if both design and build stage, and the functional modeling stage are working on the same topic at the same time. If near the middle or end of the project this is still happening then there needs to be a concern. It's a good indicator that something is wrong and the project might become never-ending.

Implementation

This too can be an iterative process with several small releases when logic is developed, tested, and ready for production. If there is any new functionality being introduced, there needs to be the normal documentation for it. Agile or any another project methodology that generates quick results should have proper project documentation done before any implementation. This includes business requirements, design, architecture, and test plan documentation. It is also necessary to think of training both business users and technical users.

I have used this process only once. It was a small-sized project but was very complex. One group had tried to implement the same functionality in another system using the traditional linear methodology. The final solution was so complicated that the project group never could get out of the analysis and design phases. Instead of working only with the 80% that they knew and starting development, they tried to uncover and solve the 20% that was unknown. They just could not ever come up with the entire solution at one time in the design phase. For our group, working only with the 80% that we knew and doing modeling based on just that 80%, we were

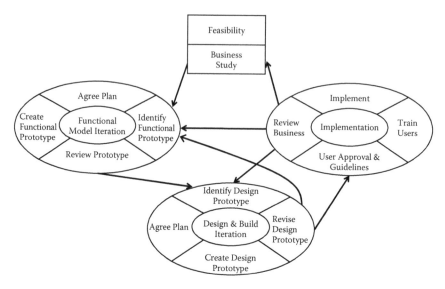

FIGURE 29.4

Dynamic Systems Development Method (DSDM) process.

able to build a prototype that business users could see the functionality of, and were able to approve because of that. At the same time modeling was being done, the requirements and design were being fine-tuned to match the needs. From that we would go back to the modeling phase and model more functionality into the solution. Over a short time we were able to come up with the complete solution for the complex functionality. Figure 29.4 demonstrates the process.

FEATURE-DRIVEN DEVELOPMENT (FDD) METHOD

I have not had any experience with FDD, another Agile methodology. FDD is supposed to be able to handle a large development effort. There are five phases to this methodology: (1) develop overall model; (2) build feature list; (3) plan by feature; (4) design for feature; and (5) build by feature.

Develop Overall Model

In the beginning, the scope of the project is defined. Both business stakeholders and technical staff work together to document the functionally for the business needs. Also created are user cases and high-level technical specifications. All this adds up to a base model or a domain of what needs to be done. After the base domain is done, then the group looks for segmentation that can occur on the base domain. Work and features on a large project can always be broken down into segmented mini projects or subdomains. As these subdomains are identified, teams can be assigned to work on them to gather detailed information on such things as requirements and deliverables. It follows the concept of breaking down a complex problem into simple items to resolve it. Each team assigned to one of these mini teams needs to produce their own documentation around the subset to which they are assigned. These end results from these smaller efforts also need to have a walkthrough with all the team members to make sure the solution fits in with all the other work that will be done.

Build Feature List

The information gathered in the first phase of modeling has now been segmented into small amounts. This information can then be used to identify a list of features that need to be done. These features include business activities along with the steps needed in each business activity. They are stated as an action, result, and object—for example, "Validate the address for a risk location for rating." Think of a feature as a business requirement. Included with each feature should be the importance of doing the feature, along with whether there are any interdependencies between other features.

Plan by Feature

The next step is to look at all the items on the feature list and group them together to produce a development plan. The first part is to look at the features that are most important and have an interdependency. After that, segmentation of work should occur based on the following criteria: balancing workload across different teams; risk factors in implementing a group of features; and complexity involved when implementing the group of features. From this a project schedule will be able to be created.

Design by Feature

For each feature there needs to be a design. At this time the lead programmer defines the fine details and estimates that are required for the feature.

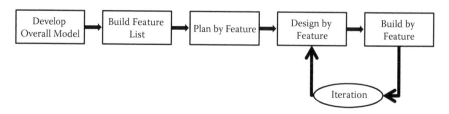

FIGURE 29.5
Feature-Driven Development (FDD) process.

Based on priority, dependency, and time frame, the programmer selects a small group of features that he or she believes can be done within 2 weeks. Naturally, this is approved by others before any development starts.

Build by Feature

At this point it's about executing the plan. Besides development, testing needs to be done. After this has all been done successfully, then it's pushed to the main build. Remember that on a large project there could be 20 other programmers, each doing their own iteration of work on different features. All must end up in one central build. With many different programmer teams working on different functionality, few will complete their work on the same day. This should not matter if the features are group independent of one another. If there no dependencies, once a team is done building their one feature they can go back to the design by feature phase to start developing a new group of features.

As you can see in Figure 29.5, the feature-driven development process is very similar to linear project methodology. The only thing that makes it Agile is the iteration that occurs in the design and build phase.

COWBOY DEVELOPMENT METHOD

We have covered some different project methods of the Agile group. Each is a structured process that always has business partners involved through all the processes. Each requires that to validate the changes documentation needs to done before development occurs. So what the business partners are requesting is defined before information technology (IT) develops it. Even though in an iterative process in the beginning there might not be much detail around *what* needs to be changed, the amount of development that occurs should match only how much of the *what* has been defined. IT cannot just go off and develop what it thinks business needs.

Cowboy development is not an official project methodology, so if you look it up as an Agile method you might not find it. Cowboy development is a term used to explain when the developers do whatever they feel is right instead of following the development process. What occurs is that IT drives the entire project and comes up with *how* things will work first and then tells business *what* they are getting, which is the opposite of how it's supposed to work. It relates to one unique entity such as IT just going off by itself and doing most of the work. You can probably look at this as a common by-product that occurs when Agile is not executed correctly.

One of the primary signs that cowboy development is occurring is to see when the business and system requirements are being made. In cowboy development analysts will be asked to create the documented requirements after the development has occurred. Instead of businesses stakeholders defining what they want, IT defines it through development and then tells the stakeholders what they will be getting.

Cowboy development usually occurs for two reasons. First, it can happen if IT does not ask their business stakeholders to participate heavily in the project. This should never happen, but many times in the real world it does. IT people believe we know what business needs better than they do. Another reason for this to occur is that many times business stakeholders have been asked but they elect not to participate. In a linear process their time requirement is only for a couple of phases to define all the business requirements. Then they are done with project until user acceptance testing occurs near the end the project. They can plan and manage their time very effectively in this process. But for spiral (Agile) project methodologies there is a requirement for business stakeholders to fully participate on a daily basis from the start of the project until the end. Because of business resource constraints or just not understanding the level of participation that is needed, business does not make the commitment to fully participate. The fast pace of Agile development requires someone within the project team to step up and make decisions around design. If the business stakeholders are not involved, that leaves only IT to do it.

Cowboy development is common when Agile is first introduced in a company. People read a couple of books or attend a seminar and hear all the benefits that Agile and iterations bring, so they implement it in their organization. Since it's not a linear process with roles and responsibility of the resources needed for each phase defined, correct staffing does not occur. Project managers are normally trained in linear process so they are unfamiliar with the spiral process. Such things as tracking financials, progress reports and resource allocations are different between spiral and linear. So project managers tend to shy away from spiral development because they don't fully understand the process. Since all methods talk about prototyping as soon as possible, IT normally takes the lead when Agile is first introduced into a company. Naturally, they run the project they way they see it, which is to develop the prototype first so that the business stakeholders can see what they are getting.

There are several negative consequences of cowboy development. The primary one is the amount of rework. At the end of each iteration there is a validation with business as to the design and project direction at the point in time. Without daily business input and participation, it's only a guess by IT as to what business wants and needs. Business stakeholders can reject all or most of the work that IT had done during that iteration. If business stakeholders has a strong stance on what they want, there will be a lot of waste in rework by IT. This increases the cost of the project and delays the delivery date of the project. If the business stakeholders has a weak stance on what they want and accepts whatever IT develops, users will end up with a solution that might not best fit their business needs nor their current processes and workflows. Again, this waste will occur with inefficient processes that end users have to work with every day.

When cowboy development does occur in the Agile process it still works most of the time. Because of the efficiency of iterations, project teams can still be successful in meeting their objectives. But to increase performance and quality and to reduce rework, cowboy development should not occur.

LEARNING ABOUT SPIRAL

I stumbled by accident on the spiral process even before it had a name. In the mid-1980s I was asked, along with another person, to develop a new front-end system that users would use to enter automobile insurance information into. We were given some high-level specifications as to what the system was supposed to look like, but the details were still being worked on. Instead of waiting for a couple of months for all the details to get defined, we started to create each empty screen with only a title at the top of each telling what the screen was reserved for. Logic was then added to navigate from screen to screen by hitting only the enter key. There was no other logic around any of it. This prototype of the system was then presented to the other team members and then to the business owners for their approval. After we got the approval, the detailed specifications were still not ready, so we started to work on the next deliverable that business wanted. We had no idea that what we were doing is now called iterations.

Within this new system there was a requirement for a feature to jump to different screens by hitting special keys on the keyboard. This ability allowed users to jump to the name and address screen, claims screen, comments screen, remarks screen, and billing screen, no matter what screen they were on. So for the next iteration, that logic was added. When that was completed, it was presented again to the team and business stakeholders for them to play with and to get their approval. The next iteration dealt with adding the feature of handling errors into every program. After completing that iteration the detail specifications were finally ready. So the last iteration was to add the functionality in each program and screen to handle the individual data fields that users would be keying.

Many benefits were realized from using this process, the first of which were speed and quality. All the programs had the same logic for the common features of screen functionality, error handling, receiving and passing data, screen jumping, and keystrokes. By having similar features in all programs, two people were able to build and test the base infrastructure that consisted of about 50 programs in about 6 months.

Since it was a new system with new concepts, in the initial design of error handling a major design flaw did not allow some functionality that business wanted. Even though there had been detailed discussions around the initial error design, only by prototyping the error handling process did the issue come to light. Since only two of us were developing at the time and since all the programs and screens consisted of base functionality only, within 3 days we were able to make major changes to the error handling logic in all 50 programs and thoroughly system test them. If the spiral project process had not been used, that design flaw would have not been found until all development was complete and system testing had started. At that point, to fix the design flaw would have been a major delay and increased the overall cost.

Initially, only two developers were needed to build the base infrastructure. After the base infrastructure was in place, several more programmers came on the project. Each was assigned to add the unique logic that was supposed to go into each program. At this point in the project each developer could work independently of one another because their coding did not depend on any other work being done. Another benefit was that new developers did not need to be trained with the complicated logic of screen jumping, passing and receiving data, general screen design, and error handling. This logic was already developed, tested, and in place. Too bad at the time nobody really understood that what we did could have been repeated. At the time the concepts of spiral development, iterations, and even project methodologies were unknown.

Much like linear methodology, spiral methodology has rules and guidelines that should be followed. The first guideline deals with who would be the best person to run a spiral project. In linear methodology it's called a team, but in reality individual tasks are first identified, and then individuals are assigned to do the tasks. Many of the individuals are brought onto the project only during a specific phase to do only a few tasks and then are moved off the project once those tasks are completed. This is not totally a dedicated team effort such as occurs in spiral.

In spiral methodology it's about a total team effort from both business and technical staff working together every day toward a common goal. Business representatives are normally assigned full time to the project so that daily they can participate in what is occurring. Many times they actually sit with the project team. Their knowledge and experience are invaluable in the first several iterations to get things going on the right track. Near the end of the project they are again invaluable in validating the design and develop functionality. They are also the best people to implement the change into the business environment.

In spiral there are few individual tasks assigned early in the project. Task assignments occur when the iteration starts and most times the team members among themselves will decide what task each person will do during the iteration. Instead of a project manager (trained in task management), a person with the skills and title of facilitator (trained in team building) should lead the team in spiral development. We talked about a facilitator when high-performance teams (HPTs) were discussed (see Chapter 11). A facilitator's first duty is to the team and not to the actual tasks. They need to be a people person and have good skills in all the disciplines of management best practices. Their duties include team building, conflict resolution, communication, negotiation, decision making, and problem solving. Here are some of the tasks that a facilitator does:

- Makes sure each iteration follows the plan-do-check-act concept.
- Makes sure project objectives or cornerstones are defined and approved in the first iteration.
- Makes sure the team defines the deadlines and deliverables for each timebox.
- If a deadline appears it might be missed, works with the team to identify and remove the least important deliverable from that timebox.
- Makes sure for the first several iterations that the team does not get bogged down in the fine details but instead stays at high levels in the beginning.
- Makes sure everyone participates, including the shy people, who need to give input, while the people with a strong personality and viewpoints don't impose their own personal solution onto the entire team.
- Functions as communication channel between the project team and the external world; unbiased, listens to what is wrong and what is right on both sides.
- Presents to and gains approval from the stakeholders in each iteration.

For spiral methodology, another new position is a scribe or historian. The same documentation that is created in a linear process needs to be created in a spiral process and before development occurs. The difference is that in a spiral project process the documentation is created right before the development is occurring. A business requirement might come up today and then be built into the prototype tomorrow. The scribe needs to capture that business requirement. When a spiral project is completed there should be a scope, solution scoping, business requirements, and technical documents, just like for a linear project. In a spiral methodology the project progresses very quickly so a separate person needs to be dedicated full time to document what is happening, and because if the team turns into an HPT, doing documentation will only slow it up if a team member needs to do it.

At the end of each iteration, the work accomplished needs to be reviewed and approved. In the later iterations there normally is a prototype to review. Even though there might be business staff on the project team, business owner and users from outside of the team need to do the review and give their approval. With the team working at a fast pace, tunnel vision can set in very easily for all the team members. The project team should be careful who gives the presentation for the review. Because of their bias of working on the project and personal pride in their work, team members might intimidate the feedback from the outside stakeholders. Let's face it: Nobody likes being told that they created something wrong. So it's important that business can give uninterrupted honest feedback. This is where the facilitator position can help in giving the presentations. This process is only for when the review of work is being done. At any time a business stakeholder can come to the project team and explain their expectation of the project. In that situation it's about getting clarification versus reviewing work that was done. It's also good in that the entire a team is getting the clarification of the same information from the same source at the same time.

Without creating and finalizing documentation early in the project process to validate the solution, spiral puts more of a responsibility back onto the business stakeholders to verify that the solution will work in their environment. The stakeholder sees it several times and has the opportunity each time to give feedback. If there is an undiscovered issue or flaw in the design, the stakeholder should find it early in the project process. When spiral is executed correctly, business stakeholders at the end of the project will never be able to make the statement: "That is not what we expected or wanted!"

The last item deals with the implementation. Most of the time it's the business's own idea or vision that is being implemented, but it's the developers ending up doing the training. Developers tend to write up the implementation documents in their words and not the user words. Sometimes the training is inaccurate because the developer does not know what currently are the processes occurring within a business department. They also rarely understand all the effects the changes will have on existing processes. Because of these factors, along with the fact that there is no reporting structure interest between a developer and business user, business users tend to complain and resist the final changes when development does the training and implementation. Sound familiar? If the business stakeholders are involved from the beginning then they can take ownership of selling the change to their own staff and doing the training. The developers are taken out of that task. In terms of quality a business stakeholder that has been heavily involved with the project since day one would be a specialist in terms of notifying and implementing the change within their area.

Spiral methodologies can be used for both large and medium-size projects. As for small projects, there really is not that much of a need for iterations or prototyping. There are just not that many unknowns when a small project starts. An example of using it for a large project was for the project that that merged the business side of two insurance companies into one. The project took 2.5 years and accomplished the following:

- Closed 5 regional offices
- Flattened the existing corporate structure by two levels by going to a team structure instead of a department structure
- Business working teams became virtual in that they could be located anywhere in the world and function correctly
- Reduced staff of around 2,300 to around 1,700 by using the team concept
- Created new job positions and titles for everyone in the business team structure; all 1,700 had to interview for a position on these teams
- Created a new web-based system to handle all daily workflow in the team environment
- Reduced processing and issuance of a new insurance application from the average time of 27 days down to 12 days

A few people drifted on and off the project, but basically only 13 people were on the core project team that accomplished these tasks. Earlier it was mentioned about business partners being part of the core team. Even though technology was a primary part of the final solution, the most important part of the project was to create quality processes, procedures, and workflow for business. To help ensure that happened, there were more business personal on the 13-member project team than IT development personal.

To the untrained, it appears that when a spiral project process is used there is no formal structure, process, or procedures. Without having all the answers before development starts, it seems like everyone is off doing whatever they want. But in reality there are processes in place to control scope, cost, time, and quality. If done correctly, the benefits from using a spiral process can be enormous versus using the linear process for the same project.

If spiral was so wonderful you are probably asking why is not everyone using it? One of the problems is that spiral is the best for some types of projects, but for other types of projects it should not be used. Later, after linear project management is discussed, the downsides and upsides of spiral will be covered and the best time to use it.

LINEAR PROJECT MANAGEMENT

This is the most common form of project methodology. It deals with taking a project and breaking it down into different phases. Depending on the actual project methodology being used it could have a dozen different phases or just four phases. We already talked about a project using the seven phases of initiation, analysis, design, development, testing, implementation, and postimplementation (see Chapter 27).

It's called linear because it gets laid out chronologically. The project starts on the left and then progresses to the right, or linearly. In each phase there are certain criteria or deliverables that need to occur because the next phase is expecting them. A phase happens only once, so there are no iterations in the linear process. Figure 29.6 shows a linear methodology that deals with only six phases. Postimplementation is part of the implementation phase for this discussion.

This is the most popular project methodology because it's easy to learn, easy to lay out the project plan, and easy to track and report the project's status. It also works for almost every type of project. Individual tasks are identified and put into the project plan. Time estimates are given for each task with start and end dates. Then resources are assigned to each task. Knowing tasks, time lengths, and resources needed, it's easy to calculate the cost of a phase. Adding up the cost in each phase will give the total cost of the project. Since there are start and stop dates on all tasks at any given time there can be a status check done on the progress of the project.

Management likes, or should I say loves, linear because they can easily see where the project is. Remember spiral? Its concept is to go through an iteration of plan-do-check-act and then do that same iteration over and over again. With starting development without having all the answers for all the unknowns, it's tough to put an exact status or overall cost on the project. Even though projects done with spiral almost always, cost less, are delivered faster and with better quality, management still prefers linear because they believe they have more control.

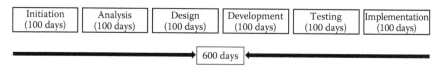

FIGURE 29.6
Timeline for true linear methodology.

Linear allows the flexibility to shorten the project phases by adding more resources. Since work is identified by tasks, the length of the project is dependent on how many tasks a person is assigned. If there are 100 tasks and each one is going to take 4 hours to do, there are 400 hours of work to be done. One worker can be assigned to do all 100 tasks. With a 40-hour work week that would mean it would take 10 weeks to complete. Or tasks can be broken down into groups of 10 with one person assigned to do each group of tasks. With a 40-hour work week this would mean that all 100 tasks, with 10 people, would be completed in 1 week. In theory the delivery of work can either be done in 10 weeks by using 1 person or in 1 week by using 10 people. When a linear project gets behind the most common process to get it back on track is to add additional resources to the project and assign tasks to them. It gets the project back on track to meet the original delivery date but increases the cost of the project. In terms of the four success benchmarks of quality, cost, delivery date, and deliverables, the project then has little chance of meeting all the criteria for success.

The purist in project management will say that one project phase cannot start until the prior one is completed (Figure 29.6). Before a phase ends all the documentation and issues for that phase must be completed and approved. In a formal project methodology there are even reviews at the end of each phase with all stakeholders before the next phase can begin. The purpose is to make sure all the documents have been created accurately that will be needed for the next project phase. These reviews are sometimes referred to as gate reviews because it controls whether the project can proceed to the next phase.

In the IT world it rarely happens that the next phase waits until the prior phase is completed. Instead the linear project process is slightly changed to what is commonly called a waterfall. In a waterfall process the phases are slightly staggered. Looking at Figure 29.7 it's easy to see why it's called a waterfall.

Instead of delaying the start of the next phase on such a small issue as the business partners deciding the color of an object, the next phase is allowed to start. This is acceptable because most always by the end of a phase only small things that have little importance or effect on the overall project are left to be defined. Normally the largest issues and questions are the first items identified and addressed. Then the next largest issues are worked on. In the end all that is left are small items. Starting the next phase before the last phase is completed follows the idea that *it is best to execute a good plan today than to have to wait weeks or months to have a perfect plan.* For this

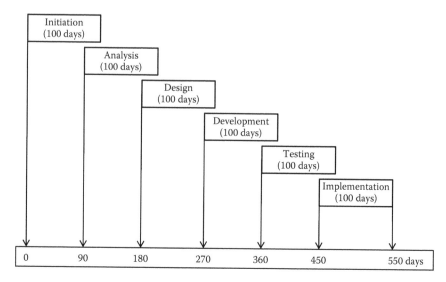

FIGURE 29.7
Linear methodology with phases staggered 10%—waterfall.

discussion let's say that each phase is supposed to take 100 days. In a true linear process the six phases will take 600 days to do. But if the waterfall is done and the phases are staggered by 10 days each, then the project is shortened by 50 days as shown in Figure 29.7.

In the real world, in a linear process there is always wrong data or bad assumptions made in the early phases. There is also the fact that requirements will need to change because business needs are always changing, or a better way of doing something is found after the project is well under way. Since there is not an iteration process to correct or change past approved documentation there needs to be a formal process to get these changes into the project plan for execution. As discussed earlier, a formal process needs to be used such as change control or request for change (RFC). Change control is a process that will get the approved changes into all the proper documents and inform everyone of what is being requested.

Changes to the linear project plan causes what is called scope creep or project creep. The word *creep* is used because every change or correction added, no matter how small, can increase the cost or lengthen the project timeline. A common mistake deals with the small changes requested. Development wants to please their business partners so normally they will just go ahead and make these small changes without going through the formal change process. One or two small changes are okay, but on large projects there can be 50 or more small changes. If each change averages adding 4 hours to the project, that equates into over 200 hours or 5 weeks of work being added to the project. If these small changes are not documented then there is no way to trace why a project got behind schedule. To control scope creep every change request, no matter the size, must be documented and approved. Nobody likes creating them because it takes additional time to create, get approval, adjust the budget if needed, add resources, or even adjust the delivery date.

The area that needs to make sure change control happens is IT. Since they control and are accountable for the last phases of a project, naturally if there are cost overruns and delivery dates are missed they get blamed for it. Project managers, business stakeholders, business analysts, solution analysts, and even architects rarely come forward and admit that maybe the cost overruns and missed delivery date were because they made more changes late in the project process than what the initial timeline and budget could handle. Only with documentation of each change can the development area validate why the original budget and delivery date changed. With linear never revisiting earlier phases again, this is the only way changes can be made to the project plan.

LINEAR WATERFALL—CRASHING THE TIMELINE

I have always told my daughters to think outside the box. You can never really tell what you can accomplish unless you try. Once in a while you will be given a deadline from upper management that you think is impossible to meet. Even without doing much research on the project you can see it's going to be a stretch goal to complete on time. We just got done talking about overlapping phases to create the waterfall affect. The question is how far can phases be overlapped? *Crashing the timeline* is a concept that answers this question.

Figure 29.7 illustrates a 10-day overlap, or 10%. As clarification, each phase that is supposed to take 100 days still takes 100 days to do the phase. But the next phase can start before the prior one is complete. Justification for doing this is based on the fact that the last 10% of each phase deals with such small issues and gaps that these things have little effect on starting the next phase.

For a small overlap of 10%, there is little risk added to the project. Very few people need to know this is occurring. But when you get into a drastic overlap, or better known as crashing the timeline, management needs to fully understand it. Upper management needs to sign off in blood that they are accepting the increased risk for the trade-off of an early delivery. We are not talking about trading quality, but only the delivery. Quality should never be negotiated or traded off.

So how far can you go with the overlap? Would you believe 80% in many of the project phases? Before your mind starts to shut down, read on.

Law of 80–20

We know 80% of what needs to be done, in the first 20% of a task.

Figure 29.8 shows what the timeline would look like if there was an 80% overlap on many of the early phases. To better understand let's look at the 80–20 rule as a bell-shaped curve in Figure 29.9.

At the very start there is nothing. But very quickly as the idea or dream evolves, the most important and largest items are the first ones that are identified and worked on. Even though small items will come up, if they cannot be resolved immediately they normally are shelved for resolution later. Building a house can be looked at as a linear process. When constructing a house the size, shape, and materials to be used are the first items that get addressed and finalized. Then later such things as electrical,

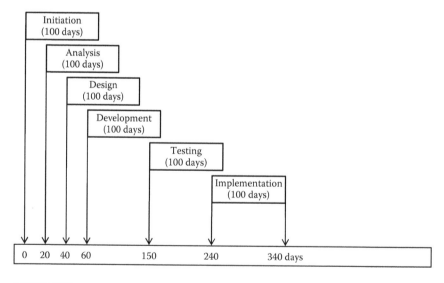

FIGURE 29.8
Linear methodology—crashing the timeline process.

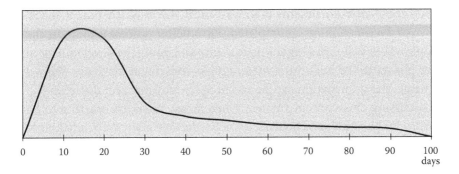

FIGURE 29.9
Percentage of knowledge acquired based on the 80–20 rule over 100 days.

heating, and plumbing get addressed. A person can start to build the house without knowing where every outlet is supposed to be. Just a general idea of where these things plan on being is good enough to start building the house. Projects are like that also in that the most important things are addressed first. A project team is not going to spend hours on discussing the color, size, or wording for a specific field, when there are more complex issues such as a new workflow that still need to be resolved. It's an automatic process in that the most important work is addressed first.

Let's go back to the diagram that shows the 80% overlap between phases (Figure 29.8). When looking at the diagram instead of thinking time and days, think of information content defined. When the analysis phase begins 80% of the initiation phase content is defined. When the design phase begins probably about 92% of the initiation phase information content is defined and 80% of the analysis phase content is defined. And when development begins, then the information content is probably 97% for initiation, 92% for analysis, and 80% for design. With this amount of content defined in each phase the risk is low if development is started on core things that are known.

When crashing the timeline, the pace of the project is so fast that the first thing that needs to be done in the initiation phase is to start to fill all the project core positions with resources, including technical and testing. For this to work a true team concept needs to be built fairly quickly. Instead of only a few working on the scope document, most everyone needs to be involved with the creation of it. What is being defined in scope gets broken down into business requirements, which in turns gets broken down into solution scoping, which in turn gets broken down into design, architecture, and technical documents. The normal process to create these later documents is to wait until the prior document in the chain of documentation is completed. But a better process is to invite the people who will be creating the documents and doing the development in later phases to the beginning meetings. As individual items are defined in scope, the information can be added to the downstream documents.

Discussing this concept further, when scope items are starting to be defined by business stakeholders, a knowledgeable analyst already knows what many of the business requirements are supposed to be with each scope item. As soon as business stakeholders are requesting new functionality or feature, IT staff are working on what needs to be done to accomplish it. Why not start to capture this information as soon as possible? So if the technical leads and architects are part of the scope and business requirements they can start to define the design documentation for the changes. We are not saying they will complete all the documentation, just that they can start it.

When using the crashing the timeline concept it becomes critical that each area is represented by a knowledgeable subject matter expert (SME). An SME understands company history and also most of the causes and effects the suggested changes are going to make. There is a very little learning curve in the beginning of a phase for a SME (see Figure 29.10). Whether it's creating business requirements from scope or technical documents from the business requirements, after the first meeting an SME can probably accurately define 80% of what needs to done. This should not be a surprise to anyone. If you assign your best, you can expect the best.

In the initiation, analysis, and design phases the most important work is always done first and follows the bell-shaped curve. I wish that could be said of development. Developers would prefer to start on the small items first and leave the most complex ones for at the end of development. To control this from happening, a priority task list needs to be created. The most complex, difficult, and critical components need to be assigned a high priority so that they get worked on first.

Testing is the second to last phase. The testing phase can be staggered but by not as much to ensure quality. In Figure 29.8 it is staggered 10%. Quality is not compromised with a 10% overlap because the first part of testing deals with setup and nothing to do with testing the changes. There is prep work in getting the test environment ready, loading data that can be used for testing, and creating the detail test plan. In defining what needs to be tested and how, test cases need to be defined with the expected results. Once development is completed then the execution of the test plan can be done. As mentioned before, the quality of testing should never be compromised.

Even the implementation process can be staggered. New functionality most times can be designed so that it's executed only when a specific situation (trigger) happens. As long as the trigger is not turned on, the new feature or function will not execute. With a trigger design, once changes are completed early and ready to be implemented they can be put through regression testing, which validates that the changes going in early have no effect in production. In technology it's very easy to check the outputs, character by character, to make sure nothing changes. The first step in regression testing is to run a large amount of data through the production programs. Then that same data is run through the changed programs with the trigger turned off. If the output files match exactly, it verifies that the changes with the trigger turned off are having no effects.

You might ask would it be better to implement everything at once? This depends on the number of changes and systems effects. For some of the large projects there could be over 500 different modules in over 100 different systems. It's impossible to coordinate everything for a one-time implementation. Plus, the programs being changed for a project are also being changed for other purposes such as routine maintenance and even other projects. All these programs have different timelines of implementation. The sooner a module or component can be put back into production, the less confusion and retrofitting of other people's changes will need to occur. There is nothing worse than checking out a component in March, making changes to it, and then when it's ready to go production in August discovering a dozen other changes that need to be manually updated because the version is outdated by 7 months. By implementing some components early it helps reduce the risk, stress, and complexity when the change is actually turned on for execution.

The trigger design and early implementation of code is also very valuable for large projects if things go wrong once the new functionality is turned on in production. The trigger allows a quick solution to turn off the new functionality until it can be discovered what is not working. Most times it's one or two pieces of logic that need to be changed for the functionality to work as planned. Without a trigger design, in order to turn off the new functionality most all logic needs to reverted back to its original state before the change. Not only is this time consuming but it can open up more errors occurring because it's not done in the correct order or things are being missed.

Once all the components are in production with the trigger turned off, it's easy to do all the final testing by simple turning on the trigger in the test environment. The negative effect is that the changes have not thoroughly been tested with the trigger turned on. So there might be some defects found in the final testing. Programs will need to be checked out of production, fixed, retested, and then put back into production.

Crashing the timeline with an 80% overlap is risky. I would not recommend it unless absolutely required. Having personally experienced it a couple of times on large projects, there were a lot of long weeks in terms of 60 to 70 hours, and the stress was at the maximum. A more realistic overlap ratio to use is 50%. At 50% overlap the project is only in two phases concurrently. Looking at the bell-shaped curve, it could be estimated that 95% is known by 50% of the way through a phase. This only leaves about 5% not analyzed (or designed) before the next phase begins. Considering there are always wrong assumptions and change requests, there is little risk added to a project if 5% is not defined before the next phase is started. The benefit of doing a 50% overlap is a much shorter timeline. Figure 29.11 shows what the linear waterfall timeline would look like at a 50% overlap. Once again quality is never compromised so the testing phase is only staggered by 10%. The implementation phase is also only staggered by 10% because the majority of changes most times can only be implemented at the end of the project.

Believe it or not, a linear run project with a 50% overlap tends to have less rework and better quality. The issue is that even though the requirements from the analysis phase could be perfect as to what business stakeholders wants, it might not fit into the design. Because of system limitations and technology barriers that exist in the company it might not be feasible to do

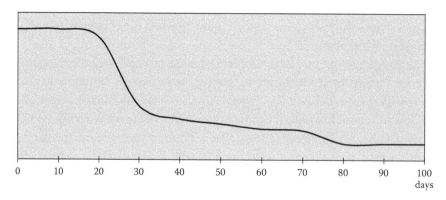

FIGURE 29.10
Percentage of knowledge acquired based on using an SME over 100 days.

what as defined. The only way to validate that it is doable is to start the next phase early and gather most of the content for the next phase. With a 50% overlap, this translates into 95% of the content for the next phase is gathered before the requirements are finally approved from the prior phase. In terms of quality, risk has been reduced for miscommunication and wrong assumptions made early. Looking at the project with 716 defects, if the phases for that project would have been staggered it would have brought to light that much of the documentation created in the analysis phase was wrong and missing critical information.

Almost always, upper management and business stakeholders want to see a linear project plan with no overlap. I'm more than willing to give that to them. But how the project is executed is with an overlap. There are two project timelines created. One timeline has phases overlapped by 50%, and that is how the project executes from. The other timeline is what management wants and sees and from what status reports are based, which is with no overlap between phases. You can say the two different project timelines define the best-case scenario and the worst-case scenario. By executing the plan with using overlapping it allows large projects to be delivered consistently early, with good quality and under budget when results are plugged into the project plan with no overlap, which is what upper management sees. Comparing the 50% overlap project in Figure 29.11 that takes 430 days to the no-overlap project in Figure 29.6 that takes 600 days,

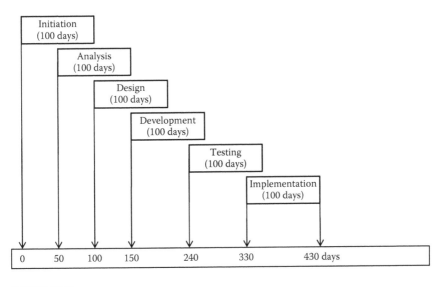

FIGURE 29.11
Linear methodology with beginning phases staggered 50%.

the difference is 170 days. In terms of improvement, it's a 28% increase by just changing the process.

The flaw that most people have when using linear is that they don't understand what the timeline represents. At the surface it appears only to be stop and start dates, but it's much more. If you look at the amount of information gathered across a time span, there is a bell-shaped curve with 80% of the knowledge needing to do the project acquired in the first 20% of the time frame for the phase. Waiting to start the next phase when the only things left in the phase are small and unimportant items is a waste of time.

If we step back, this is one of the same concepts that spiral project processes used to increase their performance. For each iteration only enough information is gathered to complete the deliverables for that specific iteration. It's not necessary to have all the project information defined before starting the next iteration. Whether linear with overlapping phases is done or spiral, both methods are covered by the statement: "It's best to start execution on a good plan today than to have to wait weeks or months to have a perfect plan."

LINEAR VERSUS SPIRAL

Linear is the most common methodology because it does work for most every type of project and is easy to execute. But it does have weaknesses when it comes to certain types of projects. Depending on the type of project, spiral will produce much better results in terms of delivery time and quality. The downfall of spiral is that it cannot be used for all types of projects. As stated earlier, spiral offers little or no benefits to a small project with few unknowns. There is not a need for iterations or prototyping.

Restating the pros and cons from before, along with adding a few additional ones, the following sections outline some of the strengths and weaknesses of both linear and spiral project processes.

Spiral Strengths

- Cost is reduced because time is spent on prototyping the product as it's being built. Does not require having all the answers and everything documented before developing can start.

- Development can be classified as a joint or collaboration venture with business. There is an active communication between development and business at all times. There are less chances of misunderstandings or miscommunication.
- Sometimes visions and dreams don't necessarily translate very well in documentation. It might seem like a great idea when talking about it and when it's documented, but when a person sees it in reality it might not be the best option, or maybe not work at all. As prototyping is being done, business stakeholders visually gets to the see it as the change is being developed.
- Once business stakeholders get their hands on what's being developed, they start to think how to make it even better. So as each iteration is being done they see how to improve on their dream. Since nothing is truly defined as to what the final product is supposed to look like, there are no problems or issues with making the improvement changes.
- Scope creep does not happen in a spiral methodology, mostly because there are no true delivery dates or detailed functionality that will be delivered. If something new comes up or a wrong assumption is made in an earlier iteration, in the next iteration the new direction can be incorporated into it. The only expectation is that for each iteration the product will be improved.
- Because of everyone's involvement at all times, a team environment is built. There is buy in from everyone.
- There is little waste in the process to create documentation. Because of the iterations and zeroing into the final solution, only enough documentation is created to get through the iteration. Even if something is missed, in the next iteration it can be documented.

Spiral Weaknesses

- Spiral only fits specific types of projects. If there are few unknowns or prototyping is not possible, then spiral offers no advantage and should not be used.
- For spiral there really are no firm deadlines. With drilling down to get the best solution nobody knows when that will happen. Even though timeboxing uses firm deadlines, there might be an early assumption that only four iterations are needed. But as the final solution is being

arrived at in the fourth iteration, it's realized that if specific changes were done business performance would be increased more. So a fifth iteration is added.

- Upper management dislikes this process because cost, functionality, and delivery are floating. Remember management deals with control through statuses and reports. They like to report during a project that it's 50% completed, and 10% under budget. For spiral it can only be reported that the project is going forward and the status of the prototyping. The final completion date and total cost can be defined with a high level of accuracy when the prototype is almost ready for production.
- With no formal plan there is a risk that nothing comes out of it. Without the proper project control installed and leadership, the team could just endlessly go into a loop with no progress.
- On a medium to large project there needs to be a specialist called a facilitator on the team. The purpose of the facilitator is to keep things going and make sure people don't jump to the quick solution. Facilitators act as a coach and referee to the team. They prevent a project from stalling or going nowhere.
- Spiral works based on the true team concept. If most of the stakeholders cannot work together as a team then spiral cannot be used. Everyone needs to work together and respects everyone else's views to end up with best possible solution.
- Teams should consist of less than 20 people. This includes both business and development. The purpose is to build a team and not a mob.

Linear Strengths

- There is structure and control. A timeline can be put on the beginning and ending date of each task and project phase. Based on that it can be reported whether or not the project is on time.
- Linear works for almost every type of project.
- Since it's a linear process that is task oriented, additional resources can be added to do specific tasks to shorten phases such as development and testing. It's not a requirement that new resources understand past discussions or decisions made. They only need to know enough information to accomplish the specific tasks assigned to them.
- With the project software programs on the market, it's really easy for project managers to create a detailed plan to follow. With all task

identified, start/stop dates, hours per task, and the reporting of percentage completed per task, in seconds reports can be created covering things from delivery dates to a countless number of reports covering the financial status of the project/phase/task.

Linear Weaknesses

- If the research in the beginning of the project is not complete or there were wrong assumptions, work in later phases will be completed based on this bad data. The success of later phases, which deals with execution and development, is critically dependent on the accuracy and thoroughness of what occurs in the first phases.
- If there is something misunderstood or missing, most times it's not found until development is well under way. There can be several reviews or checks in the project process, but until the change is being system tested it's an unknown if it will work as planned.
- If there is rework that needs to be done because of bad research or wrong assumptions, then the rework must be documented in a formal "change process." The earlier documents created needs to be updated with the changes and an approval process needs to be gone through. Communication of the changes need to be done to all team members and stakeholders of the project. Scope creep that deals with the additional work from the above affects the final cost and delivery date. All could be classified as waste in Lean management.
- It's a slow controlled process. A developer might have a good idea of what needs to be developed early in the project process. But since the project is only in the analysis phase the development phase cannot begin. There are meetings, documentation, and approvals that must be accomplished in the analysis and design phases before any development can start to occur.
- There are no incentives to complete a task early. The next task a person is assigned probably cannot be started until a specific date because of how the project plan is laid out.
- If a task's estimate is over inflated, people most likely will complete the task at the inflated hours. They will procrastinate and work at slower speeds and still be able to complete the task on time. The process, instead of pushing for high performance and early delivery, only pushes for being mediocre and meeting a date. There are a lot of wasted hours.

- Most large projects start out as a dream or vision in the business mind. In a linear process business stakeholders do not get to see anything tangible until development is almost done. What was dreamed of and how it actually fits into the business environment does not always mesh 100%. There is no chance to modify the design to make it a better fit without additional phases and cost.
- People are assigned specific roles of project manager, technical leads, architect, and solution designers. When a person is done with their assigned tasks they might have to wait and depend for others to complete their assignments before the task can be completed. Work assignments are segmented per skills, so there are naturally more resources involved.
- Even though a team is formed, because of the individual assignments in the project plan they do not work together as a team. Each person will only do the tasks he or she is assigned. Even if people want to reach out and help someone else, they could get into trouble because it was not in the project plan.
- In a linear process a great amount of documentation is created because it's unknown what will be needed in the later phases. So the business requirements, functional and non-function requirements, solution scoping, design, architecture and technical specifications are very large with content. But most of the information will never be used by development to build the functionality. Statistics from the Standish Group several years back showed that with a formal linear project methodology, about 45% of documentation created is never used, 19% is rarely used. 16% is used sometimes, 13% is used often, and 7% is used always. So about 64% of what is created is rarely or never used (Figure 29.12). Once again these numbers come from thousands of different project sizes and types. In your environment it might be better; then again it might be worse.
- Linear is generally much more costly because of the many different wastes that occur. There is the waste from unnecessary documentation being created. For linear, all large and small tasks need to be identified first and then laid out in a chorological order before development can occur. A large amount of time and resources are used to do this. Even with all that effort, on large projects that are always new tasks that need to be done while in the development stage. At that point there is waste in the re-work of the priorities of the tasks and re-scheduling of resources on assigned tasks. There is also waste

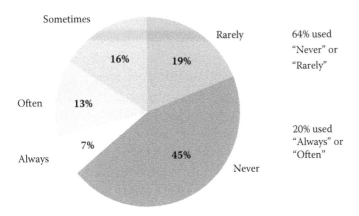

FIGURE 29.12
Documentation usage in a linear process.

in that more defects and rework occurs in the linear process than a spiral one. In linear, testing can only occur after everything is done. The defects can be large and can be caused by bad communication or bad development of large pieces of logic. For spiral, testing is done in small increments as the prototype is being built. Large defects or a large amount of rework rarely will occur because of this validation as the prototype is being built.

WORKING ENVIRONMENT

The concepts of linear and spiral has been covered and the last missing piece is the environment that the project team members should work in. For a linear process it's about first defining a task and then assigning someone to do the task. Also with a linear process there are people coming on and off the project depending on the phase. It's tough to take the team and isolate them because many of the core team members will have other duties and responsibilities outside of the linear project. There are a couple of things that can be done in order improve performance and quality.

Most linear processes talk of having a kick-off meeting when the project starts. The purpose is to communicate with all people believed to be affected by the project. It's a good idea but does not necessarily require everyone to be in one spot during the meeting. Since it's only to introduce the project to everyone and there is little detail around the project yet, a teleconference or video conference will be sufficient. The meeting at the maximum will last 2 hours.

A more important meeting is one that should occur after the business requirements are completed and midway through the design phase. If the project is large and complex, then all stakeholders involved and affected by the project should be invited to the meeting. Even though it adds cost, everyone needs to attend face to face in one spot. Attendees are dedicated to the meeting that at the maximum will last for 2 days. The purpose is a checkpoint to make sure everyone is on the right path. At this point there are still many unknowns open and many more that still have not even been found. The goal of the meeting is to identify and address as many of them as possible. Sometimes I have attended these meetings that have had up to up to 50 people in them. The consequences of not doing it are endless numbers of small meetings with only getting the information to a small group of people each time. It ends up being more costly in terms of time and consistency. For linear once in development there is little that can be done that will have a large performance increase. From that point on it's about execution of the plan and tasks. The development can occur all at one specific location or, since it's individual tasks, the work can be scattered to many different locations, including overseas.

For a spiral process it's a true team effort. People are dedicated full time during the duration of the entire project. The team works together on everything. The best environment for spiral development is an isolated one for the team members. This includes both business and IT staff. Sometimes these are called labs or development centers.

A lab is a reserved area segmented away from the daily work world. Most times the layout of the lab is an open area with no cubicles in it. In the center of the lab many times is a large table that all lab members can meet at quickly. Also in the lab are flip charts, whiteboards, and a projector that can be used to quickly display information. Away from the lab is one to two meeting rooms that private meetings and conversations can occur at. Not all meetings need to involve everyone, nor do people need to eavesdrop.

I have personally experienced working in a lab a couple of times and it's different. Both times changes were made to the initial design to make the lab environment more friendly and productive. First change dealt with the openness. The labs are just a rectangle box with no walls to make individual spaces. So something as simple as hanging a coat cannot be done, nor is there any room to place personal pictures or things. Imagine working in a high-performance area with lots of stress and not being able to have any personal things around you to remind you why you are there. There is almost no privacy. There will be people in the lab that are going to receive personal phones calls that others should not hear. With no walls to make an individual space or barrier, all personal phone conversation within the lab became a topic of conversation. One change we made was the size of the outside walls. The short walls or no walls were what management wanted for visibility. It served the project team no benefit and actually took away from their productivity. People would freely wander over or through the area just being curious. It also allowed members to easily wander off. A modification was to make the external walls taller and only have one entrance into the lab. Another modification was to put up small cubicle walls between individual work places. With small walls on both sides there was twice as much room for each lab member. It also gave a sense of being an individual.

This brings up another modification, or more of how to think about how the labs work. Even though spiral (Agile) concepts talk of the team concept, when it gets down to the execution a task it is mostly done on an individual basis—especially from the middle of the project until the end of the project where it's no longer around discussions on *what* needs to be done, but instead it's about executing *how* things will be changed. Only one person can code a piece of logic at one time, just as only one person at a time can update documentation. The way labs need to be designed is to have a defined external barrier to isolate the project team. Inside the lab there needs to be openness so that at any time within seconds a meeting with all team members can occur. Last, the individual work place must be designed to allow individual work. This does not mean to create cubicles as we are accustomed to but instead a smaller version with smaller side walls to define a personal work place.

Sometimes people misunderstand what a team concept is. In sports it's a group of unique individuals that each has strengths and weakness that work together as a team. Each has individual assignments to complete and different roles to play on the team. The better that each does on their individual assignments on the team, the better the overall team performance will be during the game. Project teams are much like sports team. It's the unique performance of each individual in the project team that makes the team performance increases. Having each team member do the exact task as everyone does nothing to increase performance, nor improve quality.

Having project team members work in an environment that does not allow individuality takes away the purpose of team. It's not about creating clones, but instead it's about leveraging the strengths of each individual on the team to increase performance and quality.

In the very beginning of the book there was a statement made about reducing expenses by 15% and also decreasing delivery time of all projects by 25% across the enterprise. Obtaining those results are accomplished by selecting the best tools for the right needs. Most tools will still accomplish the task, but a combination of the best tools will accomplish the task faster and with better quality. One tool is the selection of the right team based on behavior characteristics. Another tool is to apply the concepts of HPTs to improve the team's performance even further. Having the right leadership for the task can be thought of as another tool. And yet another tool is to use the best process, linear or spiral, to complete the task. When the best tools end up being selected and executed for a type of task, then the impossible can be accomplished as Jack Welch mentioned in one of his points. When that happens, performance and quality increases can then be measured in factors and not fractions.

30

Project Management Improvement

What should have been learned by now is that most everything can be improved upon with knowledge and processes—even existing project management methods. Let's assume that project process can be modified to improve the results. Going back to the 80–20 rule, 80% of the project methodology is rock solid and can be used for all types of projects and all type of business. It's the other 20% of it, that can probably be changed to better fit the type of business and project it's being used for to ensure success.

I have been with two large companies as they implemented project methodology for the first time. Both companies made no modifications to the project methodology when they implemented it. What was taught or read in a book became the only project process that was used in the company. All projects had to adhere to the new processes. Naturally, some projects ended up with a challenged or failure final status only because they did not fit well into the process. Instead of researching why things were not working, they just kept making the same mistakes over and over again. Both companies initially made no attempt to modify the process. They never realized they could get better results out of the project process if they would modify it to the type of project being done. Over time though they made changes to the project process for the type of project being done.

Another company I was with had a formal project methodology in place for some time. They had the same project team structure and titles that exist today. There were project managers, business analysts, architects, tech leads, and testers. The skill level for project managers had evolved to three different levels. Each project manager level had strict guidelines as to what project types they could do. To try and improve the possibility of success even more, the top projects of the company were also assigned an outside consultant that specialized in project management.

Even with all this in place, the company still consistently had issues with delivering large complex projects. Descoping was a common tool used to meet deadlines, which in turn tied resources up longer than originally expected, which in turn meant there was never enough staff. Long-term information technology (IT) resource planning was impossible. A small team was put together to research why a company with all the latest project methodology in place still could not deliver large projects consistently.

The research revealed that project management knowledge is very important to every project. A project manager is required to have excellent knowledge in the areas of scope, time, cost, communication, integration, human resource allotment, quality, and risk. These are all tangible items that can be shown with spreadsheets, reports, or graphs. But for a large complex project to succeed based on the success criteria of cost, performance, delivery time, and quality, it also needed someone with excellent skills in the six management best practice knowledge disciplines discussed at the beginning of the book (see Chapter 2). As a refresher these are the intangible disciplines of leadership, negotiation, problem solving, decision making, the ability to influence the organization, and communication,

KNOWLEDGE AREAS OF A PROJECT

In Chapter 27 we covered the different project phases of initiation, analysis, design, development, implementation, and postimplementation that make up a project. The next layer of knowledge to understand is finding the best person to lead or manage the different parts of the project. It's surprising that many times the reason a project is not successful is because key leaders on the project are not doing their duties and responsibilities. It's not that they do it on purpose but that they just don't know how to work together. Earlier we suggested who would be best, but there was no justification around it. To get justification we need to understand the different knowledge areas that every project has.

A project can be defined as having three distinct knowledge areas. One knowledge area consists of managing the project process itself and is called the *form* part of the project. Another knowledge area consists of managing people and the work they do and is called the *art* part of the project. The last knowledge area is referred to as the *substance* and is where all the work is being done. This last knowledge area is managed by the first two knowledge areas (Figure 30.1).

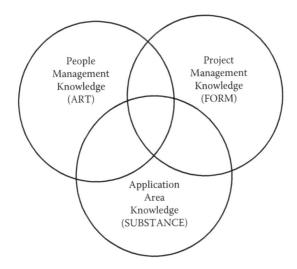

FIGURE 30.1
Project knowledge areas.

Managing the form knowledge area deals with such things as monitoring scope, business requirements, time estimate, communication on the project status, cost control, project phase control, human resource acquisitions, and risk identification. It's called *form* because it relates to tangible items that can be produced. In the project phases most of these items are in the early project phases of initiation, analysis, and design. Looking at the form knowledge area requires someone who is trained in the science of projects and managing the overall project structure. They need to know how to gather a team, prepare a budget, and make sure the necessary deliverables in each phase are done. It's not so much that the person needs to understand what exactly is changing and how it will be changed but instead how to manage that the correct project steps are being followed. A project manager fills all these requirements.

Managing the art knowledge area deals with the six management best practice disciplines. It involves understanding the resource capabilities along with understanding somewhat of the environment that is changing. It's called the *art* because there is nothing tangible with this knowledge area. It's about making sure everyone has the right tools, instructions, and guidance to work effectively and efficiently. The art is important in the later project phases of design, development, and implementation, which is where the execution of the project plan occurs. The best person to manage this knowledge area is someone with people management skills. They also need to have company knowledge and system knowledge, and it would

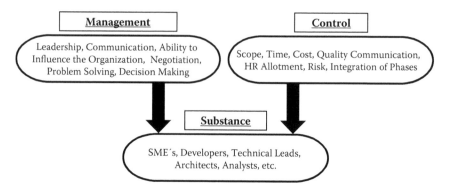

FIGURE 30.2
Project knowledge areas attributes.

greatly help to have a network of people throughout the enterprise. A technical manager fills all these requirements.

The last knowledge area of a project is called the *substance*. This is the part of the project where the actual work is done. To do this part there needs to be subject matter knowledge and experience. The business partners, system analysts, developers, and architects fall into this category. This knowledge area does not have to manage anything related to the overall running of the project. Their knowledge is used to build the project plan. Then their skills are used to develop the changes requested.

Figure 30.2 shows visually what the knowledge areas of a project looks like. Stop and spend some time thinking about this diagram and the material covered on projects, management best practices, and quality. If you have any experience with medium-sized to large projects, things should be starting to come together.

With the project manager responsible for the *form* and the technical manager responsible for the *art*, there are specific duties and responsibilities that each must perform for performance and quality to increase. This can best be explained by applying this concept to a football game, something most people can relate to.

To start with, let's say the form part is controlled by the football officials. It's their responsibility to make sure the defined rules of the game are followed. They report on such tangible things as time, score, and when infractions occur during the game. They know what the overall structure of a football game is supposed to be, and they have controls to make sure it happens. They have no control over what plays get run and which players get to play or what defenses to run. These items are controlled by the coaches. Much like the football officials, the project manager understands all the deliverables that are required for a project to be successful.

We can say the coaches do the art of a football game. They make decisions as to what offense and defense will be run. If there is a problem with the other team scoring too many touchdowns, it's up to the coaches to make changes to fix the problems. The coach's responsibility is to understand each player's capability (resource) along with the fine details (system knowledge) that make each football game unique. Technical managers are much like football coaches in that they are the only ones who can truly understand how to get peak performance out of the resources. They are also the only ones who can identify early when things are starting to go wrong and make changes.

Football players are the substance. They don't need to be an expert on all the rules. They only need to know enough to do their job successfully. Much like on a football team where there are unique skills such as running backs, quarterbacks, linemen and wide receivers, for a project their equivalent would be analysts, developers, architects, testers, and business stakeholders.

You might be thinking that football games are nothing like a project. A football game is about competing against another team and scoring more points than the other to win. But for a project, don't we do the same thing? Deadlines, deliverables, cost estimates, and quality thresholds are set. We compete to meet these thresholds or to be under them. If we do, then the project is classified as a winning project.

Running through the project and management knowledge areas for a project called "An NFL Football Game," this is how it can be explained even better.

Scope and Integration

These are very similar in that they deal with the structure and rules of the game. Most of this is already in place because the football rule book is already created. But in some stadiums the rules are changed specifically to fit unique possibilities. One example is that in a dome stadium there are rules around what occurs when the football hits the roof or maybe a scoreboard hanging over the field. Many things also can be done (in scope), and a lot of things cannot be done (out of scope). If the out-of-scope things occur, normally there is a penalty. The rules and structure also lay out the duration of the game, number of timeouts, minutes per quarter, and when the game clock starts and stops. The football officials (referees) are responsible for controlling these things.

Normally a project methodology is already in place in the company, but how it gets executed can be different from project to project. Because of project size and project needs, different processes can be used. There can be some unique changes such as merging some phases to ensure the project is completed on time. Or special equipment needs to be purchased so procurement needs to occur. Once in a while an area will go off and start to work on something that has been defined as out of scope. It's the project manager's responsibility to make sure the project team follows the rules and guidelines of the project methodology. If someone is not following the guidelines of the project methodology or the rules for a specific project, it's up to the project manager to enforce them.

Time

Football officials control when different phases of the game start and end. The game does not start until officials blow their whistle. At the end of each play they blow their whistle to signal play has ended. They do not let the next play start until everything is in place and ready to go. Many times they stand over the ball to stop play until everything is ready. Football officials also control when the game clock starts and stops by blowing their whistles and signaling with their arms. By doing that they control when the quarters end, along with the game.

In a project the project manager controls when the project starts by building a project team and having initial project kickoff meetings. They control when different project phases are supposed to start and end. If something is not right or ready, they will stop the project until things are. This could be because documentation is missing or incomplete, funding is not ready, or resources are not available. A project manager is responsible for laying out all the phases chronologically.

Communication

This is in both project management and technical management, but the two are different types of communication. The football officials are responsible for communicating the score of the game, time of the game, and which quarter (phases) it's in. If someone is not following the rules, officials notify everyone by throwing a penalty flag and telling what was done wrong. They are responsible not for fixing the problem but only for reporting it.

In a formal project methodology the project manager is responsible for making sure everyone involved and affected by the project receives communication on what is occurring. Normally one of the pieces of documentation that the project manager creates to control this is a communication plan. It defines all the stakeholders that need to be informed. It also defines what each person needs to be informed of and the frequency of the communication. A chief executive officer (CEO) might want to know only of the overall status in terms of meeting the budget and delivery date, whereas a front-line business manager will want more detailed information on the exact changes occurring, the phase the project is in, and the training that will occur. The project manager defines and controls all of this in the communication plan.

Human Resource Allotment

Once again, this ties back to the rulebook for which officials are responsible. It's stated how many players can be on the field and what positions they will be in. There are rules dealing with how many players can be in the backfield and rules with how many offense players can go downfield on a pass play. It's the football official's duty to make sure the correct number of players are on the football field and in the correct positions.

For a project the project manager makes sure correct resources are on the project. The project might require one architect, two technical leads, and six developers, with three developers needing to understand internet web development. The project manager is responsible for acquiring these resources for the project. If the estimates are 400 hours and the business needs the new functionality in 1 week, then 10 resources need to be assigned. If business does not need the functionality until 10 weeks or more into the future, then only one resource is needed. Depending on the business delivery date and the estimates of the work needing to be done, the project manager decides how many resources are needed.

Quality

The quality of the game would be bad if the football officials are slow in starting the clock or placing the ball wrong after each play or don't call penalties when infractions occur. If coaches were responsible for this, they would cheat as much as possible to win the game. Quality would not exist.

On a project if the project manager does not do a good job on the creation or monitoring of the tangible items of scope, cost, time, and communication, it leads to poor quality. When there is poor quality in the project plan then there are misunderstandings, confusion, and lack of direction from the project team. All this greatly increases the possibility that the project will fail at some level.

Risk

Once again the football official controls risk by making sure players are wearing the proper equipment and that the field of play is safe. Certain type of tackles and blocks are forbidden because of the risk of injury to the players. When things are out of place or infractions occur, the officials take actions to eliminate or reduce the risk. The most common way they do this is by throwing a flag and penalizing the person or team that is increasing the risk. If the actions are causing a really high risk, officials will go so far as to eject players and coaches from the game.

On a project some of the risks that arises could be lack of qualified staff, task not completed on time, or lack of funding. The project manager controls the risk by first documenting and raising a concern about it. If the risk can be reduced, someone will be assigned to work on doing that. To reduce a risk of lack of qualified staff, the project manager might replace the team member or ask for additional resources to meet the deadline. Another way to reduce risk is to move the completion date further into the future to get more time to get things done. Only the project manager has the final control over risk and the final say in how to reduce it.

The purpose of this analogy is to present an alternative way to understand the roles and duties of a project manager. Most people have problems understanding what is and is not a project manager's responsibility, especially the technical side. Just like the football official, who is responsible for administrating a football game, the project manager is responsible for all aspects dealing with administrating a project.

The next knowledge level is to look at the intangible items dealing with general management, or the art. In the same way we compared officials for a football game to project managers, we can compare football coaches to technical managers.

Leadership

Football coaches are the primary people who bring leadership to the team. The secondary source of leadership would come from players. The coaches set the tone and expectations of the team. They possess the capability of providing leadership because they have a direct relationship with each and every team member. The coaches are primarily concerned with the development of the players and the team. A football official is concerned only with the game itself and does nothing to help develop an individual. At best an official might have the respect of players because of how they officiated a game.

Looking at project roles, once a project gets into design and development the technical manager is the primary source of leadership. They mentor and develop developers through the project life cycle. They are interested in the individual's improvement. Players look toward coaches for leadership because of these things. The only thing a project manager can do is explain what is expected as well as the rules that need to be followed for the project. Since project managers have no official people reporting to them, they are not interested in skill improvement.

Negotiation

Football coaches are always negotiating. Their purpose is not only to win the game but also to make the right choices and bring out the best in everyone so that the team is successful. During the game at times you can see quarterbacks, defensive and offensive teams huddled around their coaches on the sideline. In these conversations there is negotiating going on. The players are telling the coaches what is occurring on the field, and the coaches are negotiating changes to the players to try to make things better. The coaches can do this because they have experience and knowledge in playing the game.

Project managers do some negotiating; it's mostly done during the first part of the project when the project plan, staffing, and budget are being set up. But in the later project phases where the technical stuff is being done the project manager is not the best for negotiating. In these later phases negotiating requires knowing the subject material that is being talked about, which are changes to systems and workflows. Unless the project manager came from the technical side, he will have no idea what is being negotiated. A better resource for the negotiating would be a technical manager. They normally have a better understanding of the effect of changes (both long- and short-term) and should understand the effect on users. This same reasoning also goes with the disciplines of problem solving and decision making.

Problem Solving

If something is not working during the game it's the coaches who are held accountable in solving the problem. Coaches know that if an opponent player is always beating the block and sacking the quarterback before he can throw or hand off, they need to tell their players to double-team the person or call plays away from the person. Because of their knowledge and coaching the players directly, they can solve team problems that are occurring during the game. Even though some of the things a team is doing wrong are obvious enough that officials know how to correct, they still cannot problem solve because players do not report to them, nor is it any of their duties or responsibilities. The duties and responsibilities are to only administrate the game.

A technical manager with their knowledge and skills can quickly recognize when things are not going as planned. Their knowledge can help the person get back on track. Even if they do not know the answer immediately on how to fix something, they can at least know how to contact someone who does. A project manager can report and document that a problem exists. They can even go so far as to document that a problem has been closed. To come up with the solution for the problem requires technical background and system knowledge. Most times the developer has this, but sometimes even they need to turn to someone else for help, which would be a technical manager.

Decision Making

Football coaches make the decisions on what plays to run and what defenses to run during the game. They select what players get to play and in which situations. When a player is not performing they make the decision to replace the player with someone else that they believe can perform better.

Just as stated for negotiation and problem solving, a technical manager is the best person to make a technical-related decision because of their skills, experience, and knowledge. A project manager can make many decisions around how the project is being run, but when it comes to making decisions around the actual work, design, and layout of the work, a technical manager is the best option.

Influencing the Organization

Football officials' only concern is running the game. Once the game is over they really have no more concerns dealing with that game, except how to run the next game better. On the other hand, a football coach is concerned about winning not only the single game but also the rest of the games in the season and also future seasons. A coach will not stay in the job long unless he succeeds both short- and long-term. Coaches will strongly recommend certain types of new players so that they can run their type of offense and defense. Does a football coach have the final decision on all these things? Absolutely not! Normally, a team's general manger and the owner need to be influenced for this to happen.

The technical manager has the same concerns as the football coach. It's important that the changes being made work for both short-term and long-term. They use their technical knowledge, experiences, and people network to try to influence the company so that the solution selected is the best one. Job security for the technical manager is dependent on this. As for selecting resources for a project, they would love to have nothing but the best resources on their project. But because of other projects and company needs they negotiate who is going to work on the project. For complex items that require complex development, a SME might be assigned. Logic that is simple and affects very little might be assigned to someone new. These correct assignment of skills with the task are best negotiated by someone with resource and system knowledge, which is a technical manager.

Communication

Earlier we mentioned the communication that the football official and project manager are responsible for. It dealt more with informing through documentation. The communication being covered here is more the instruction communication that comes from the football coach. It deals with working with the players to make them better. It can also be on how the game will be played. The coach might call nothing but running plays. The coach could even delegate that all play calling is done by the quarterback. If someone is always being penalized, it's the coach's responsibility to communicate to the player what's being done wrong. If there is not a coach to do this, then the player would probably continue with the bad behavior.

This is similar to projects. One of the major gaps continuously seen on projects is that when the developer gets into trouble or has issues, there is nobody there to help or recognize it. The developer believes they themselves can work through it. Valuable time is wasted as the developer becomes more and more frustrated and stressed. The best scenario is that the developer can actually work their way through the problem. When this happens, the only thing that is lost is time. But then again in a project, time is the most valuable thing.

Earlier in the book it was mentioned about a good manager being able to be proactive versus reactive. Before the resource starts to spend too much time struggling, a good technical manager can recognize this and get the person help and guidance. Image how much sooner a project could be completed that as soon as a delay or issue comes up it gets fixed. A project manager does not have system knowledge or resource skill knowledge to see when someone starts to struggle. The only thing they can do is to keep checking with the technical staff so see if things are going as planned and when the task will be done. A project manager can effectively manage the task but cannot effectively manage the resource. Only a technical manager can effectively manage the resource.

LEADERSHIP OF THE DIFFERENT PROJECT PHASES

By now there should be an understanding of the separation of roles, duties, and responsibilities between the project management position and technical management position for a project. In summary, project managers manage the tasks that make up the project, whereas technical managers manage the resources that accomplish the task.

Earlier we discussed generalist versus specialist. If applied to the project process, this concept helps to validate the best person to fill each of these project knowledge areas. And if we incorporate the different phases in a linear methodology, the graph would look like Figure 30.3.

Another common issue that sets a project up for failure is the assignment of a technical person to lead the effort. Normally in a project methodology there is only a technical lead and not a technical manager. The issue with this is that on a large complex project it requires more than a lead in this

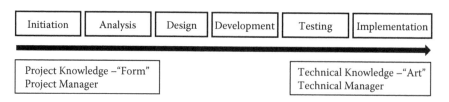

FIGURE 30.3
Aligning project knowledge area with project phases.

key position. It requires someone who is good in the six management best practices. So calling it a manager instead of a lead makes more sense. A lead most times has never had people report to them directly. Their duties in the past probably have been around only managing their own time and assigned tasks to complete things. They also are accustomed to having their manager looking over their shoulder to give them guidance in tough situations. Even though a lead might be very good on the system knowledge, the other management disciplines are needed to get things done and manage other technical people through tough situations. Does the person officially need to be a manager? No. I know of several architects and senior developers who excel in most of the disciplines. Because of their ability to work with people and their knowledge of systems they have no problems with handling the responsibilities and duties of the technical manager position in a project.

PROJECT SIZES AND THE AMOUNT OF FORM AND ART NEEDED

The project team structure also affects the outcomes of a project. The characteristics and needs of a small project are different from a medium-size project, which is different from a large project. But companies tend to put all three project types into a project structure similar to what is shown in Figure 30.4.

Companies instead need to have several different project structures. Each structure has different levels of knowledge for project management form and technical management art. The size and complexity would dictate which project structure would be used. For a small project the tangible *form* and intangible *art* items needed are fewer and fairly simple. A small project will have few requirements, stakeholders, decisions, unknowns, and resources assigned. So the amount of documentation, project administration, leadership, decision making, problem solving, communication, and negotiating is minimal. On a large project everything is just the opposite. Using the same project structure for both small and large projects not only is there a waste of performance for many projects, but it also increases the risk that certain types of projects will fail. Let's take a detailed look at the type of projects classified as small, medium, and large in the real world.

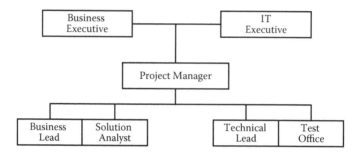

FIGURE 30.4
Common project structure led by project manager.

SMALL PROJECT CHARACTERISTICS

Resources

Normally there is not both a project manager and a technical manager or lead assigned. It's an overkill on skills that only adds unnecessary cost. Only a few resources are needed. Resources that get assigned tend to have skills and knowledge that are average to below average. The reason for this is because smaller projects most always have a low priority. The above average resources mostly get assigned to the larger higher priority projects. All that is left are average and below average resources.

Areas Affected

Business stakeholders and development areas affected are only one or two.

Documentation

Business requirements are small in number and simple.

Simple Design and Development

There are very few unknowns that have to be worked through. There ends up being no major decisions that need to be made. Minimal project documentation is needed for the project to be completed successfully. There is more technical work then project management work.

GOOD: Project manager leads the project.

Projects most of the time will be delivered successfully based on meeting all four criteria: quality, deliverables, delivery date, and cost. The success, though, is dependent on skill level and knowledge of the team resources. The risk is that, with few resources and lower skills that normally get assigned, when there are technical questions or problems there is nobody on the team to address them. There are a couple negative effects that can happen when this occurs. First is that without addressing issues and problems immediately, it slows up the work, which affects the speed to market. The other negative effect is that since lower skilled and less knowledgeable people were assigned there is a chance the final outcome will be of poor quality. Too many times it's the small simple projects that cause the most damage.

BEST: Technical manager or leader leads the project.

Projects almost always will be delivered successfully based on meeting all four success criteria. Naturally, having a manager run the project would be better than a skilled technical lead, but still not required for success. If a resource is having issues or does not understand something, the technical manager or lead normally sees this early because of her technical background. Knowing the system the technical manager or lead usually can supply the needed information or find the correct person to help the resource. There is a risk that the documentation and budget might not be the best since the technical manager is not trained. But with everything smaller on this size of project, number of tasks, and costs, perfect documentation is not required. Even though it's nice to have detailed administration around a small project, it's not a requirement. For the factors of cost, quality, delivery time, and deliverables, someone with the technical and people knowledge are the best people to lead a small project (Figure 30.5).

MEDIUM PROJECT CHARACTERISTICS

Resources

There are probably less than 30 people that work on a medium-sized project during its duration. This might seem high, but it includes the test office staff, developers, analysts, and business resources.

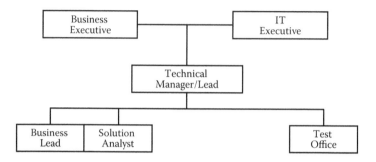

FIGURE 30.5
Small project structure led by technical manager/lead.

Resources that get assigned tend to have skills and knowledge that are average or above average. A medium-size project can be a top-priority project, or it can be low-priority project.

Areas Affected

Business areas affected can be one or several. Development area required can be one or several.

Documentation

What best classifies the project as medium sized is the documentation and the number of unknowns. There can be many pages of business requirements but few unknowns in them. Or there can just be a few pages of requirements but many unknowns because of the complexity.

Design and Development

There can either be a great deal of design changes that are fairly simple to do, or the project can have complex changes that go into only one to two modules. An example of the first situation is that one project it was required to capture statistical data on all files in the enterprise that were being passed from one system to another. It sounds complicated, but it was the same small simple module that was placed in over 200 different locations. It was easy to design but time-consuming to implement it into the 200 different locations across the organization. Most of the unknowns were to identify all the places the small module needed to be added. Proper and accurate project documentation is needed for the project to be completed successfully because of the number of people involved, financial planning, along with documentation around the unknowns.

BAD: Technical manager or leader leads the project.

Projects most of the time will have issues meeting all four success criteria. The success is dependent on the project process being defined and administrated. So there is a high risk when the technical manager does not have a high level of project administration knowledge. Most technical managers don't know how to set up a complex budget or set up processes such as the communication plan. Without this project management knowledge, the beginning of the project will be slow, and key information that needs to be gathered at the start of the project will be of poor quality. No matter how talented the technical staff is at the end of the project, it will not overcome the bad requirements, budget, and project processes. There is a high risk the project will end up in the failure category.

GOOD: Project manager is assigned without a technical lead or technical manager.

Projects most times will be delivered successfully. The key to success when working without a technical manager/lead is to make sure the project team has at least one expert from each area affected. The experts in each system can get together on their own to address the unknowns, document them, and report back to the project manager. The risk is that if just one area does not assign an expert to do the changes, then the entire project is at danger of failing.

BEST: Project manager leads with a technical lead assigned.

Projects most always will be delivered successfully. A project manager understands how to set up and administrate a project from the beginning to the end. There is structure around the process with tasks being defined and administrated. As for risk there is very little with this structure as long as the process is followed and the technical lead is skilled and knowledgeable in the areas affected. A technical manager could be assigned instead of a technical lead, but that would be overkill in knowledge and skills. If the work is really complex but occurs only in one to two modules, a technical lead from the area where the modules are changing has enough knowledge to complete the project. If the project is simple but across many different systems, the work is more about identification of where the changes need to go and not so much about how they will work. Again, this is something a technical lead can handle. Figure 30.4 is an example of the project structure.

LARGE PROJECT CHARACTERISTICS

Resources

A large number of resources are assigned. Large projects most always have a high priority because of the large cost in both money and resources involved. Because of that normally at least one average or above average resource from each area affected gets assigned to work on the project.

Areas Affected

There are many business areas affected. Many times there are major changes that need to be made in a couple of areas and minor changes in most of the rest of the areas. The minor changes can be as simple as changing reports to handling different data being passed. Part of the changes that need to occur are new processes and procedures that need to be implemented.

Documentation

There are a large number of different documents: from the initial scope document that gives a high vision of what the project is and what it hopes to accomplish, to the detail business requirements that explains the *what,* and the technical specifications that explains the *how.*

Complex and Difficult Design and Development

Many unknowns have to be worked through, along with many major decisions to be made. For the project to be successful there needs to be financial and resource planning, control, monitoring, and administration of the project.

BAD: *Project manager leads the project with a technical lead assigned.*

Projects most of the time will have issues in meeting all four criteria of quality, delivery date, deliverables, and cost. With the large number of areas affected and needing to know how the change is going to affect each area, the correct skill and knowledge assigned to this position can make a major difference between a large project succeeding and failing. The risk with a technical lead is that they are familiar with only a couple of areas and work with only a few resources. Most times their overall management disciplines could be measured as average or below. When it comes to motivating and coordinating work with other resources in other areas, they may get lost in how to get that accomplished.

**BEST: *Project manager leads the project
with a technical manager assigned.***

For large projects it was covered what not to have for a project structure, but for the best solution there are several options depending on the type of large project. All the options have strengths and weaknesses.

The first project structure is where the project manager and a technical manager colead the project. This project structure works for large projects that cannot be easily broken into subprojects. Even though the changes are required in several different systems, each system is dependent on work the other systems are doing. I mention colead. With both their skills they understand how to set up and administrate a project from the beginning to the end.

The project manager can concentrate solely on the administration (form) part of the project, while the technical manager can concentrate on the technical (art) part of the project. On a large project there normally is enough work to keep both busy. Also on the very large projects the technical work might be so much that it needs to be segmented out and a technical lead assigned to handle each segment of work. These technical leads then report up through the technical manager. Sometimes on the really large projects there might be 10 technical leads reporting to 1 technical manager.

Another key reason for coleadership is that there is not a single person for failure. Many times I have seen project managers just get up and leave a company in the middle of a project. When a large project is going bad the first thing that goes is normally the project manager. So another project manager then gets thrown in and has to learn quickly what is

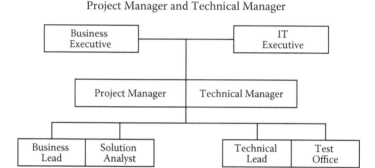

FIGURE 30.6

Project structure co-led by project manager and technical manager.

occurring. With coleadership, if one leaves, gets sick, takes vacation, or gets promoted, the project can continue somewhat normally. The manager who did not leave can temporarily do the other person's task until another manager is brought on the project. The existing manager can help the new manager get up to speed quickly on where the project is. It would not be perfect, but at least there would be some continuity during the change-over. Figure 30.6 is a project structure showing co-leadership.

The project methodology purist will argue against these different structures. They will say that the technical manager is not needed on a large project. They will say the technical architect or technical lead can handle everything that a technical manager does. They can provide the leadership, negotiation, problem solving, decision making, organizational influence, and communication needed for the project. Stop and think about this for a minute. What is being asked of the IT architect and technical lead is to provide management levels of input, when they have never been in management. And that is the problem. A good manager will have the contacts, skill, knowledge, experiences, and intuition. Earlier it was mentioned that I get called into projects to help get them back on track. All that is done is to supply the technical management knowledge at the project manager level to get the project back on track.

Another project structure for large project projects is to have several project managers who report to a program manager. A program manager has not been talked about before, but these are just experienced project managers. Large projects that cover many different systems often can be segmented into smaller subprojects because there are few dependencies between each part that is being done. These subprojects can be run as individual projects. They have their own requirements, system design, and even financials. All of these things get rolled up to the program project plan. The primary reason for doing the segmentation is that there is just so much project administration work that needs to be done that it would be impossible for just one project manager to do it all.

On the technical side, a technical manager is still assigned and coleads with the program manager. Much in the same way a project manager is assigned to lead each subproject, in each subproject a technical lead is assigned, who will report to the technical manager (Figure 30.7). The reason for this structure again goes back to the intangible management best practice disciplines of leadership, negotiation, problem solving, decision making, ability to influence, and communication. When a subproject requires one of these disciplines to address an issue, the technical lead can turn to the technical manager. Remember when we covered the disciplines (see Chapter 2): It's never about stepping in and taking over by dictating; instead it's about working with the group in helping them to arrive at their own decisions and to solve their own problems. A good technical manager can give that guidance and mentoring to the technical lead and their team.

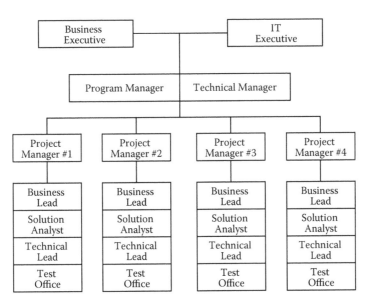

FIGURE 30.7
Large project structure led by program manager with several project managers.

The last reason is knowledge transfer. Over many decades and in various companies, I have met very few people that could be classified as the best of the best in terms of being a technical manager and the management disciplines. Yet with so few, there was never a process put in place to off-load their knowledge. These very good technical managers always get assigned to the most complex large projects, and because they are so good and can get things done with little help, no other technical resources are assigned to learn from them, which is a waste of knowledge.

Will a project fail if this is not followed? No! What is being talked about is a project team structure and knowledge that will reduce the risk of failure to ensure the project has the best chance of success. What is being talked about is reengineering the project process and structure so there is improvement in terms of quality and speed to market.

In large companies it's very easy to have a budget of over $100 million for large project work annually. By looking at the current project processes and making changes the return on investment can increase drastically. If by making changes to the existing large projects they could be delivered sooner and have better quality, which would equate into a 10% performance gain, financially this would translate into over $10 million in savings in 1 year. Customers would be happier because more items promised to them would be delivered on time and at the cost promised. Upper management of both business and technical like this because more is getting done with less. It's a win–win situation for everyone.

I have been in two organizations that implemented project methodology, and both took the same path. Because of the low cost and shorter time frame, they started out with testing the project methodology on several small projects. It worked successfully. Then they applied the project methodology to some medium-size projects, and it worked there also. At this point the companies made a wrong assumption that the project methodology structure would work for all projects, including large ones. What occurred on the first large projects in both companies was failure on a large scale. What was sad is that the companies did not go back and analyze why it did not work on large projects. Instead they just accepted the failure rate and the cost overruns, missed deadlines, and descoping that goes with it. After many years of high failure rates on large projects, both companies started to make slight modifications to their project methodology to improve their results. By that time tens of millions of dollars had been wasted.

NEVER ASSUME, ALWAYS VALIDATE

The last step is to find a solution specific for your environment. As mentioned several times already, this book is about giving a person the understanding of 80% of what is occurring. The other 20% a person needs to modify to their specific environment. The following is a process that can be used to help figure out the 20% that is unknown and that will work in your environment.

Following the Lean management process of looking at the entire process and product that needs to be improved, build a small team that consists of the best project manager, analyst, technical manager, business stakeholder, and technical lead. Four or five members are all that is needed on the team. Make sure everyone understands the three knowledge areas that make up a project: project knowledge, management knowledge, and subject knowledge. Along with that the team needs to understand the subparts that make up the project knowledge area and management knowledge area. The team needs to define the criteria for a project to be classified as successful in tangible terms such as cost, deliverables, quality, and delivery date. If there are other easy benchmarks that can be acquired, add them as well. Last, create categories such as success, challenge, and failure. There can be more categories, but the recommendation is to not go over five, because then the results start to be sliced too fine and add no value. On a scale of 0–10, what is the difference between a 6 and 7?

After this prework is done, have the team review past projects. Review the documentation and the final results in terms of the criteria defined for success. A key part of the research is to go out and talk to the actual team members who were on the project. It should be easy to get the names of the core team members of a past project and meet with them one at a time. Do not meet with the entire core project at once because it will not be an open conversation. People will hold back because they are afraid to offend someone. Ask the hard questions. What worked, and what did not? When there were issues, who addressed them, and what skills and knowledge did they use to address them? Then go find that person and ask them the same questions. Get to the root cause of why things happened. Also ask how things could have been improved. Was a technical lead good enough, or would a technical manager have been better? Was the project manager overworked? Was the documentation accurate and complete? The purpose is to find the waste that occurred in the project process. In

Lean management terminology, it would be called value stream mapping (VSM) of the product called projects.

The topics covered in this book have been laid out to get you to this point in the process. There should be an understanding of such concepts as management best practices, quality, process engineering, Lean management, and several different project methodologies. By presenting these different concepts, the hope is that you can start to understand them and how they come into play in the everyday world of IT and will know what to look for as you are researching and analyzing in your specific environment.

Once the research is complete, it's time to turn the data into an action using one of the many processes covered. Most all follow W. Edwards Deming's wheel, discussed earlier. Using the continuous quality improvement of PDCA it might look like this:

- **Plan** the product. Revise the existing project methodology to return better results on large projects. The objective of the changes should be a performance increase reflected in time and budget. If it appears a technical manager would increase performance, add one.
- **Do** it. Identify a couple of large projects. On these projects make the changes.
- **Check** the results. As the projects go through the different phases, gather information on the negatives and positives of the change. Most large projects take over 6 months, so do not expect overnight results.
- **Act** on the results. Review the data as they are being gathered to see if there is a noticeable improvement with the changes. It's not always necessary for the project to be completed to come up with an accurate conclusion that there is a major benefit with the changes. Compare the old results from before the change with the current results at the different project phase end points. There should be some noticeable differences before the project is over. Once there is evidence that the change has resulted in a benefit or may have created a negative effect, start the cycle over with the plan stage. Thinking of the log chain concept, the goal is to identify the weakest links in the process to get the most increased productivity.

The improvement processes is not about making large gains instantly overnight, nor is it about making major changes. If 20 things are identified that could be improved, only a few that show the most return should be changed at one time. It's about making small changes and measuring those changes to obtain improvement increases. After those changes are in production, then look for the next couple of enhancements that can be done and repeat the process.

31

Conclusion

In examining what makes a company unique, it is not the product that they create. Even if a company happened to create something unique that customers wanted, within a couple of months competitors would spring up all over the world to take market share away. One of the primary distinctions between companies are the processes. A company with effective and efficient processes will be able to create their product cheaper, faster, and with better quality than its competition. A company with these characteristics can also make quicker changes than the competition.

Efficient processes just don't suddenly appear. Even if they did they need to be continuously improved upon as the company, resources, product, market, and technology changes. The culture of the company needs to be changed so that everyone looks for ways to improve things. The best way to improve things is to identify and reduce the waste that occurs in a process. The best way to do this is through small increments by using a continuous improvement process such as the Deming wheel. Probably the most critical part of any improvement effort is the ability to measure the results accurately. Before the changes occur, research is needed to make sure the current items are being measured accurately. After that is done and enough historical data are captured, then the change can occur. With measurements taken after the change, a comparison can be made to see if the changes are adding value or decreasing value to the company.

For the continuous evolution of processes, people are needed to lead this effort. The best people for this responsibility are management team members. However, many managers are cave dwellers and fence sitters, so unless they are forced they will most likely not get involved with continuous improvement. Processes such as the annual review need to be modified. The normal review process is somewhat of a rubber stamp. Common objectives are given to the managers no matter what type of work they do or their management style. The process needs to be changed so a few objectives are specific to the manager and the environment they manage in. Having subordinates help set some of the improvement objectives for their manager for the coming year is a very easy change to make this happen.

To improve management, an understanding is first needed of what management means in the company. So there needs to be definitions such as the six disciplines of management best practices: leadership, negotiation, problem solving, decision making, ability to influence, and communication. Next, tangible action items need to be defined that managers can use to improve. Most managers know what their weaknesses are but have little idea what actions they can do to improve them. Also, with a tangible action item list that all the managers can select improvement items from, management would become more consistent across the company. Consistency of any type is equated with performance increase.

There are other tools and knowledge such as quality, high-performance teams, technology, using contractors, distractions, and project methodology. Companies that understand these topics and concepts can transform from a reactive mode to a proactive mode. These companies will continuously get better and faster than their competition. If they can stay on track at some point they will be at or near the top of their market.

I end the book as it began. Most companies have very skilled and knowledgeable employees, but processes and procedures often prevent employees from achieving maximum performance, even if they try. It's like a taking a race car with a skilled driver down a gravel road. Even though the driver and car have the capability of going over 200 mph, the gravel road limits how fast the car can go without having an accident. Business is much like this. Companies need to remove the processes and procedures that are causing waste and robbing employees of maximum performance. Only then can they have a chance of being market leader instead of market follower.

Bibliography

Books

Bossidy, Larry & Charan, Ram. *Execution: The Discipline of Getting Things Done*. New York: Crown Business, 2002.

Deming, Edward. *Out of the Crisis*. Cambridge, MA: Massachusetts Institute of Technology/Center for Advanced Engineering Study (MIT/CAES), 1986

Greenleaf, Robert K. *The Servant as Leader*. Assay, The Robert K Greenleaf Center, 1970

Kouzes, James & Posner, Barry. *The Leadership Challenge: How to Keep Getting Extraordinary Things Done in Organizations*. San Francisco, CA: Jossey-Bass, 1997.

Michael Hammer & James Champy, *Reengineering the Corporation*, New York: HarperCollins Publishers, Inc, 1993.

Project Management Institute, *A Guide to the Project Management Body of Knowledge, Fourth Edition*, Newtown Square, PA: Project Management Institute, 2008.

Scott, Jim. *Good to Great*. New York: HarperCollins, 2001

Senge, Peter. *The Fifth Discipline*. New York: Doubleday/Currency, 1990

Smith, Adam. *The Wealth of Nations*. United Kingdom, London: Strahan & Cadell, 1776.

Websites

1000Ventures.com, "25 Lessons from Jack Welch" by Vadim Kotelnikov, accessed June 1, 2011, http://1000ventures.com/business_guide/mgmt_new-model_25lessons-welch.html.

ABC News, "White House Crashers" by Pierre Thomas, Yunji de Nies, and Devin Dwyer, accessed October 18, 2011, http://abcnews.go.com/GMA/white-house-crashers-michaele-tareq-salahi-past-secret-service/story?id=9202817

Agile Diary, Agile Introducion, Agile Implementation: Experiences in Transistion to Agile Project Management, "Is Agile Software Development Equal to Cowboy Coding?", accessed June 1, 2011, http://agilediary.wordpress.com/2008/12/30/is-agile-software-development-equal-to-cowboy-coding/.

AgileManifesto.org, "History: The Agile Manifesto" by Jim Highsmith, accessed June 1, 2011, http://www.agilemanifesto.org/history.html.

AgileModeling.com, "Feature Driven Development (FDD) and Agile Modeling", accessed June 1, 2011, http://www.agilemodeling.com/essays/fdd.htm.

AllFamousQuotes.com, "The Most Famous Henry Ford Quotes of All Time", accessed June 01, 2011, http://www.all-famous-quotes.com/Henry_Ford_quotes.html.

BCS: The Chartered Institute for IT, "A Study in Project Failure" by Dr. John McManus and Dr. Trevor Wood-Harper, last modified June 2008, http://www.bcs.org/content/conWebDoc/19584.

Businessballs.com, "Tuckman Forming Storming Norming Performing model", accessed June 1, 2011, http://www.businessballs.com/tuckmanformingstormingnorming-performing.htm.

CoachWooden.com, "Pyramid of Success", accessed October 18, 2011, http://www.coachwooden.com/index2.html

Encyclopedia Britannica, "W. Edward Deming", accessed on October 18, 2011, http://www.britannica.com/EBchecked/topic/157093/W-Edwards-Deming.

ExtremeProgramming.org, "Pair Programming", accessed October 18, 2011, http://www.extremeprogramming.org/rules/pair.html.

Ford Motor Company, "Henry Ford $5-a-Day Revolution", accessed June 1, 2011, http://corporate.ford.com/about-ford/heritage/milestones/5dollaraday/677-5-dollar-a-day.

GE, "Past Leaders – John F Welch, Jr", accessed June 1, 2011 http://www.ge.com/company/history/bios/john_welch.html.

General Motors, "Company: History & Heritage—Creation 1897–1909", accessed June 1, 2011, http://www.gm.com/company/historyAndHeritage/creation.html.

Los Angeles Times, "John Wooden's pyramid stands test of time" by Robyn Norwood, accessed October 18, 2011, http://articles.latimes.com/2010/jun/04/sports/la-sp-adv-woodenpyramid-20100605.

MedicineNet.com, "10 Tips to Reduce the Common Cold" by Melissa Conrad Stoppler, MD, last modified on October 7, 2008, http://www.medicinenet.com/script/main/art.asp?articlekey=53472

ReferenceForBusiness.com, "Traditional Organizational Structure" by Howard Distelzweig, accessed June 1, 2011, http://www.referenceforbusiness.com/management/Ob-Or/Organizational-Structure.html.

Ronald LeRoi Burback, "The Boehm-Spiral Methodology", last modified December 14, 1998, http://infolab.stanford.edu/~burback/watersluice/node53.html.

The Standish Group, "Standish Newsroom–CHAOS 2009," accessed June 1, 2011, http://www1.standishgroup.com/newsroom/chaos_2009.php.

The W. Edwards Deming Institute "W. Edward Deming", accessed June 1, 2011 http://deming.org/index.cfm?content=61.

ToyotaGeorgetown.com, "The Production System – Ask Yourself Why Five Times", last updated October 8, 2003, http://www.toyotageorgetown.com/tps.asp.

WelchWay.com, "The People Part", accessed June 1,2011, http://www.welchway.com/Principles/Differentiation.aspx.

WelchWay.com, "The Case for 20-70-10", last modified October 2, 2006, http://www.welchway.com/Principles/Differentiation/The-Case-for-20-70-10.aspx.

Wikipedia, "A Guide to the Project Management Body of Knowledge/ History" , accessed October 18, 2011, http://en.wikipedia.org/wiki/A_Guide_to_the_Project_Management_Body_of_Knowledge

Wikipedia, "Lean Manufacturing", last modified on May 25, 2011, http://en.wikipedia.org/wiki/Lean_manufacturing.

Wikipedia, "Six Sigma", last modified on May 24, 2011, http://en.wikipedia.org/wiki/Six_Sigma.

Wilfrid Hutagalung, "Extreme Programming", accessed October 18, 2011, http://www.umsl.edu/~sauterv/analysis/f06Papers/Hutagalung/.

Index

Author Biography

I'm a great believer in luck, and I find the harder I work, the more I have of it.

Thomas Jefferson

Tom Witt has a B.S. in mathematics, with a minor in coaching, from the University of Wisconsin–Platteville. He has worked in the information technology (IT) environment for almost 30 years. The first half of his career held varies management titles that involved development and management of staff and systems. In the second half of Tom's career he moved into solely the project environment, in which he has held the titles of office automation manager, project manager, technical manager, technical lead, architect, and system analyst. Most of Tom's experience has been in the insurance industry in addition to 3 years in the magazine fulfillment business and 3 years at an institute of higher education. Tom has worked on a wide range of projects; he has been a part of the development of new mainframe systems, new web systems, and vendor-purchased imaging systems, as well as being part of a small team that reengineered a business division for a major insurance company. Many of the projects on which Tom has been involved have effected changes—as many as 200 different systems—throughout the entire enterprise. Project costs have ranged from $200,000 into the millions of dollars. Tom has acquired knowledge not only through personal experiences but also from outside sources such as external consultants, seminars, books, and a personal network of people. More importantly, he was put into many different types of project and situations that allowed him to apply the many different concepts and knowledge acquired to see the results from a front-line perspective, where work is executed in an organization.